NEW ESSAYS ON UNCLE TOM'S CABIN

D0024188

★ The American Novel ★

GENERAL EDITOR

Emory Elliott, Princeton University

Other books in the series:
New Essays on The Scarlet Letter
New Essays on The Great Gatsby
New Essays on Adventures of Huckleberry Finn
New Essays on Moby-Dick
New Essays on The Red Badge of Courage

Forthcoming:
New Essays on Chopin's The Awakening (ed. Wendy Martin)
New Essays on Ellison's Invisible Man (ed. Robert O'Meally)
New Essays on Light in August (ed. Michael Millgate)
New Essays on The Sun Also Rises (ed. Linda Wagner)
New Essays on James's The American (ed. Martha Banta)

New Essays on
Uncle Tom's Cabin

Edited by

Eric J. Sundquist

CAMBRIDGE
UNIVERSITY PRESS

813.3
5892 v Z5
C.1

Published by the Press Syndicate of the University of Cambridge
The Pitt Building, Trumpington Street, Cambridge CB2 1RP
40 West 20th Street, New York, NY 10011-4211, USA
10 Stamford Road, Oakleigh, Melbourne 3166, Australia

© Cambridge University Press 1986

First published 1986
Reprinted 1993

Printed in the United States of America

Library of Congress Cataloging-in-Publication Data is available
A catalogue record for this book is available from the British Library

ISBN 0-521-30203-X hardback
ISBN 0-521-31786-X paperback

Contents

v

METHODIST COLLEGE LIBRARY
Fayetteville, N.C.

Contents

Series Editor's Preface

In literary criticism the last twenty-five years have been particularly fruitful. Since the rise of the New Criticism in the 1950s, which focused attention of critics and readers upon the text itself – apart from history, biography, and society – there has emerged a wide variety of critical methods which have brought to literary works a rich diversity of perspectives: social, historical, political, psychological, economic, ideological, and philosophical. While attention to the text itself, as taught by the New Critics, remains at the core of contemporary interpretation, the widely shared assumption that works of art generate many different kinds of interpretation has opened up possibilities for new readings and new meanings.

Before this critical revolution, many American novels had come to be taken for granted by earlier generations of readers as having an established set of recognized interpretations. There was a sense among many students that the canon was established and that the larger thematic and interpretative issues had been decided. The task of the new reader was to examine the ways in which elements such as structure, style, and imagery contributed to each novel's acknowledged purpose. But recent criticism has brought these old assumptions into question and has thereby generated a wide variety of original, and often quite surprising, interpretations of the classics, as well as of rediscovered novels such as Kate Chopin's *The Awakening*, which has only recently entered the canon of works that scholars and critics study and that teachers assign their students.

The aim of The American Novel Series is to provide students of American literature and culture with introductory critical guides to

American novels now widely read and studied. Each volume is devoted to a single novel and begins with an introduction by the volume editor, a distinguished authority on the text. The introduction presents details of the novel's composition, publication history, and contemporary reception, as well as a survey of the major critical trends and readings from first publication to the present. This overview is followed by four or five original essays, specifically commissioned from senior scholars of established reputation and from outstanding younger critics. Each essay presents a distinct point of view, and together they constitute a forum of interpretative methods and of the best contemporary ideas on each text.

It is our hope that these volumes will convey the vitality of current critical work in American literature, generate new insights and excitement for students of the American novel, and inspire new respect for and new perspectives upon these major literary texts.

Emory Elliott
Princeton University

1

Introduction

ERIC J. SUNDQUIST

CLEAR judgments of the merits of *Uncle Tom's Cabin* will never be easy to make. Even though the Civil War novelist John De Forest, inaugurating the search for "The Great American Novel" in an 1868 essay in *The Nation*, thought Harriet Beecher Stowe's novel the best candidate to date, the book's phenomenal popularity in its own day and in the century following the Civil War has served to cast suspicion on it among those who define the artifacts of high culture by excluding works that seem to cater to the tastes of the masses. The novel's characterization of black Americans, whether slave or free, has often rendered it objectionable to modern sensibilities. Even Stowe's broad depiction of the role of women in society, because it appears to restrict their moral influence to the circumscribed arena of home and family, has struck some feminist readers as constrained or demeaning. Despite such problems, redefinitions of the place of popular literature, of blacks, and of women in American political and cultural history witnessed over the last several decades have focused new attention on Stowe's masterpiece, illuminating again its complicated and sometimes contradictory powers.

Like any great work of literature, *Uncle Tom's Cabin* may well transcend the issues and events of its own era but must nonetheless be seen to be firmly anchored in them. This is emphatically true of Stowe's novel, which is so deeply *political* in nature – despite seeming at times oblivious to crucial realities in America's great debate over slavery – that it has often been considered a strange hybrid of polemic and sentimental melodrama, a work that helped instigate the Civil War and then ceased to have value once its purpose had been accomplished. But it is also a sign of

1

prevailing twentieth-century notions of literature in America that both polemicism and sentimentality, especially in the heated union of the two forged by Stowe, could discredit the novel. Many major critical studies of American literature in this century have found no place for Stowe, and only recently has she been considered at all central to the great flowering of native literature before the Civil War known as the American Renaissance. The early assessment of Carl Van Doren in *The American Novel* is perhaps typical of most modern critical response: "Leave out the merely domestic elements of the book – slave families broken up by sale, ailing and dying children, negro women at the mercy of their masters, white households which at the best are slovenly and extravagant by reason of irresponsible servants and at the worst are abodes of brutality and license – and little remains."[1]

One might as well say of *Moby-Dick* (as some readers have), "leave out the whales and little remains." The comparison is not entirely idle. Both Stowe and Herman Melville, at almost exactly the same time, wrote epic novels that drove to the heart of American democracy by infusing everyday materials with highly charged political purpose. Melville's novel went largely unrecognized by readers and critics until this century; Stowe's novel, although retaining a popular audience, was progressively lowered in scholarly estimation almost in exact proportion to Melville's ascent – in part because it lacks the complex philosophical intent and dense literary allusiveness of *Moby-Dick* and in part because it is in direct opposition to the rich American tradition of masculine confrontation with nature (the frontier tradition of the "American Adam") that Melville helped to define. Add to this Nathaniel Hawthorne's condemnation of popular female writers as a "damned mob of scribbling women," along with the influential novelistic canon opening out of *The Scarlet Letter*, based on the narrative introspection and nuanced dramatic plotting found, for example, in the works of William Dean Howells, Henry James, and Edith Wharton, and the main terms by which Stowe has been excluded are evident.[2]

Against the standards defined by Hawthorne and Melville (and despite the fact that both Howells and James found the novel something of a landmark in American fiction), *Uncle Tom's Cabin* has appeared to be awkwardly plotted, overly melodramatic, and naively visionary – a book for children and (what could be thought to amount to the same thing) those women readers who, from Stowe's day on into the twentieth century, have formed the largest part of the popular reading public. "It literally wallows in tears," writes one critic. "There is no subterfuge and no artistry about appealing to the simplest emotions of the reader."[3] At the same time, however, Edmund Wilson wrote in an important reassessment in 1962 that Stowe's work is comparable to that of Dickens and Zola (as readers in her own day recognized); and the novel has often been read in Europe, both in the original and in numerous translations, as the masterpiece of social realism George Sand, George Eliot, Turgenev, Tolstoy, Hugo, and Heine found it to be.[4] Moreover, contemporary scholars have begun to see in the novel's astute manipulation of the strategies of sentimentality a careful artistry and an engagement of striking, if neglected, political powers. The tradition of the domestic novel to which *Uncle Tom's Cabin* belongs, writes Jane Tompkins, "represents a monumental effort to reorganize culture from the woman's point of view," an effort that is "remarkable for its intellectual complexity, ambition, and resourcefulness" and that "offers a critique of American society far more devastating than any delivered by better-known critics such as Hawthorne and Melville." In this view, the novel's "tearful episodes and frequent violations of probability [are] invested with a structure of meanings" that draw on important nineteenth-century patterns of individual emotion, social equality, and religious belief in order to fix the work, "not in the realm of fairy tale or escapist fantasy, but in the very bedrock of reality."[5]

The redefinition of the canon of classical American literature that has accompanied the rise of feminist scholarship in the last twenty years has had to confront a still greater, and less easily resolved, problem in the case of *Uncle Tom's Cabin*. It is a problem defined with abrupt succinctness in the title of J. C. Furnas's book, *Goodbye to Uncle Tom*. Appearing in 1956, Furnas's thorough study of the novel's relationship to the realities of slavery, its popularized versions, and its derivative cultural stereotypes revealed in great detail what he saw to be Stowe's role in perpetuating "the misconceptions, Southern and Northern, the wrongheadednesses, the distortions and wishful thinkings about Negroes in general and American Negroes in particular that still plague us today." What Furnas wrote then is without doubt true, perhaps more true, thirty years later: Many black Americans "have made her titular hero a hissing and a byword," such a hated epithet connoting meek servility and offensive minstrel-like traits that many of them "would rather be called 'nigger' than 'Uncle Tom.' "[6]

Although Tom's appellation, "Uncle," is a conventional sign of kinship and familiarity in slave life, and although he is portrayed by Stowe as a young, broad-chested, powerful man, his passive martyrdom at the hands of Simon Legree has become an unfortunate image for the entire novel. In the same vein, James Baldwin's famous claim that the novel is activated by a "theological terror" in which "black equates with evil and white with grace" trenchantly defined the appeal to a race-prejudiced Calvinism latent within Stowe's best intentions.[7] Like the attempts by black individuals or groups such as the National Association for the Advancement of Colored People (NAACP) to proscribe the novel or ban its dramatizations, the brilliant critiques by Baldwin and Furnas recognized disturbing elements in the novel that cannot be explained away. Any reformation of the canon of American literature that sets out to give *Uncle Tom's Cabin* the central place it deserves cannot afford to take lightly, much less ignore altogether, such problems in the book itself or in the cultural images it has engendered.

Upon its publication, the novel immediately produced a flood of imitative drama, poetry, and songs that capitalized upon its most saccharine scenes. The melodramatic apotheosis of Eva and bowdlerized scenes of minstrel humor appeared in consumable artifacts – dioramas, engravings, gift books, card games, figurines, plates, silverware, and needlepoint. Stage versions and the traveling "Tom troupes" that performed them purged any radical messages from the blackface drama: Topsy became a star, singing "I'se So Wicked" and "Topsy's Song: I am but a Little Nigger Gal"; the famous minstrel performer T. D. Rice "jumped Jim Crow" in the role of Uncle Tom; the South appeared as an arena of light-hearted fun (in the P. T. Barnum version, Tom was rescued from Legree by

George Shelby); Tom and Eva were reunited in cardboard heavens; and abolitionism itself was attacked in such songs as "Happy
Are We, Darkies So Gay." The increased popularity of Tom troupes
following the Civil War – some 400 by 1899 in one estimate – was
not diminished by the fact that blacks finally played a few leading
roles. Blackface white actors returned again in the earliest of many
film depictions, beginning with a twelve-minute version in 1903;
but Sam Lucas starred as Tom in the first black film lead in 1914.
Harry Pollard's monumental 1927 remake had a $2 million budget
($20,000 for real bloodhounds, a staple of stage versions); an
animated Uncle Tom starred Felix the Cat; Shirley Temple performed as the Eva of a Tom troupe in *Dimples* (1936) and was
paired with Bill "Bojangles" Robinson as Tom in *The Littlest Rebel*
(1935); Judy Garland was Topsy in *Everybody Sing* (1938); Betty
Grable and June Hoover were twin Topsies (also a tradition on
stage) in *The Dolly Sisters* (1945); and Abbott and Costello mas-
queraded as Simon Legree and Eva in *The Naughty Nineties*
(1945).[8]

Given this extraordinary record of cultural abuse, it is little wonder that Richard Wright satirically entitled his collection of stories
about black life in the Jim Crow South *Uncle Tom's Children* (1940)
or that Ishmael Reed has burlesqued Stowe's novel and its fictive
descendents in *Flight to Canada* (1976). *Uncle Tom's Cabin* can now
barely be read with an open mind. Leaving aside the post–Civil War
versions of Stowe's melodrama (which belong to the continued
history of American racism in popular culture epitomized by films
like *The Birth of a Nation* or *Gone With the Wind* and the novels that
spawned them), one might note that the popular reaction of the
1850s may well have *concealed* the novel's guarded subversive
power by containing it within ostentatiously marketable forms that
would reaffirm the basic prejudices of Stowe's audience. The author
herself wrote a dramatic version entitled "The Christian Slave" that
was never staged; and she too derived crude sentimental verse from
her own fiction (based on such themes as "Eliza Crossing the
River," "Eva Putting Flowers Round Tom's Neck," and "Topsy at
the Looking Glass").[9] However, these efforts keep central what the
minstrel versions either suppressed or rendered irrelevantly comic
or absurdly pious: namely, that in its most fundamental sense, the

novel (as Stowe later put it) was "written by God," that its message was an apocalyptic judgment upon America's worst continuing sin.

Underlying Stowe's portrayal of women in society and her depictions of black character is an acceptance of the power of Christianity that may seem equally alien to modern readers. The model of Christian virtue that Stowe – like the vast majority of her readers – grew up with underwent important changes between the American Revolution and the Civil War. The separation of sacred and secular realms of experience that accompanied the rise of liberal ideology (which asserted the primacy of man's own capacity to define the just nature of society, and valued individual conscience and democratic political ideals above the community of God defined by institutional religion) accounts to a great degree for the book's unusual combination of effects. As a recent critic has noted, "the radical democracy of *Uncle Tom's Cabin* is at once liberal and conservative – liberal in its determination to extend humanity into the excluded slave population, and conservative in its direct insistence upon reasserting the sacred as the essence of social justice."[10] Because abolitionists had to override the historical justification of slavery on the basis of biblical scripture and the Calvinistic claim that all human institutions were forms of bondage to the "darkness" of sin, while at the same time retaining a clear sense of chattel slavery as particularly evil, they often sought to fuse the rhetoric of human depravity and the rhetoric of regeneration according to enlightened liberal ideals. Stowe's novel is itself revolutionary in demanding that the sacred and secular realms be reunited, that the role of God be reinserted into an American political system that paid lip service to Christian ideals and constantly invoked them in its discourse but failed to act upon them seriously.

What might thus be termed the "radical conservatism" of *Uncle Tom's Cabin* can be seen to lie behind its elevation of domestic, Christian virtues associated with women over the failed political, secular virtues associated with a patriarchal society. It also helps to clarify the fact that Stowe could contemplate a potentially revolutionary assault on American social institutions – epitomized by a legal form of slavery that became emblematic for her of other forms of enslavement – while adopting simplistic or reactionary views of the black slave experience. The triangular entanglements among the role of women, the place of blacks in American history and society, and the radical powers of Christianity cannot be pulled apart or reduced to easy schematic interpretations. Precisely their knotted complexity reveals instead how inadequately *Uncle Tom's Cabin* has been understood and how central it is, as a literary and political document, to the American experience.

By the time *Uncle Tom's Cabin* began to appear in serial installments in the abolitionist journal *The National Era* in June 1851, the crisis over slavery in the United States had reached a high pitch. Although Stowe's own account of the novel's inception took different forms, she undeniably wrote in reaction to the Compromise of 1850, the main provisions of which admitted California to the Union as a free state and abolished the slave trade in Washington, D.C., but organized the New Mexico and Utah territories without prohibiting slavery and enacted a Fugitive Slave Law requiring northerners to aid in the return of escaped slaves to their southern masters. Among antislavery forces, the Compromise was seen as a capitulation to the demands of the southern "Slave Power," and the Fugitive Slave Law in particular seemed a hateful extension of the brutalities of slavery beyond its legal borders. Already a published author of light sketches and short domestic stories, Stowe wrote a first tentative response for the *Era* in August 1850 entitled "The Freeman's Dream; A Parable," which told the story of a white man who dreamed he was damned for refusing shelter to a fugitive slave and his family.[11]

Once the Compromise was passed at the end of the year, the fictive dream took palpable form in Stowe's own life. When challenged in a letter from her sister-in-law to "write something that will make this whole nation feel what an accursed thing slavery is," Stowe is said to have risen to her feet and declared, "I *will* write something. I will if I live." In early 1851, she confided to her famous brother, the Reverend Henry Ward Beecher (whose ministry at Plymouth Church in Brooklyn was marked by vigorous antislavery crusading) her desire to write a series of sketches, called "Uncle Tom's Cabin," "to illustrate the cruelties of slavery"; and in a letter to her husband she wrote that she was "projecting a sketch for the *Era* on the capability of liberated blacks to take care of themselves." A month later, during communion service at her church in Brunswick, Maine, Stowe experienced a dramatic awakening, later described by her son: "Suddenly, like the unrolling of a picture, the scene of the death of Uncle Tom passed before her mind. So strongly was she affected that it was with difficulty she could keep from weeping aloud. Immediately on returning home she took pen and paper and wrote out the vision which had been as it were blown into her mind as by the rushing of a mighty wind."[12]

The scene that became the rhetorical climax of *Uncle Tom's Cabin* thus seemed to arise from a deep well of conscience, to be *visionary* in the most exact sense of the term. As Stowe later wrote in an 1879 preface to the novel (speaking of herself in the third person), "she was perfectly overcome by it, and could scarcely restrain the convulsion of tears and sobbing that shook her frame." When she read the scene to her two young sons, "the little fellows broke out into convulsions of weeping, one of them saying, through his sobs, 'Oh! mamma, slavery is the most cursed thing in the world!'"[13] Such a response to the cruelties of slavery would be repeated in various forms throughout the novel – for example, in the scene in which Mrs. Shelby, after her husband has sold Tom to the slave trader Haley, enters the cabin of Tom's family to tell him goodbye:

> "Tom," she said, "I come to – " and stopping suddenly, and regarding the silent group, she sat down in the chair, and, covering her face with her handkerchief, began to sob.
> "Lor, now, Missis, don't – don't!" said Aunt Chloe, bursting out in her turn; and for a few moments they all wept in company. And in those tears they all shed together, the high and the lowly, melted away all the heart-burnings and anger of the oppressed. O, ye who visit the distressed, do ye know that everything your money can buy, given with a cold, averted face, is not worth one honest tear shed in real sympathy? (Chap. 10)[14]

The scene is instructive in that it defines the book's ability to ground a moral lesson in a concrete reality, the tragic destruction of a slave family. Typically, Stowe's own address to the reader is continuous with the implied audience response symbolized by Mrs. Shelby's tears, which break down barriers between lowly slaves and their properly sympathetic masters. In addition, it illustrates the strategy she spoke of when writing in March 1851 to Gamaliel Bailey, the editor of the *Era:* "My vocation is simply that of a painter, and my object will be to hold up in the most lifelike and graphic manner possible Slavery, its reverses, changes, and the negro character, which I have had ample opportunities for studying. There is no arguing with *pictures,* and everybody is impressed by them, whether they mean to be or not."[15]

Uncle Tom's Cabin is filled with such pictures, and there is no doubt that Stowe's readers were impressed by them. When the serial version of the novel began to appear under the title *Uncle Tom's Cabin, Or the Man That Was a Thing* (the subtitle in volume form would be *Life Among the Lowly*), her audience was given to expect a tale that would run about fourteen weekly installments. In the end, it ran for ten months, gaining a steadily larger audience, as new characters and events came to life and as Stowe discovered the pleasures and suspense of serial publication. There is little evidence that the *Era*'s circulation increased much on account of *Uncle Tom's Cabin*, but numerous issues must have been passed from hand to hand. Immediately, fan letters appeared in the *Era* or were addressed to Stowe, claiming to identify the originals of her characters, expressing anguish about the exposed evils of slavery, or berating her for permitting the death of little Eva. Despite the growing demonstration of popular support, book publishers were wary of contracting for an antislavery tale appearing in an obscure journal by a very minor author. The firm Stowe finally found, Jewett and Company of Boston, then had to wait anxiously from September 1851 until April 1852 for the relentless cascade of her story to reach its conclusion. The explosion of sales that followed the publication of *Uncle Tom's Cabin*'s slightly revised two volumes in 1852 shocked everyone except her reading public. Thousands of copies were sold within weeks, and the newly famous author received congratulations from already famous authors like Henry Wadsworth Longfellow and John Whittier, and from politicians like William Seward and Charles Sumner. Although her faulty royalty and copyright arrangements prevented her from making a fortune on the book, Stowe's name and Tom's story were already immortal.

Despite the fact that *Uncle Tom's Cabin* is in important respects a complex work built on complex issues, its popularity owed much to the surface simplicity of its story and to the wealth of moving and detailed pictures the "painter" Harriet Beecher Stowe had promised her editor. Yet Stowe had not had the wide experience with slavery and blacks that her letter suggests, and she appeared willing to ignore a problem of which critics of sentimental literature had long been aware – that simple pictures are easily reduced to stereotypes and, as the scene in Tom's cabin makes clear, might possibly lead to emotional indulgence and a cathartic dispersal of "heart-burnings and anger" in her audience (as in the potentially rebellious slaves in Tom's cabin) rather than to mobilizing action on behalf of the oppressed. The risk lay in the fact that, although Christianity "made it possible for abolitionists to find solace and salvation in the lowly condition of black people," as Ronald Walters has written, it might require a psychological and geographical distance "that allowed abolitionist imaginations to see slavery abstractly, as a moral drama rather than as interaction among real human beings."[16] It is one of the most marked features of *Uncle Tom's Cabin* that its greatest and most effective scenes constantly waver between picture and abstraction. Even so, Stowe understood the inherent power of melodrama to move an audience. And when almost a year later she wrote the final installment of the serial version of the novel, she made no mistake in addressing her readers in a surprising way: "Farewell, dear children, till we meet again." It was not that Stowe imagined children as her only audience (there was ample testimony to the contrary), but rather that she accurately gauged the emotive level at which the story would do its work. As Forrest Wilson has remarked, she had of necessity been writing a "violent and tragic tale, spattered with murder, lust, illicit love, suicide, sadistic torture, profanity, drunkeness [and] barroom brawls" that would "condition a whole generation of children to march in the spirit of crusaders ten years later up to the cannon's mouth."[17]

The untenable claim that *Uncle Tom's Cabin* in any way "caused" the Civil War (Abraham Lincoln is reported to have remarked upon meeting Stowe in 1863, "so this is the little lady who made this big war") must be considered in relation to Stowe's artistic strategies. It must take account as well of the fact that the Christian tradition in which Stowe was raised – as the daughter of one minister, the sister of six, and the wife of yet another – often rendered experience of the temporal world in terms of timeless allegorical or parabolic images whose immediacy and simplicity could conceal complex meanings and require complex responses. *Uncle Tom's Cabin* employs biblical quotation, hymns, sermons, and scriptural emblems to enforce its deepest levels of significance. As Tompkins puts it, Stowe "rewrites the Bible as the story of a Negro slave." If little Eva is represented as a type of Christ, it is because the life of Jesus, properly understood, requires a radical "femininity" and innocence that the institutions of American society have buried under a load of oppression and sophisticated theology; if Tom is represented as a type of Christ, it is because Stowe's story, she later wrote, is meant "to show how Jesus Christ, who liveth and was dead, is now alive and forever-more, has still a mother's love for the poor and lowly, and that no man can sink so low but that Jesus Christ will stoop to take his hand."[18]

The significant events of Stowe's life up to the publication of *Uncle Tom's Cabin* may not appear to have destined her to write the novel, even though the fiery process of her composition sounds apocalyptically conditioned. Born in Litchfield, Connecticut, in 1811, Harriet was the seventh of Lyman Beecher's nine children by his first wife, Roxanna (he had four more with a second wife after Roxanna's death in 1816, an event that affected Harriet deeply and led her to speak often of the important influence of her mother as a moral model). Lyman Beecher was a well-known Presbyterian minister whose moderate antislavery stance emphasized moral suasion, not violent activism, and looked to colonization of freed blacks in Africa as the best solution to America's crisis. Beecher's beliefs grew out of the Calvinistic theology of Jonathan Edwards, which held that man was depraved and dependent upon God's grace for salvation but stressed as well the importance of emotion and the awakening of benevolent human feelings in the process of Christian conversion. Lyman Beecher's lifelong quarrel with the rising liberal theology of New England Unitarians like Ralph Waldo Emerson, Theodore Parker, and William Ellery Channing, the radical abolitionists led by William

Lloyd Garrison, and the more extreme midwestern evangelistic revivalism sparked by Charles Grandison Finney made him representative of battles fought during the shift in American theology away from the more rigid doctrines of Puritanism. Stowe would later chronicle these intellectual and social changes in her father's and her own generation in such novels as *The Minister's Wooing* (1859) and *Oldtown Folks* (1869), which portray the historical decline of New England Puritanism. Rejecting her father's strict adherence to the doctrines of original sin and election while retaining his sense that slavery was representative of man's earthly damnation, Stowe sided finally with the liberals and the revivalists, whose theology demanded active social reform in the service of God. Although the thirteen-year-old Harriet underwent the religious conversion experience required by her father's beliefs in 1824, her devotion to his creed was never rigid. Her letters over the next several years, in fact, reveal melancholy doubts about her own salvation and, at times, overt reaction against the "vehement and absorbing intensity" of the "devotional thought and emotion" that led her to feel that "my mind is exhausted, and seems to be sinking into deadness."[19]

From 1824 to 1832 young Harriet assisted her sister Catharine, a pioneer in women's education, at the Hartford Female Seminary; and she later contributed to several of Catharine's important textbooks when they taught together in Cincinnati, where Lyman Beecher had moved in 1832 to take over the Lane Theological Seminary. Cincinnati during the 1830s and 1840s was a hotbed of antislavery activity and the scene of several bloody race riots. Although a brief visit to Kentucky in 1833 constituted Stowe's only direct experience of the slave South, her family and friends had regular contact with men and women active in the underground railroad, and the Cincinnati press was full of reports about and advertisements for escaped slaves. A number of the stories connected with these experiences would find their way into *Uncle Tom's Cabin*. More significantly, the Lane Theological Seminary was wracked by antislavery controversy. When he found Lyman Beecher's position too moderate, a student named Theodore Weld, influenced by Finney's radicalism, formed the Lane Anti-Slavery Society and, in the face of opposition from Beecher and other Lane conservatives, led away a large number of students to Finney's new divinity school at Oberlin in 1833, a divisive action from which Lane never fully recovered. Prompted in part by the increasingly vocal antislavery beliefs of her brothers William, Edward, and Henry, and even her sister Catharine, and by the family's friendships with influential abolitionists such as James G. Birney, Salmon Chase, and the editor Gamaliel Bailey, Harriet gradually turned against the ineffective and often abstract views of her father and her husband, Calvin Stowe, a Lane professor of religion whom she married in 1836 after the death of his first wife, Eliza, one of Harriet's best friends.

Besides bearing and caring for six children during her years in Cincinnati (and one more in Maine), Stowe became active in local literary clubs, continuing her girlhood readings, which mixed rigorous theology with writers like Milton, Byron, and Scott, and developing writing talents that had been evident in her early life. By the late 1830s she was contributing sketches to annual gift books, as well as to periodicals such as the *Western Monthly Magazine*, the New York *Evangelist*, the *Ladies Repository*, and *Godey's Lady's Book*. In 1843 a group of her New England tales was collected in a volume entitled *The Mayflower*, and in 1845 she wrote a piece on "Immediate Emancipation" for the *Evangelist*. If none of these literary efforts gave an indication of the great power that would be unleashed in Stowe's response to the Fugitive Slave Law, they demonstrated her gradual psychological release from the harsh introspection of Lyman Beecher's Calvinism. Also, the very facts of her career chronicle the double burden faced by a woman writing in the nineteenth century. Her obligations to her family inevitably took first place in her life; her letters are a record of her struggle to find time for writing amid the seemingly endless series of pregnancies and the illnesses and depression that often accompanied them. As though recasting her painful conversion experience of childhood in secular terms, Stowe's desire (echoing Anne Bradstreet and anticipating the more famous expression of Virginia Woolf) to have for her writing "a room for myself, which shall be *my* room," was figured in terms of bondage: "I have determined not to be a mere domestic slave, without even the leisure to excel in my duties. I mean to have money enough to have my house kept in the best manner and yet to have time for reflection and that preparation for the education of my children which every mother needs." In early 1847, burdened by domestic duties to the point of a severe depression of the kind that afflicted a number of women in the nineteenth century, Stowe underwent hydrotherapy at a sanitarium in Brattleboro, Vermont. The treatment improved her physiologically; it also led her to demand of Calvin Stowe more freedom from family cares.[20] Along with the Cincinnati cholera epidemic that carried off their son Charles in 1849 (an event of great personal pain that would be portrayed by Stowe in the scenes of childhood death in *Uncle Tom's Cabin*), the therapeutic cure of Stowe's "hysteria" eventuated in Calvin's resettlement in 1850 at Bowdoin College in Maine and must be seen to lie behind the feminine release from domestic enslavement that her great novel would initimate – even if, like Stowe herself, it remained committed to the ideal of maternal nurture and care.

Surrounded by a family of ministers, Stowe was a first-hand witness to the declining political power of the clergy and its post–Revolutionary War displacement into the growing fields of evangelistic and secular social reform.[21] Although Christianity is at its heart, *Uncle Tom's Cabin* attacks the explicit or implied support of slavery by institutionalized religion in its allusion to the Beecher family friend Joel Parker, the "American divine" who tells us that slavery "has *'no evils but such as are inseparable from any other relations in social and domestic life' '*"; and then again in the example of Marie St. Clare's clergyman, who preaches the standard pro-slavery line that "some should be high and some low, and that some were born to rule and some to serve" (Chaps. 12, 16). It was such views, North and South, that Frederick Douglass had in mind when he wrote in the blistering appendix to *Narrative of the Life of Frederick Douglass* (1845): "Revivals of religion and revivals in the slave-trade go hand in hand together. . . . The clanking of fetters and the rattling of chains in the prison, and the pious psalm and solemn prayer in the church, may be heard at the same time. The dealers in the bodies and souls of men erect their stand in the presence of the pulpit, and they mutually help each other." Stowe wrote Douglass in 1851, during the serialization of *Uncle Tom's Cabin*, that she found his view rather harsh; she also asked Douglass for information about slave life that might prove useful to her novel, a request that apparently went unanswered.[22] But there are no portraits of the church in *Uncle Tom's Cabin* that run counter to Douglass's charges.

That the role of the church in the antislavery movement was vexing is evident enough in Stowe's novel. But her response to the problem was also troubled by the advocacy of nonviolence. Even Garrison, the prime advocate of nonviolent tactics, who once nominated Jesus Christ for president, found in her book a replica of his own confusion:

> We are curious to know whether Mrs. Stowe is a believer in the duty of non-resistance for the white man, under all possible outrage and peril, as well as for the black man. . . . When [slaves] are spit upon and buffeted, outraged and oppressed, talk not then of a non-resisting Savior — it is fanaticism! . . . Talk not of servants being obedient to their masters — let the blood of the tyrants flow! How is this to be explained or reconciled? Is there one law of submission and non-resistance for the black man, and another law of rebellion and conflict for the white man? When it is the whites who are trodden in the dust, does Christ justify them in taking up arms to vindicate their rights? And when it is the blacks who are thus treated, does Christ require them to be patient, harmless, long-suffering, and forgiving? And are there two Christs?[23]

Because Garrison and other radical social reformers tended to distrust or reject the institutions around them, however, their efforts risked utopian isolation from reality. Like many of them, Stowe, in attacking existing institutions while disavowing violent resistance, emphasized an appeal to individual conscience as the source of eventual collective perfection. Yet such a strategy threatened to make slavery a guilt-ridden conundrum admitting of no clear political solution.[24] In *Uncle Tom's Cabin*, Stowe's focus on individual acts of conscience primarily ascribed to women is an attempt to surmount such barriers by finding in the feminine perfection of the heart an elementary path beyond the reasoned abstractions of the head.

As Stowe's experiences of underground railroad activities in Cincinnati and her pursuit of sentimental literature proved, the individual act of conscience could be united with public action — perhaps in a more fruitful way than many of her more famous literary peers in the antebellum years realized. Even though she was active in local literary circles before her fame in the 1850s, Stowe appears to have been largely unaffected by the antislavery opinion of other major literary figures. But this is due in part to their relative reticence on the subject. Emerson spoke out in important addresses like "Emancipation in the British West Indies" (1844) and "The Fugitive Slave Law" (1851); and Thoreau attacked the Mexican War as a proslavery ruse in "Civil Disobedience" (1849), excoriated the Compromise in "Slavery in Massachusetts" (1854), and celebrated John Brown's assault on Harper's Ferry in "A Plea for Captain John Brown" (1859). Longfellow, Lowell, Holmes, and especially Whittier wrote important antislavery verse, as did Whitman, whose brilliant war poems collected in *Drum-Taps* (1865) were a record of America's deep wounds, healed and purified in the terrible war for reunion. In several short stories and in *The Narrative of Arthur Gordon Pym* (1838), Poe wrote ambiguously about racial hysteria. Hawthorne's views, as in his campaign biography of Franklin Pierce (1852) or his essay "Chiefly About War Matters" (1862), can only be interpreted as moderately proslavery, whereas Melville, both in his later war poems collected in *Battle-Pieces* (1866) and in the explosively enigmatic story "Benito Cereno" (1855), vehemently attacked slavery but concealed his vision in complicated allegory.

In contrast to the "inner civil war" waged by northern intellectuals and the paucity of major literary works produced by this strangely "unwritten war" (to cite the titles of two important studies of the subject),[25] the tradition of antislavery literature to which Stowe would be assigned has until recently played only a minor role in definitions of the period's great literature; but it too seems to have offered Stowe few resources for her own process of composition. Aside from family experience and discussion, and her own inspired vision, the major source for the details of *Uncle Tom's Cabin* was probably Weld's *American Slavery As It Is* (1839), a widely read collection of statements by slaveholders and extracts from advertisements, newspapers, and legal documents on which Stowe drew extensively when she wrote her documentary defense of the novel, *A Key to Uncle Tom's Cabin,* in 1853. In the *Key* and elsewhere, Stowe herself noted parallels to her work in the lives and slave narratives of Henry Bibb, William Wells Brown, Solomon Northup, Frederick Douglass, Josiah Henson, and Lewis Clarke; the last two men built careers on the now dubious claims that they were Stowe's models for Uncle Tom and George Harris. Although their exact influence on Stowe is equally open to question, there were at least a dozen antislavery novels and many shorter tales published before *Uncle Tom's Cabin*. Some texts, like John Greenleaf Whittier's *The Narrative of James Williams* (1838), nearly became fiction when the slave's story was fashioned into a narrative by the white writer. The most famous novel (taken by many at the time to be an authentic narrative), Richard Hildreth's *The Slave, or Memoirs of Archy Moore* (1836), offers a number of potential parallels in plot and character to *Uncle Tom's Cabin* that are, if anything, watered down and undermined by Stowe. The mulatto Archy and his wife Cassy may lie behind George and Eliza Harris, but their lives end in tragic separation. The black slave Tom, at first religious and obedient, becomes a fugitive rebel after witnessing the flogging death of his wife at the hands of an overseer; tracked down by the overseer, Tom calmly murders him. In Hildreth's novel, as in most authentic slave narratives, the Christianity and domesticity valued by Stowe are shown to be thoroughly corrupted by plantation life.[26]

Whatever the sources of Stowe's novel in previous antislavery fiction or slave narratives, it is evident that works that followed hers often responded directly to it. For example, Northup, in *Twelve Years a Slave* (1853), and Douglass, in his revised autobiography, *My Bondage and My Freedom* (1855), explicitly invoke (and implicitly criticize) the novel and its main character. Northup writes:

> Men may write fictions portraying lowly life as it is, or as it is not — may expatiate with owlish gravity upon the bliss of ignorance — discourse flippantly from arm chairs of the pleasures of slave life; but let them toil with him in the field — sleep with him in the cabin — feed with him on husks; let them behold him scourged, hunted, trampled on. . . . Let them know the *heart* of the poor slave — learn his secret thoughts — thoughts he dare not utter in the hearing of the white man . . . and they will find that ninety-nine out of every hundred are intelligent enough to understand their situation, and to cherish in their bosoms the love of freedom, as passionately as themselves.[27]

Douglass presents an even more striking case. As though in response to Stowe's request for information about slave life, both the heightened drama of his violent resistance to the slave breaker Covey and his harsher attack on the corruption of the black family under slavery in *My Bondage and My Freedom* seem deliberately to take Stowe's main themes in a more aggressive direction. When he remarks that "scenes of sacred tenderness, around the deathbed, never forgotten, and which often arrest the vicious and confirm the virtuous during life, must be looked for among the free," or that because the "image of [my mother] is mute, and I have not striking words of her's treasured up . . . I had to learn the value of my mother long after her death, and by witnessing the devotion of other mothers to their children,"[28] Douglass suggests the limitations of Stowe's vision even as he gives further ammunition to her attack on the destruction of the family. Douglass's turn toward an advocacy of violent slave rebellion by the 1850s and Stowe's lukewarm response to his 1853 letter requesting aid in establishing a black educational program in manual arts (a project in which she had claimed to be interested) further indicate the differences between the two greatest literary figures of the antislavery crusade.

If the sources of *Uncle Tom's Cabin* are open to debate, its instrumental role in the abolitionist cause is beyond question. When it appeared in book form in 1852, 50,000 copies were sold within eight weeks, 300,000 within a year, and 1 million in America and England combined by early 1853. It added an entirely new dimension to a campaign that had often bogged down in internecine quarrels and useless theorizing. By giving flesh-and-blood reality to the inhuman system for which the Fugitive Slave Law now required the North, as well as the South, to be responsible, it became a touchstone for antislavery sentiment. Stowe was hardly the first to call attention to slavery's destruction of both black and white families, but her novel perfectly combined the tradition of the sentimental novel and the rhetoric of antislavery polemic. In scene after scene, the fragmentation of black households and the corrosive moral effect on white conscience is her focal point. When Lucy's child is sold by the unfeeling Haley, for example, Stowe writes bitterly: "You can get used to such things, too, my friend; and it is the great object of recent efforts to make our whole northern community used to them, for the glory of the Union.'' And when Lucy then commits suicide, Stowe adds: ''the woman had escaped into a state which *never will* give up a fugitive, – not even at the demand of the whole glorious Union'' (Chap. 12).

The irony, which Stowe well understood, was that the Compromise of 1850 was itself founded on a notion of ''sentiment'' in that the preservation of the Union – in the face of increasing demands on the part of the South for slavery's extension – was seen to be critical to America's still young experiment in democracy. Whereas antislavery radicals such as Garrison demanded that the North adopt a policy of disunion from the South, more practical northern leaders like Daniel Webster were willing to sacrifice the revolutionary ideals of freedom to ward off the social and economic chaos of a political division of the country. Webster and others appealed to the founding fathers, whose views on slavery embodied in the Constitution (despite the vision of equality announced in the Declaration of Independence) were ambiguous, open to both proslavery and antislavery interpretation. In doing so, they conceived of America as a social family presided over by benevolent fathers, one in which an inevitably hierarchical structure of white men ruling over women, blacks, and children was the norm. Still, the national cult of the fathers centered on George Washington, which developed around the popular ideal of mothers instructing their children in the virtues of America's greatest father figure (even Uncle Tom's cabin contains his rude portrait over the fireplace), presented ambiguities of parental power open to antislavery exploitation. The sketch concerning liberated blacks about which Stowe had written her husband in early 1851 turned into ''The Two Altars, or, Two Pictures in One,'' which ironically compared the sacrifices of a family for the Revolutionary cause at Valley Forge to the 1850 sacrifice of a fugitive slave on the ''altar of liberty'' in accordance with the Fugitive Slave Law. All sides appealed to the wisdom of the founding fathers on the question of slavery, and all found support for their views, not least because Washington and Jefferson, among others, had been slaveholders themselves. Not until Abraham Lincoln broke the impasse by preserving the Union and at the same time destroying slavery was the paralyzing ambiguity of the American Revolutionary tradition, now passed through the furnace of civil war, overcome.[29]

Uncle Tom's Cabin unites the uses of sentiment in literature and in politics; in doing so, it provisionally challenges the patriarchal model on which the sentiment of union was based. The domestic tradition in fiction and in social thought declared women to be the moral superiors of men but at the same time attributed to them specific characteristics of sensitivity, docility, and weakness. Drawing into itself the faltering powers of the clergy, the domestic tradition separated the "woman's sphere" of homemaking and the moral instruction of children from the masculine world of commerce and politics. However, it also risked providing a new rationale for the subordination of women. Because the sentimental family acted as an ordering structure in place of the "natural hierarchy" that had been shaken by the birth of liberal individualism and bourgeois capitalism, the home itself could become a kind of prison, and by the same token the rebelling woman could appear a traitor to the values and needs of her family. *Uncle Tom's Cabin* hangs on this paradox. For if it acts out (in the words of Constance Rourke) "deep-laid patterns of escape, bondage, and rebellion" that included for Stowe not just slavery and the Calvinist dogma of her father, but also the bondage of women within the domestic ideal, the novel is in each case ambivalent about the limits and means of such rebellion.[30]

From the 1820s to the 1840s, the domestic ideal merged with rising social reform movements, tentatively seeking a moral role for women that would move beyond the confines of the home and utilize their seemingly greater access to Christian virtue to correct the ills of society evident in drinking, gambling, prostitution, crime, and – most of all – slavery. Not only men but women themselves were divided over the proper limits of their role in reform causes, fearing corruption of their delicate sensibilities. Catharine Beecher, for example, eschewed women's direct involvement in politics. In her *Essay on Slavery and Abolitionism* (1837), she denounced abolitionist societies for their public stridency; and carefully separating the duties of men from those of women, she warned that woman's deviation from the place she "is appointed to fill by the dispensations of heaven" would deprive children of their proper moral instruction and subvert the cause of reform: "For the more intelligent a woman becomes, the more she can appreciate the wisdom of that ordinance that appointed her subordinate station, and the more her taste will conform to the graceful and dignified retirement and submission it involves."[31] Angelina and Sarah Grimké, southern Quaker sisters who were vocal abolitionists, wrote powerful replies to Stowe's sister, advocating women's public activism in the antislavery cause. In 1840, a quarrel over Garrison's proposal to place a woman on the executive committee of the American Anti-Slavery Society so splintered abolitionist ranks, some historians have argued, that the campaign against slavery was set back by a decade. Later in the year, the World Anti-Slavery Convention in London refused to admit women delegates from the United States; but two of them, Lucretia Mott and Elizabeth Cady Stanton, immediately resolved to launch a women's rights movement, and the 1848 Seneca Falls convention was the eventual result.[32]

The place of Stowe and her novel in the argument over women's role in reform is not perfectly clear. During debate about the Kansas-Nebraska Act (which was passed in 1854 and seemed a further conciliation of southern slavery interests) she announced her position thus:

> Women of the free States! the question is not shall we remonstrate with slavery on its own soil, but are we willing to receive slavery into the free States and Territories of this Union? . . .
>
> And now you ask, What can the *women* of a country do?
>
> O women of the free States! what did your brave mothers do in the days of our Revolution? Did not liberty in those days feel the strong impulse of woman's heart? . . .
>
> The first duty of every American woman at this time is to thoroughly understand the subject for herself, and to feel that she is bound to use her influence for the right. Then they can obtain signatures to petitions to our national legislature. They can spread information upon this vital topic throughout their neighborhoods. They can employ lecturers to lay the subject before the people. They can circulate the speeches of their members of Congress that bear upon the subject, and in many others ways they can secure to all a full understanding of the present position of our country.
>
> Above all, it seems to be necessary and desirable that we should make this subject a matter of earnest prayer.[33]

If Stowe's appeal stops somewhat short of the full activism Mott and Stanton proposed (will women, or only men, be employed as lecturers?), it nevertheless appears to surpass the concluding chapter of *Uncle Tom's Cabin*, which answers the question of what a woman or any individual can do: "they can see to it that *they feel right*" (Chap. 45). Although she also calls for the education of free blacks and escaped slaves in her final chapter, it is certain that the influence of women in the novel is largely restricted to the "woman's sphere" of Christian example and moral instruction.

From the perspective of feminist activism, *Uncle Tom's Cabin* is moderate. Stowe would probably not have agreed with Susan B. Anthony, who once counseled a mother to steal her child from its abusive father: "does not the law of the United States give the slave holder the ownership of the slave? And don't you break the law every time you help a slave to Canada? Well, the law which gives the father the sole ownership of the children is just as wicked, and I'll break it just as quickly." But the great emotive power of her novel arises time and again from its capacity to equate the victimization of slaves and women (with children, a third supposedly oppressed group, linking the two), to play upon the potential conversion of sentiment into action adumbrated by another abolitionist, Lydia Maria Child. Both women and blacks, Child wrote, "are characterized by affection more than intellect; both have a strong development of the religious sentiment; both . . . have a tendency to submission; and hence, both have been kept in subjection by physical force, and considered rather in the light of property, than as individuals."[34] Child's characterization pinpoints those attributes that radical feminists rejected and that led Stowe to depict some of her black characters in postures of submissiveness, but it also clarifies the moral role ascribed to women and blacks in the novel. Although the ethical influence of wives and mothers often fails in *Uncle Tom's Cabin*, it sometimes succeeds as well. The recent critics who have designated Tom himself as the novel's primary Victorian "suffering heroine" have done so in order to locate in Stowe's protagonist her basic argument "that home and mother must not figure as sanctuaries from the world but as imperative models for its reconstruction."[35] Were such a reconstitution to succeed throughout the Union, Stowe implies, not only slavery but the whole host of problems attributable to male "lust" and patriarchal governance in politics and in the family itself would disappear. The book must therefore be located midway between the moderate position of woman's "influence" and the more radical position of feminist "power."

Stowe's presentation of a range of home models – on a scale running from Rachel Halliday's ordered, maternal Quaker home and kitchen down through the disordered chaos of Dinah's kitchen at Marie St. Clare's (which Ophelia must set aright) to the drunken hell of Legree's virtual house of prostitution, its walls defaced by "slops of beer and wine" and the arithmetical sums of his slaveholding commerce (Chaps. 13, 18, 35) – shows the progressive failure of maternal influence. In each instance, the domestic model projects a political model of nationhood and implies a final refuge with, or judgment by, God. In a remarkable essay entitled "Can the Immortality of the Soul Be Proved by the Light of Nature?", composed when she was twelve years old, Stowe herself had written that the Gospel reveals that man is "destined, after this earthly house of his tabernacle is dissolved, to an inheritance incorruptible, undefiled, and that fadeth not away, to a house not made with hands, eternal in the heavens."[36] For St. Clare and for Tom, such a heaven is the "home" to which they escape from the house of earthly bondage (Chaps. 28, 33). Purified of evil, the American home would create a millennial heaven on earth; at the least, it would stop slavery and repair the "House Divided," in the popular New Testament image Lincoln invoked in a famous speech on the destructive sectional conflict over slavery.

The division in Stowe's houses rests both on slavery and on sexual roles. In extremity, the two are yoked together in the problem of slaveholding sexual abuse and its resulting miscegenation. The southern diarist Mary Chesnut was perhaps right when she sarcastically remarked that "Mrs. Stowe did not hit the sorest spot. She makes Legree a bachelor," but Stowe's exploitation of the already conventional "tragic mulatto" theme (whatever questions it can be seen to raise for her depiction of George Harris) went to the heart of bondage.[37] Like a slaveholding version of Poe's House of Usher, Legree's decayed mansion symbolizes tragic sexual perversion. In her story of Cassy's mistreatment at the hands of white masters (leading even to infanticide as the ultimate act of rebellion against slavery) and its climax in escape through her terrorizing of Legree in the ghostly garments of his "mother's shroud," Stowe makes the gothic novel the primary stage of antislavery sentiment (Chap. 42). Along with the fiction of other white writers, novels by black women, such as Harriet Wilson's *Our Nig* (1859), set in the North, and Harriet Jacobs's *Incidents in the Life of a Slave Girl* (1860), set in the South, testified as well to the rape and abuse of black women. Like *Uncle Tom's Cabin,* they supported the abolitionist charge that slavery and sexual violation were inseparable and that the plantation could become an arena of erotic dissipation and male lust, a "cage of obscene birds"[38] that scandalized the most intimate affections of the domestic ideal by revealing the painful hierarchy upon which it was built.

There is more to be said about Stowe's handling of the question of miscegenation. But we may note again that although *Uncle Tom's Cabin* conforms to the model of moral instruction (especially as it is directed toward an audience of children), its gothic exploration of licentious behavior surpasses "influence" in a decidedly public act that can be construed, at least provisionally, as a revolutionary attack on the masculine world. In this respect, Stowe's divergence from her sister must be thought of in the context of Beecher's *Treatise on Domestic Economy.* Appearing in 1841, the *Treatise* joined the moral influence of woman in the home to the millennial regeneration of the world American democracy promised. Women would play a crucial role in that regeneration by subordinating themselves to men and thus contributing to the civil and political stability necessary to build "a glorious temple, whose base shall be coextensive with the bounds of the earth, whose summit shall pierce the skies, [and] whose splendor shall beam on all lands."[39] Beecher's domestic version of "manifest destiny," because it promotes the central claims of America's male Anglo-Saxon superiority, sidesteps just those issues Stowe attempted to meet head-on.

If "New World slavery," as David Brion Davis has written, "provided Protestant Christianity with an epic stage for vindicating itself as the most liberal and progressive force in history,"[40] America's moral mission, as antislavery forces insisted, would have to begin at home – home in the sense of nation and in the sense of family as its proper model. "You see the men, how they are willing to sell shamelessly the happiness of countless generations of fellow-creatures, the honor of their country, and their immortal souls, for a money market and political power," wrote Margaret Fuller in *Woman in the Nineteenth Century* (1845). In thus attacking the annexation of Texas and the extension of slavery it would promote, Fuller took a stance similar to Stowe's: "Do you not feel within you that which can reprove them, which can check, which can convince them? You would not speak in vain; whether each in her own home, or banded in unison. . . . Let not slip the occasion, but do something to lift off the curse incurred by Eve."[41] An advocate of "power" rather than "influence," Fuller is ambivalent (not to say schizophrenic) in her allusion to Eve (not Adam) as the source of original sin and its purported contemporary embodiment in the curse of masculine aggression and slavery. Bypassing the question of original sin and the Calvinistic tradition of her father, Stowe embraces the New Testament and takes literally the saving power of Jesus – but depicts him, in essence, as a woman. Besides Tom, her critical Christ figure is Eva: a child, a female, a typological figuring of Christ descended not from Adam but from Eve, and – as her full name, Evangeline, implies – the book's most powerful evangelist.

In Eva are united the ministerial leader of evangelistic social reform and the prime actor in sentimental literature, the child. The proliferation of children in antislavery literature – and in books and journals specifically directed at children, such as *The Child's Anti-Slavery Book* and *Anti-Slavery Alphabet* – assumed that, instead of needing moral instruction, children were perhaps best equipped to give it. Asexual and uncorrupted, the child, like Eva, was often imagined to be the "only true democrat" (Chap. 16), and its innate morality would, like Eva's, offer a perfect Christian example. As Ronald Walters has suggested, the figure of the child could enact a tension "between the human nature to be liberated and that to be repressed. . . . the spirituality of the slave matched against the lustful tyranny of the master [could be dramatized in] the innocent good will of the child played off against the brutal insensitivity of the adult."[42] If the child and the slave (and women) were imagined to be "imprisoned" in the family, the most conventional, conservative domain of sentiment could appear as the primary locus of needed reform. Consider Topsy's minstrel catechism with Ophelia:

> "You mustn't answer me in that way, child; I'm not playing with you. Tell me where you were born, and who your mother and father were."
>
> "Never was born," reiterated the creature, more emphatically; "never had no father nor mother, nor nothing. I was raised by a speculator, with lots of others. . . ."
>
> "Have you ever heard anything about God, Topsy? . . . Do you know who made you? . . ."
>
> "I spect I grow'd. Don't think nobody never made me." (Chap. 20)

Hidden within this comic scene is one of Stowe's most incisive critiques of the holding and raising of the slave family as property and its degradation of childlike innocence and faith. The antislavery tradition of "benevolence," which elevated feeling above reason and advocated the democratic extension of rights to the lowliest members of society, sought to put into practice the radical doctrines of equality generated in the age of revolution by bridging what David Brion Davis has called the "immense gulf between literary pathos and dedicated reform, between the ideal of moral refinement and a willingness to liberate the uncultivated forces of nature." As Davis notes as well, the conventional antislavery symbols of heartless master and lamenting slave depended upon "attitudes which had first been learned in the theater or in an idle hour of reading [being] transferred to the grim stage of reality."[43] Mediating between master and slave is the figure of the child – a "slave" itself, but morally superior to its parents and masters.

Eva's pious life and death, then, are not simply ornamental melodrama; as an emblem of the novel's incorporation of popular narratives of religious conversion, they are central to Stowe's evangelistic message. Although it would become ludicrously stylized in later stage versions of *Uncle Tom's Cabin* (a sign of its great popularity with readers), the scene of Eva's death is the primary example of Stowe's attempt to construct a bridge between pathos and reform. The scene is therapeutic in that it *might* only burn off the reader's charged sympathies or direct them away from the issue of slavery into the cul-de-sac of sentimental indulgence; but it *may* also provide, in the only way possible, a suitable representation of the reader's transfiguration of emotion into antislavery action of the kind Eva's Christlike role would entail. Significantly, when St. Clare and Ophelia watch the dying Eva enact the conversion of Topsy ("a ray of heavenly love had penetrated the darkness of her heathen soul! . . . while the beautiful child, bending over her, looked like the picture of some bright angel stooping to reclaim a sinner"), they do so by lifting a "curtain," as though the room were a children's stage, its edifying actions witnessed by morally flawed adults. And the later gathering of family and slaves around Eva's deathbed to hear her final sermon ("You must remember that each one of you can become angels forever. . . . If you want to be Christians, Jesus will help you") enforces the fact that the readers of Stowe's story and the audience encircling the child evangelist have been fused (Chaps. 25, 26). Subsuming the failed power of institutional religion into the realm of sentimental social reform, Eva's death belongs to the period's enormous literature of mourning and consolation[44] but transcends its simple pieties as Stowe seeks out a new world of power by reconceiving Christian man in the image of a beatific child–woman.

Because he dies before he can act on his daughter's advice and free his slaves, Augustine St. Clare may be the book's most tragic white figure. Embodying the South's spiritual enervation, he fails to heed the example of his mother, refigured now in the ministerial Eva, and inadvertently sets in motion the climactic horrors of Tom's life under Legree. The range of violent probabilities explored in the last third of the novel is also anticipated in St. Clare's discussion with his brother of the question of revolution. Invoking the "divine law" behind the rise of oppressed "masses" — whether European peasants or American slaves — St. Clare forecasts a rebellion in the South comparable to the revolt of Haitian slaves in the late eighteenth century. In mixing Christian millennialism with the liberal ideology of revolution, however, St. Clare subscribes to the split between *African* docility and *mulatto* aggressiveness that Stowe's own differing characterizations of Tom and George Harris

27

demand. When his brother rejects the model of the revolt in Haiti (San Domingo), remarking that "the Anglo Saxon is the dominant race of the world, and *is to be so,"* St. Clare responds that "there is a pretty fair infusion of Anglo Saxon blood among our slaves, now, [and] . . . if ever the San Domingo hour comes, Anglo Saxon blood will lead on the day. Sons of white fathers, with all our haughty feelings burning in their veins, will not always be bought and sold and traded. They will rise, and raise with them their mother's race" (Chap. 23).

St. Clare's statement brings into focus a number of the main themes and questions of *Uncle Tom's Cabin*. To the South, the San Domingo revolt was an event of bloodshed and horror that prompted periodic discussions of the possibility of a similar fate for American slaveholders. After Nat Turner's murderous slave rebellion in Virginia in 1831, southern attitudes became increasingly reactionary, and rigid measures designed to prevent slave unrest increased.[45] Stowe's own novel *Dred* (1856) modeled its black titular hero on Turner (but failed to reenact his revolt), and Turner's purported "Confessions," the primary source of Stowe's novel, depicted him as a fanatical religious prophet emboldened by bloody heavenly visions of "white spirits and black spirits engaged in battle."[46] However, such a characterization worked both to inflame and to quiet southern apprehensions, for Turner could easily be seen as a freak and his rebellion as a deviation from the normal docility of the slave population. Likewise, if the mulatto George Harris is a potential Nat Turner, the black Tom certainly is not.

The seemingly polarized slave types represented in Nat Turner and Uncle Tom have recently received more subtle consideration by John Blassingame, who argues that many slaves developed what amounted to a double personality. Refining upon the arguments of an often acrimonious debate over whether southern slaves, dehumanized by a brutal regime, developed a "Sambo" personality (that is, an ingrained personality of weakness and submissiveness), Blassingame suggests that the Sambo role was a mask or ritual act often adopted by slaves to guard against brutality, and that the willingness of masters to accept the slave's masked behavior at face value grew from deep psychological and social necessity. Southerners, Blassingame writes, were

> compelled to portray the slave as Sambo because of their need to disprove the allegations of antislavery novelists. Facing the withering attack of abolitionists, they had to prove that slavery was not an unmitigated evil. The loyal contented slave was a *sine qua non* in Southern literary propaganda. . . . With Nat Turner perennially in the wings, the creation of Sambo was almost mandatory for the Southerner's emotional security. . . . This public stereotype only partially hid a multitude of private fears, which reached the proportion of mass hysteria at the mere mention of the word "rebellion."[47]

Leaving aside for the moment Stowe's own acceptance of the stereotype, we can note that the numerous novelistic replies to *Uncle Tom's Cabin* claimed that Stowe had misconceived the benevolent paternalism of southern slaveholding and pointed out that Legree was a northerner (and thus an exception to the norm of kind southern masters). Southern novelists and essayists often maintained as well that northern wage labor was far more vicious than southern chattel slavery. Drawing on this contrast, novels such as Mary H. Eastman's *Aunt Phillis' Cabin* (1852), Caroline Rush's *North and South* (1852), William Smith's *Life at the South* (1852), John Page's *Uncle Robin in His Cabin in Virginia and Tom Without One in Boston* (1853), and Thomas Thorpe's *The Master's House* (1854) depicted slaves as content with their lot. The deathbed scene of the old slave Phillis in Eastman's novel, for example, shows Phillis telling her master *not* to free her children, who are well cared for on the plantation and will suffer in the North or in Liberia. Because the tearful scene also forecasts a reunion of slave and master in heaven, where "the distinctions of this world will be forgotten," it testifies to the planters' need to rationalize slavery but at the same time mitigate the sin that they implicitly recognized to lie within it.[48] In William Gilmore Simms's *Woodcraft* (1854), a novel set in the aftermath of the American Revolution but alluding to the potential civil conflict between South and North, the relationship between the main character, the planter Porgy, and his trusted slave, Tom, is one of benevolent affection. Porgy says he will shoot Tom "in order to save him" from the

29

hostile forces that would carry him off (he even tells Tom to kill himself to prevent capture), and Tom says to Porgy: "Ef I doesn't b'long to *you*, *you* b'longs to *me!* . . . so, maussa, don't you bodder me wid dis nonsense t'ing 'bout free paper any more. I's well off whar' I is I tell you."[49]

Such fictional replies to Stowe entirely buried the potential Nat figure beneath the Sambo facade. Proponents of slavery as a political and economic system took a similar tack. Thomas R. Dew, writing in the wake of Turner's revolt, argued that abolitionist calls for emancipation were "based upon false principles, and assumptions of the most vicious and alarming kind, subversive of the rights of property and the order and tranquillity of society. . . . They are admirably calculated to excite plots, murders, and insurrections," and will prompt in the slave a desire "to gain that fatal freedom whose blessings he does not comprehend." Similarly, William Harper maintained that "the virtues of a freeman would be the vices of slaves. To submit to a blow, would be degrading to a freeman, because he is the protector of himself. It is not degrading to a slave – neither is it to a priest or woman." In demanding rhetorically whether one would "do a benefit to the horse or the ox, by giving him a cultivated understanding or fine feelings," Harper echoed George Fitzhugh's *Cannibals All!*, which carefully argued that the labor system of northern capitalism was less free and more inhumane than southern slavery: "It invades every recess of domestic life, infects its food, its clothing, its drink, its very atmosphere, and pursues the hireling, from the hovel to the poorhouse, the prison and the grave." Citing the fact that God had authorized slavery and that "human law cannot beget benevolence, affection, [or] maternal and paternal love," Fitzhugh summed up the hierarchical principles that supported slaveholding paternalism:

> Within the family circle, the law of love prevails, not that of selfishness.
>
> But, besides wife and children, brothers and sister, dogs, horses, birds and flowers – slaves, also, belong to the family circle. Does their common humanity, their abject weakness and dependence, their great value, their ministering to our wants in childhood, man-

hood, sickness, and old age, cut them off from that affection which everything else in the family elicits? No; the interests of master and slave are bound up together, and each in his appropriate sphere naturally endeavors to promote the happiness of the other.[50]

Such a view takes the separation of sexual and racial "spheres" to an extreme, revealing both the great suppression of the facts of slave life to which the South could be driven and the deepest source of southern anxieties about *Uncle Tom's Cabin*. Stowe's novel, at least from the southern point of view, appeared to assault not just slavery but the hierarchy of the family and the economic structure of America itself, both of which could be seen (as Fitzhugh suggested) as requiring differing forms of "enslavement." Because "exponents of domesticity defined the home as a peaceful order in contrast to the disorder and fluctuations occasioned by competitive economic activity in the marketplace," Gillian Brown points out, the "ultimate adversary to mothers and housekeepers is not slavery, not even capitalism, but the masculine sphere of the marketplace . . . not only the patriarchal institution, but nineteenth-century patriarchy."[51] Requested by the editor of the *Southern Literary Messenger* to write a review "as hot as hell fire, blasting and searing the reputation of the vile wretch in petticoats who could write such a volume," George Holmes responded with an attack on Stowe's novel that reached the heart of the matter:

> If it was capable of proving anything at all, it would prove too much. It would demonstrate that all order, law, government, society was a flagrant and unjustifiable violation of the rights and mockery of the feelings of man. . . . The fundamental position, then, of these dangerous and dirty little volumes is a deadly blow to all the interests and duties of humanity, and is utterly impotent to show any inherent vice in the institution of slavery which does not also appertain to all other existing institutions whatever.[52]

At the same time, however, a moderate essay in the *North American Review* suggested that the novel implicitly proved that kind masters like Shelby and St. Clare were the southern norm; that although the abolition of the holding of slaves as property was desirable, freedom for slaves "would be like freedom to children, or to domestic animals," and a governmental paternalism that recognized the slave's right "to be governed for his own benefit" was the only answer.[53]

Between these conflicting interpretations of Stowe's novel lies the burden of its ambiguity on the question of the family as a model. Does *Uncle Tom's Cabin* in fact subvert all patriarchal and paternalistic order, or does it – rephrasing the distinction between women's influence and women's power in other terms – allow for a different, less harsh form of paternalistic governance? The majority of northerners were apprehensive about the effects of emancipation. Like the Free Soil Party (which became the basis for the Republican Party in the 1850s and eventually propelled Lincoln into the White House), they often wanted to *limit* the spread of slavery in order to protect free white labor in newly organized territories and often feared that freedom for blacks would provoke a wave of miscegenation and social and economic chaos. Like Stowe, they tended to be "romantic racialists" who believed blacks innately inferior to whites in political and social terms, but perhaps superior to them in their affections and natural Christian virtues; as a result, they often endorsed colonization schemes to deport freed slaves to their "own" nations in Africa or the Caribbean.[54] The limits of abolitionist idealism must be seen in these terms, not least because *Uncle Tom's Cabin* itself is infused with them.

When Tom is sold to Haley, he advises George Shelby, his young master, to "be a good Mas'r, like yer father; and be a good Christian, like yer Mother." This scene, along with Stowe's depiction of the African race (especially Tom) as "home-loving and affectionate," "naturally patient, timid and unenterprising," and typified by "much kindliness and benevolence," opens precisely the possibility that many southern (and some northern) critics seized upon in claiming that Afro-Americans could not survive outside the paternalistic protection of slavery unless they were shipped off to another country (Chaps. 10, 4). Young George, of course, later becomes an even better master than Tom had advised. Even though he arrives at Legree's plantation too late to save Tom from death, he releases the contained rage that Stowe's portrayal of Tom's agony has instilled in the reader: "George turned, and, with one indignant blow, knocked Legree flat on his face; and, as he stood over him, blazing with wrath and defiance, he would have formed no bad personification of his great namesake triumphing over the dragon" (Chap. 41). George goes on to free his family's slaves (who stay on the plantation as free laborers); but the gap between the violent act and the benevolent liberation is one that Stowe's novel can bridge in only a limited way, and George Shelby's wrath, like George Harris's violent patriotic sentiments, is not allowed to become a primary model for the reader's own potential actions.

Tom's own martyrdom is not by any means a Sambo act. For one thing, he is murdered for refusing to betray Cassy and Emmeline and for refusing to capitulate to Legree's demand that he renounce his Christian beliefs. His death results from his aggressive nonviolence, and Stowe's figuring of him as the book's second Christ figure alerts us once again to the extraordinary power she intended the Christian ideal to offer. At the same time, however, Tom cannot help but be seen in contrast to the mulatto George Harris, whose infusion of "white blood" (as St. Clare puts it in speaking of San Domingo) makes him at once rebellious and patriotic. Harris conforms to the dictates of romantic racialism, which ascribed to Anglo-Saxons characteristics of leadership and the desire for freedom. From his white father, Stowe writes, "he had inherited a set of fine European features, and a high, indomitable spirit" that leads him to invoke the Revolutionary fathers as a source of righteous power: "I'll fight for my liberty to the last breath I breathe. You say your fathers did it; if it was right for them, it is right for me!" (Chap. 11). At the novel's conclusion, however, when he renounces his father's race and embraces his mother's in leading a colonization movement that will found a new millennial Christian nation in Africa, George Harris speaks to the novel's grave anxieties about emancipation even as he crowns Stowe's argument on behalf of a feminine, maternal world vision.

As we have seen earlier, Stowe found sexual abuse and *southern* miscegenation one of slavery's terrible abominations. Yet she also responded to *northern* fears about the mixing of the races emancipation might entail. The scene of Eva's death, played out in a glaringly "white" setting, symbolic of her angelic purity, contains this fear in the charged intimacy of the Anglo-Saxon Eva and the "dark heathen" Topsy:

> St. Clare, at this instant, dropped the curtain. "It puts me in mind of mother," he said to Miss Ophelia. "It is true what she told me; if we want to give sight to the blind, we must be willing to do as Christ did, – call them to us, and *put our hands on them.*"
>
> "I've always had a prejudice against negroes," said Miss Ophelia, "and it's a fact, I never could bear to have that child touch me; but, I don't think she knew it." (Chap. 25)

Although she is clearly satirized here and elsewhere as a representative of northern prejudice up against the barriers of its own purported sympathy with slaves, Ophelia exposes Stowe's recognition of her own, and the novel's, unwillingness to face the ultimate question of freedom. As she tells St. Clare in an earlier scene, the thought of "kissing niggers" revolts her (Chap. 15). If abolitionists conceived of the southern plantation as a place of rampant sexual vice, they were hardly prepared to endorse miscegenation among races made free and equal. The issue is not tangential. In his famous 1858 debates with Stephen Douglas, for example, Lincoln continually had to defend himself against charges that the Republican Party advocated miscegenation: "Judge Douglas is especially horrified at the thought of the mixing of blood by the white and black races. Agreed for once – a thousand times agreed. . . . [But] I do not perceive that because the white man is to have the superior position the Negro should be denied everything. I do not understand that because I do not want a Negro woman for a slave I must necessarily want her for a wife."[55] Nonetheless, proslavery attacks on Lincoln often brought up the issue; once he had issued the Emancipation Proclamation, moreover, hysterical rebuttals were unleashed, with some southern pamphleteers asserting that a sexual holocaust would ensue. In the description of Forrest Wood, one reply was built around the "true" enactment of " 'Uncle Tom's Drama,' a play in which white maidens with 'quivering limbs' and 'snow-white bosoms, that ever throbbed in angelic purity,' suffered 'untold outrage, woe and wrong' at the hands of 'Black Ourang-Outangs,' who dragged them down to 'gratify their brutal instincts.' "[56]

Uncle Tom's Cabin, to be sure, is not "Uncle Tom's Drama." But the novel itself, like the racist thought and fiction of the post–Civil

War years and like the minstrel versions of the novel, which cleansed the relationship between Eva and Tom in comically stylized ways, conceals a hesitation about black freedom that unfolded along sexual lines. If the ideal "home" symbolized by a race of mothers was to redeem the world, it would do so without the most intimate human passion and would, in an imaginary world of abstract images, unite the maternal docility of *blackness* with the redeemed paternal ideals of revolutionary, millennial *whiteness*. George Harris is a George Washington (even an Abraham Lincoln) purified in the tradition of maternal moral instruction, and Tom is the martyred prophet without Nat Turner's murderous intent. Even though colonization was endorsed by many whites (including Lincoln) and by some blacks (James Holly, for example, imagined that Haiti could become a new "Eden of America" and "the Fatherland of the [black] race"),[57] it was absurdly impractical, as even Stowe must have recognized. The novel employs it as a safety valve for northern anxiety about both slave rebellion and miscegenation. But as though admitting its inadequacy as an answer to the question of slavery *and* the question of emancipation, Stowe reveals a further possibility in the last remarks of her novel:

> This is an age of the world when nations are trembling and convulsed. . . . Every nation that carries in its bosom great and unredressed injustice has in it the elements of this last convulsion. . . . Christians! every time that you pray that the kingdom of Christ may come, can you forget that prophecy associates, in dread fellowship, the *day of vengeance* with the year of his redeemed? . . . [and obeys] that stronger law, by which injustice and cruelty shall bring on nations the wrath of Almight God! (Chap. 45)

She returned, that is, to a paternal revolutionary tradition bound up in the wrath of God the Father, to the suppressed Calvinistic vengeance of Lyman Beecher's religion to which the novel's immense moral work of mothers may finally give way. In this respect, Stowe's millennial colonizationist vision, with all its racialist overtones, must be seen to be rooted, as Cushing Strout notes, in "her messianic view of history, in which all persons tend to lose their individual reality in the great cosmic drama of God's plan."[58]

When civil war was imminent, Stowe wrote that it "was God's

will that this nation – the North as well as the South – should deeply and terribly suffer for the sin of consenting to and encouraging the great oppressions of the South. . . . that the blood of the poor slave, that had cried so many years from the ground in vain, should be answered by the blood of the sons from the best hearthstones through all the free States."[59] Lincoln's famous conception of the Civil War, in his Second Inaugural speech, as an act of divine judgment more eloquently represents this view:

> If we shall suppose that American slavery is one of those offenses which, in the providence of God, must needs come, but which, having continued through His appointed time, He now wills to remove, and that He now gives to both North and South this terrible war, as the woe due to those by whom the offense came, shall we discern therein any departure from those divine attributes which the believers in a living God always ascribe to Him? . . . if God wills that it continue until all the wealth piled by the bondsman's two hundred and fifty years of unrequited toil shall be sunk, and until every drop of blood drawn with the lash shall be paid by another drawn with the sword, as was said three thousand years ago, so still it must be said, "The judgments of the Lord are true and righteous altogether."[60]

The apocalyptic language of Lincoln and Stowe indicates the manner in which the Civil War could seem a purifying redemption of America's greatest sin, accomplished only through violent purgation. America's mothers, Stowe implies, would work pacifically to overthrow slavery, but they would not turn away from the last solution – the sacrifice of the very sons *Uncle Tom's Cabin* was intended to reform. Influence would become power one way or another; unthinkable slave rebellion would become a liberating Christian war on their behalf; domesticity would release its restrained violent action in the name of freedom.

Intimating but suppressing until the final moment the fury latent within her vision, Stowe's novel could in its own day appear reluctant to go the full distance on behalf of American slaves. In later years, given the terrible price of the war and the nation's consequent failure to actualize freedom for blacks in meaningful ways, the novel could seem one more flawed instrument of liberation, a well-meant but inadequate indictment of America's racial sins as they assumed more complicated and explosive forms in the twentieth century. Those forms would be measured and clarified in the endless entanglements of legal proscription and social theory, in the violence of country roads and city streets, and in the literary visions of writers as diverse as Mark Twain, Charles Chesnutt, Zora Neale Hurston, William Faulkner, Ralph Ellison, Robert Penn Warren, Chester Himes, Alice Walker, and Ishmael Reed, to name but a few.

The essays in this volume take up the novel's central and enduring critical problems in a variety of forms. Two, those by Elizabeth Ammons and Jean Fagan Yellin, are focused on the role of women in *Uncle Tom's Cabin*, both as that role is examined in the context of the domestic ideology that Stowe herself sought to incorporate and revise in her novel and as it became illuminated by developments in women's writing in the later nineteenth and early twentieth centuries. Inseparable from the question of gender, as both essays show, is the question of race, not least because some of the most influential and controversial abolitionists were women or, in notorious cases, made an issue of whether women could properly contribute to the antislavery cause. Most important of all, perhaps, black women were doubly victimized by slavery and therefore spoke from a position of particular power. The essays by Robert Stepto and Richard Yarborough are devoted more explicitly to the relationship between Stowe's novel and black cultural history. Stepto examines the role slave narratives may have played in Stowe's composition and the role of response by black writers that *Uncle Tom's Cabin* necessitated. Yarborough follows this response into the later decades of the nineteenth century and, like Ammons, shows that Stowe's novel only began to reach the full effects of its influence after, not on the eve of, the Civil War. Both essays demonstrate that the black response to Stowe was or has been by no means unanimous. Only in its depth of argument, in fact, is the novel's full meaning clarified. The two pivotal traditions out of which Stowe wrote — the Calvinistic religious tradition exemplified in different ways in the works of her father and her brother, and the tradition of the gothic novel, the source of much fictional reform writing — are the subject of Karen Halttunen's essay. Her interpretation of Stowe's relation to these traditions serves to tie together, in specific contexts, the larger and more comprehensive problems of gender and race as they are represented in *Uncle Tom's Cabin*. The renewed interest in the novel that these essays represent, and its appearance now in a series devoted to classic American texts, indicate how startlingly long it can take for an important cultural work to achieve recognition, however controversial our assessments of it may remain. Both the history of race relations in America and the wealth of imaginative literature devoted to it testify as well not only to the long struggle for freedom, black and white, but also to the role played by *Uncle Tom's Cabin* in a rich, complex tradition at the heart of our national experience.

NOTES

1 Carl Van Doren, *The American Novel* (New York: Macmillan, 1922), pp. 118–19.

2 On Hawthorne, Stowe, and canon formation, see, for example, Henry Nash Smith, *Democracy and the Novel: Popular Resistance to Classic American Writers* (New York: Oxford University Press, 1978); Jane Tompkins, *Sensational Designs: The Cultural Work of American Fiction, 1790–1860* (New York: Oxford University Press, 1985); Ellen Moers, *Harriet Beecher Stowe and American Literature* (Hartford, Conn.: Stowe-Day Foundation, 1978); and Larzer Ziff, *Literary Democracy: The Declaration of Cultural Independence in America* (New York: Viking, 1981).

3 Russell Blankenship, *American Literature as an Expression of the National Mind* (London: Routledge & Sons, 1931), p. 322.

4 Edmund Wilson, *Patriotic Gore: Studies in the Literature of the American Civil War* (New York: Farrar, Straus and Giroux, 1962), pp. 3–58.

5 Tompkins, *Sensational Designs,* p. 127; on the domestic tradition, see also Herbert Ross Brown, *The Sentimental Novel in America, 1789–1860* (Durham, N.C.: Duke University Press, 1940); Frank Luther Mott, *Golden Multitudes: The Story of Best Sellers in the United States* (New York: R. R. Bowker, 1947); Nina Baym, *Women's Fiction: A Guide to Novels by and about Women in America, 1820–1870* (Ithaca, N.Y.: Cornell University Press, 1978); and Mary Kelley, *Private Woman, Public Stage: Literary Domesticity in Nineteenth-Century America* (New York: Oxford University Press, 1984).

6 J. C. Furnas, *Goodbye to Uncle Tom* (New York: William Sloane, 1956), pp: 8–10 and passim; see also William L. Van Deburg, *Slavery and Race*

in American Popular Culture (Madison: University of Wisconsin Press, 1984).

7 James Baldwin, "Everybody's Protest Novel," in *Notes of a Native Son* (1955; rpt. New York: Bantam, 1964), p. 13.

8 See Stephen A. Hirsch, "Uncle Tomitudes: The Popular Reaction to *Uncle Tom's Cabin*," in *Studies in the American Renaissance*, ed. Joel Meyerson (Boston: Twayne, 1978), pp. 303–30; Robert C. Toll, *Blacking Up: The Minstrel Show in Nineteenth-Century America* (New York: Oxford University Press, 1974); Harry Birdoff, *The World's Greatest Hit: Uncle Tom's Cabin* (New York: S. F. Vanni, 1947); Furnas, *Goodbye to Uncle Tom*, pp. 259–84; and Donald Bogle, *Toms, Coons, Mulattoes, Mammies, and Bucks: An Interpretive History of Blacks in American Films* (New York: Viking, 1973).

9 *Collected Poems of Harriet Beecher Stowe*, ed. John Michael Moran, Jr. (Hartford, Conn.: Transcendental Books, 1967).

10 James M. Cox, "Harriet Beecher Stowe: From Sectionalism to Regionalism," *Nineteenth-Century Fiction*, 38, no. 4 (March 1984):444–66.

11 For Stowe's life and her writing of *Uncle Tom's Cabin*, I have drawn primarily on Forrest Wilson, *Crusader in Crinoline: The Life of Harriet Beecher Stowe* (Philadelphia: J. B. Lippincott, 1941), and E. Bruce Kirkham, *The Building of Uncle Tom's Cabin* (Knoxville: University of Tennessee Press, 1977). See also *The Life of Harriet Beecher Stowe Compiled from Her Letters and Journals*, ed. Charles Edward Stowe (Boston: Houghton Mifflin, 1889); *Life and Letters of Harriet Beecher Stowe*, ed. Annie Fields (London: Samson Low, 1898); *The Autobiography of Lyman Beecher*, ed. Barbara Cross (Cambridge, Mass.: Harvard University Press, 1961); Constance Mayfield Rourke, *Trumpets of Jubilee: Henry Ward Beecher, Harriet Beecher Stowe, Lyman Beecher, Horace Greeley, P. T. Barnum* (New York: Harcourt, Brace, 1963); Milton Rugoff, *The Beechers: An American Family in the Nineteenth Century* (New York: Harper & Row, 1981); Lyman Beecher Stowe, *Saints, Sinners, and Beechers* (Indianapolis: Bobbs-Merrill, 1934). On Stowe as a writer, see also Charles H. Foster, *The Rungless Ladder: Harriet Beecher Stowe and New England Puritanism* (Durham, N.C.: Duke University Press, 1954); Edward Wagenknecht, *Harriet Beecher Stowe: The Known and the Unknown* (New York: Oxford University Press, 1965); Alice C. Crozier, *The Novels of Harriet Beecher Stowe* (New York: Oxford University Press, 1969); *Critical Essays on Harriet Beecher Stowe*, ed. Elizabeth Ammons (Boston: G. K. Hall, 1980); Margaret Holbrook Hildreth, *Harriet Beecher Stowe: A Bibliography* (Hamden, Conn.: Archon Press,

1976); and Jean W. Ashton, *Harriet Beecher Stowe: A Reference Guide* (Boston: G. K. Hall, 1977).

12 Stowe, *Life of Harriet Beecher Stowe*, p. 148.

13 Fields, *Life and Letters*, pp. 146–7.

14 All quotations are from *Uncle Tom's Cabin or, Life among the Lowly*, ed. Kenneth S. Lynn (Cambridge, Mass.: Harvard University Press, 1962); the same text is reprinted in a paperback edition by Ann Douglas (New York: Penguin, 1981).

15 Kirkham, *Building of Uncle Tom's Cabin*, pp. 66–7.

16 Ronald G. Walters, *The Antislavery Appeal: American Abolitionism After 1830* (Baltimore: Johns Hopkins University Press, 1976), p. 59.

17 Wilson, *Crusader in Crinoline*, p. 278.

18 Tompkins, *Sensational Designs*, p. 134; Stowe, *Life of Harriet Beecher Stowe*, p. 154.

19 Wilson, *Crusader in Crinoline*, p. 67.

20 Wilson, *Crusader in Crinoline*, pp. 213, 204. Cf. Barbara J. Berg, *The Remembered Gate: Origins of American Feminism* (New York: Oxford University Press, 1978), pp. 112–42, and Carroll Smith-Rosenberg, "Beauty, the Beast and the Militant Woman: A Case Study in Sex Roles and Social Stress in Jacksonian America," *American Quarterly* 23, no. 4 (October 1971):562–84.

21 On the clergy and social reform, see Alice Felt Tyler, *Freedom's Ferment: Phases of American Social History from the Colonial Period to the Outbreak of the Civil War* (1944; rpt. New York: Harper & Row, 1962); Cushing Strout, *The New Heavens and New Earth: Political Religion in America* (New York: Harper & Row, 1974); Barbara Welter, *Dimity Convictions: The American Woman in the Nineteenth Century* (Athens: Ohio University Press, 1976); Nancy F. Cott, *The Bonds of Womanhood: "Woman's Sphere" in New England, 1780–1835* (New Haven, Conn.: Yale University Press, 1977); and Ann Douglas, *The Feminization of American Culture* New York: Alfred A. Knopf, 1977).

22 Frederick Douglass, *Narrative of the Life of Frederick Douglass* (New York: Signet, 1968), p. 121; Stowe, *Life of Harriet Beecher Stowe*, pp. 151–2.

23 *The Liberator*, March 26, 1852, in *Documents of Upheaval: Selections from William Lloyd Garrison's The Liberator, 1831–1865*, ed. Truman Nelson (New York: Hill and Wang, 1966), pp. 239–40.

24 On slavery and the limits of social reform, see John L. Thomas, "Antislavery and Utopia," in Martin Duberman, ed., *The Antislavery Vanguard: New Essays on the Abolitionists* (Princeton, N.J.: Princeton University Press, 1965), pp. 240–69; Stanley M. Elkins, *Slavery: A Problem*

in American Institutional and Intellectual Life, rev. ed (Chicago: University of Chicago Press, 1976), pp. 27–37, 140–92; and John Demos, "The Antislavery Movement and the Problem of Violent 'Means,'" *New England Quarterly* 37, no. 4 (December 1964):501–26.

25 George M. Fredrickson, *The Inner Civil War: Northern Intellectuals and the Crisis of Union* (New York: Harper & Row, 1965); Daniel Aaron, *The Unwritten War: American Writers and the Civil War* (New York: Oxford University Press, 1973). See also Howard R. Floan, *The South in Northern Eyes, 1831 to 1861* (Austin: University of Texas Press, 1958).

26 See Kirkham, *Building of Uncle Tom's Cabin,* pp. 80–103; Robin Winks, ed., *An Autobiography of the Reverend Josiah Henson* (Reading, Mass.: Addison-Wesley, 1969); Lorenzo Dow Turner, *Anti-Slavery Sentiment in American Literature Prior to 1865* (1929; rpt. Port Washington, N.Y.: Kennikat Press, 1966); Jean Fagan Yellin, *The Intricate Knot: Black Figures in American Literature, 1776–1863* (New York: New York University Press, 1972); Nicholas Canaday, Jr., "The Antislavery Novel Prior to 1852 and Richard Hildreth's *The Slave* (1836)," *CLA Journal* 17, no. 2 (December 1973):175–91; and Evan Brandstadter, "Uncle Tom and Archy Moore: The Antislavery Novel as Ideological Symbol," *American Quarterly* 26, no. 2 (May 1974):160–75.

27 Northup, *Twelve Years a Slave,* in *Puttin' On Ole Massa,* ed. Gilbert Osofsky (New York: Harper & Row, 1969), p. 338.

28 Douglass, *My Bondage and My Freedom* (New York: Dover, 1969), pp. 57, 60.

29 See George B. Forgie, *Patricide in the House Divided: A Psychological Interpretation of Lincoln and His Age* (New York: Norton, 1979); R. A. Yoder, "The First Romantics and the Last Revolution," *Studies in Romanticism* 15, no. 4 (Fall 1976):493–529; Kenneth M. Stampp, *The Imperiled Union: Essays on the Background of the Civil War* (New York: Oxford University Press, 1980), pp. 3–36; and Eric J. Sundquist, "Slavery, Revolution, and the American Renaissance," in *The American Renaissance Reconsidered,* ed. Walter Benn Michaels and Donald Pease (Baltimore: Johns Hopkins University Press, 1985), pp. 1–33.

30 Rourke, *Trumpets of Jubilee,* p. 107; cf. Susan Moller Okin, "Women and the Making of the Sentimental Family," *Philosophy and Public Affairs* 11, no. 1 (Winter 1982):65–88.

31 Beecher, *An Essay on Slavery and Abolitionism* (Philadelphia: Henry Perkins, 1837), pp. 88–89, 97, 107–8.

32 On abolitionism in general and the role of women, see Tyler, *Freedom's Ferment;* Louis Filler, *The Crusade Against Slavery, 1830–1860* (New York: Harper & Row, 1960); James Brewer Stewart, *Holy War-*

41

riors: The Abolitionists and American Slavery (New York: Hill and Wang, 1976); Walters, *The Antislavery Appeal;* Blanche Glassman Hersh, *The Slavery of Sex: Feminist-Abolitionists in America* (Urbana: University of Illinois Press, 1978); Jane H. Pease and William H. Pease, *They Who Would Be Free: Blacks' Search for Freedom, 1830–1861* (New York: Atheneum, 1974); and Lawrence J. Friedman, *Gregarious Saints: Self and Community in American Abolitionism, 1830–1870* (Cambridge: Cambridge University Press, 1982).

33 Stowe, *Life of Harriet Beecher Stowe,* pp. 257–60.

34 Susan B. Anthony quoted in Tyler, *Freedom's Ferment,* pp. 459–60; Lydia Maria Child quoted in Ronald G. Walters, *American Reformers, 1815–1860* (New York: Hill and Wang, 1978), p. 105.

35 Elizabeth Ammons, "Heroines in *Uncle Tom's Cabin,*" in Ammons, ed., *Critical Essays,* p. 160; cf. Leslie Fiedler, *What Was Literature?: Class Culture and Mass Society* (New York: Simon and Schuster, 1982), pp. 145–78.

36 Stowe, *Life of Harriet Beecher Stowe,* p. 21.

37 *Mary Chesnut's Civil War,* ed. C. Vann Woodward (New Haven, Conn.: Yale University Press, 1981), p. 168; on the "tragic mulatto" and miscegenation, see Severn Duvall, *"Uncle Tom's Cabin:* The Sinister Side of Patriarchy," in *Images of the Negro in American Literaure,* ed. Seymour L. Gross and John Edward Hardy (Chicago: University of Chicago Press, 1966), pp. 163–80; Jules Zanger, "The 'Tragic Octoroon' in Pre–Civil War Fiction," *American Quarterly* 18, no. 1 (Spring 1966);63–70; and Judith R. Berzon, *Neither White Nor Black: The Mulatto Character in American Fiction* (New York: New York University Press, 1978).

38 Harriet Jacobs [Linda Brent, pseudo.], *Incidents in the Life of a Slave Girl* (New York: Harcourt Brace, 1973), p. 53.

39 Beecher quoted in Kathryn Kish Sklar, *Catharine Beecher: A Study in American Domesticity* (1973; rpt. New York: Norton, 1976), pp. 157–60.

40 David Brion Davis, *Slavery and Human Progress* (New York: Oxford University Press, 1984), p. 129.

41 Margaret Fuller, *Woman in the Nineteenth Century* (New York: Norton, 1971), pp. 166–7.

42 Walters, *The Antislavery Appeal,* p. 99.

43 David Brion Davis, *The Problem of Slavery in Western Culture* (Ithaca, N.Y.: Cornell University Press, 1966), p. 357; cf. Philip Fisher, *Hard Facts: Setting and Form in the American Novel* (New York: Oxford University Press, 1985), pp. 87–127.

44 See Ann Douglas, *The Feminization of American Culture*, pp. 200–26, and Karen Halttunen, *Confidence Men and Painted Women: A Study of Middle-Class Culture in America, 1830–1870* (New Haven, Conn.: Yale University Press, 1982), pp. 124–52.

45 On slave revolts and southern apprehensions, see Clement Eaton, *The Freedom-of-Thought Struggle in the Old South* (1940; rpt. New York: Harper & Row, 1964), pp. 89–117; Herbert Aptheker, *American Negro Slave Revolts* (1943; rpt. New York: International Publishers, 1974); and Eugene D. Genovese, *From Rebellion to Revolution: Afro-American Slave Revolts in the Making of the New World* (1979; rpt. New York: Vintage, 1981).

46 *The Confessions of Nat Turner*, in Herbert Aptheker, ed. *Nat Turner's Slave Rebellion* (New York: Humanities Press, 1966), pp. 128–31.

47 John W. Blassingame, *The Slave Community: Plantation Life in the Antebellum South*, rev. ed. (New York: Oxford University Press, 1979), pp. 223–48, 284–322, quotation at p. 230; see also Ann J. Lane, ed. *The Debate over Slavery: Stanley Elkins and His Critics* (Urbana: University of Illinois Press, 1971).

48 Eastman, *Aunt Phillis' Cabin: Or, Southern Life as It Is* (Philadelphia: Lippincott, Grambo, 1852), pp. 257–63; cf. James Oakes, *The Ruling Race: A History of American Slaveholders* (New York: Alfred A. Knopf, 1982), pp. 96–122.

49 Simms, *Woodcraft* (New York: Norton, 1961), pp. 113, 184, 509; on proslavery replies to *Uncle Tom's Cabin*, see Jeannette Reid Tandy, "Proslavery Propaganda in American Fiction of the Fifties," *South Atlantic Quarterly* 21, nos. 1–2 (January–April 1922):41–50, 170–8; Brown, *The Sentimental Novel in America*, pp. 241–80; and Barrie Hayne, "Yankee in the Patriarchy: T. B. Thorpe's Reply to *Uncle Tom's Cabin*," *American Quarterly* 20, no. 2, pt. 1 (Summer 1968):180–95.

50 Dew, "Abolition of Negro Slavery" (1831) in *The Ideology of Slavery: Proslavery Thought in the Antebellum South, 1830–1860*, ed. Drew Gilpin Faust (Baton Rouge: Louisiana State University Press, 1981), pp. 27, 57; Harper, "Slavery in the Light of Social Ethics," in *Cotton Is King*, ed. E. N. Elliott (Augusta, Ga.: Pritchard, Abbott, and Loomis, 1860), pp. 588–9; and Fitzhugh, *Cannibals All!* (1857), ed. C. Vann Woodward (Cambridge, Mass.: Harvard University Press, 1960), pp. 202–5.

51 Brown, "Getting in the Kitchen with Dinah: Domestic Politics in *Uncle Tom's Cabin*," *American Quarterly* 36, no. 4 (Fall 1984):511; cf. William R. Taylor, *Cavalier and Yankee: The Old South and the American National Character* (1961; rpt. New York: Harper & Row, 1969), pp. 308–10.

52 Quoted in Duvall, *"Uncle Tom's Cabin:* The Sinister Side of Patriarchy," p. 175, and Thomas, "Antislavery and Utopia," p. 242.

53 "Uncle Tom's Cabin," *North American Review* 77, no. 151 (October 1853):477, 482.

54 George M. Fredrickson, *The Black Image in the White Mind: The Debate on Afro-American Character and Destiny, 1817–1914* (New York: Harper & Row, 1971), pp. 97–129.

55 Lincoln, *The Life and Writings of Abraham Lincoln,* ed. Philip Van Doren Stern (New York: Modern Library, 1940), pp. 425, 493.

56 Forrest G. Wood, *Black Scare: The Racist Response to Emancipation and Reconstruction* (Berkeley: University of California Press, 1968), pp. 64–5.

57 Holly, "A Vindication of the Capacity of the Negro Race for Self-Government and Civilized Progress" (1857), in Howard H. Bell, ed., *Black Separatism and the Caribbean, 1860* (Ann Arbor: University of Michigan Press, 1970), pp. 64–5.

58 Strout, *The New Heavens and New Earth,* p. 58.

59 Stowe, *Life of Harriet Beecher Stowe,* p. 363.

60 Lincoln, *Life and Writings,* pp. 841–2; see also Ernest Lee Tuveson, *Redeemer Nation: The Idea of America's Millennial Role* (1968; rpt. Chicago: University of Chicago Press, 1980), pp. 187–214; and Tompkins, *Sensational Designs,* pp. 133–46.

2

Strategies of Black Characterization in *Uncle Tom's Cabin* and the Early Afro-American Novel

RICHARD YARBOROUGH

> Poor Uncle Tom,
> The faithful, honest, brave
> Poor Uncle Tom!
> The patient captive slave,
> Poor Uncle Tom!
> —"Poor Uncle Tom!", a song from *The Uncle Tom's Cabin Almanack*[1]

> Mrs. Stowe has *invented* the Negro novel.
> —George Eliot[2]

IN lectures, journals, pamphlets, newspapers, and sermons throughout the first half of the nineteenth century, pro- and antislavery forces debated not only the place of the black in the United States but also the very physical and psychological nature of the transplanted Africans. When the abolitionist journal *National Era* began the serial publication of a tale by Harriet Beecher Stowe called *Uncle Tom's Cabin; or, Life among the Lowly* in June 1851, fiction immediately became a major weapon in the arsenals of both sides. Appearing in two-volume book form in March 1852, Stowe's novel set off an astounding public response unique in the history of American publishing. Frederick Douglass reported that the first edition of 5,000 was gone in four days and that in one year *Uncle Tom's Cabin* sold more than 300,000 copies.[3] This figure is

Funding from the National Endowment for the Humanities, the U.C.L.A. College Institute, the U.C.L.A. Academic Senate Research Committee, and the U.C.L.A. Institute of American Cultures supported my work on this essay. I am also indebted to the U.C.L.A. Center for Afro-American Studies and to the staffs of the libraries at Fisk University, Harvard University, Howard University, and U.C.L.A.

particularly astonishing when one considers that out of a population of roughly 24 million in the United States, much of the South
has to be exluded from any serious estimation of Stowe's read-
ership – both because of the huge slave population and because
the novel was banned in many communities. Furthermore, one
must forget neither the degree of illiteracy in mid-nineteenth-century America nor the widespread practice of passing books from
hand to hand. Another indication of the reading public's infatua-
tion with Stowe was the reception accorded *The Key to Uncle Tom's
Cabin* (1853), a ponderous compilation of the factual material she
claimed to have used in composing her best-seller: In the space of
a month, roughly 90,000 copies were sold.

Uncle Tom's Cabin was the epicenter of a massive cultural phenomenon, the tremors of which still affect the relationship between
blacks and whites in the United States. Articulating most contem-
poraneous arguments regarding the Afro-American and endorsing
a response to the race problem that has haunted black thinkers for
over a century, Stowe's novel has had a particularly powerful
artistic impact as well. As the black critic William Stanley Braithwaite observes, not only was *Uncle Tom's Cabin* "the first conspic-
uous example of the Negro as a subject for literary treatment," but it
also "dominated in mood and attitude the American literature of a
whole generation." In so doing, Stowe's work played a major role
of establishing the level of discourse for the majority of fictional
treatments of the Afro-American that were to follow – even for
those produced by blacks themselves. This is not to underestimate
the crucial prototypical role the slave narratives played in shaping
the Afro-American fiction tradition, especially through their impact
on white abolitionist writers (like Stowe), who, in turn, influenced
black authors. A further important intergeneric connection can be
discerned in the work of the ex-slaves William Wells Brown and
Frederick Douglass, both of whom published narratives before turning to fiction. Finally, as Benjamin Quarles points out, "the vast
audience that responded to [Stowe's] classic tale of Uncle Tom . . .
had already been conditioned and prepared by the life stories of
runaway slaves." Nonetheless, the lasting effect of Stowe's master-
work on popular American culture dwarfs that of the slave nar-

ratives. With its extraordinary synthesizing power, *Uncle Tom's Cabin* presented Afro-American characters, however derivative and distorted, who leaped with incredible speed to the status of literary paradigms and even cultural archetypes with which subsequent writers – black and white – have had to reckon. The grandeur of Leslie Fiedler's claim that "for better or worse, it was Mrs. Stowe who invented American Blacks for the imagination of the whole world" does not belie its essential truth.[4]

Although Stowe unquestionably sympathized with the slaves, her commitment to challenging the claim of black inferiority was frequently undermined by her own endorsement of racial stereotypes. And it could hardly have been otherwise, for as Thomas Graham contends, "the Negro remained an enigma to her." Of necessity, Stowe falls back upon popular conceptions of the Afro-American in depicting many of her slave characters. As one result, the blacks she uses to supply much of the humor in *Uncle Tom's Cabin* owe a great deal to the darky figures who capered across minstrel stages and white imaginations in the antebellum years. The black pranksters Sam and Andy, for instance, provide a comic counterpoint to the melodramatic flight of Eliza and Harry from the slave trader Haley. And although the two slaves play a critical role in Eliza's escape by leading the white man astray, they ultimately seem little more than bumptious, giggling, outsized adolescents. Further, Stowe never attributes their tricksterlike manipulation of Haley to any real desire to help the fugitives to freedom. Rather, Sam and Andy realize that Mrs. Shelby does not want Eliza captured; eager to please their mistress, they are only too glad to oblige. Stowe's attitude toward these slaves is also revealed in Sam's remaining appearances, which are wholly comic. Primarily concerned with his own image, he is a pompous, philosophizing amateur politician, and his speeches are fraught with the tortured syntax and strained malapropisms that Stowe intends to be amusing.[5]

Other frequent sources of humor for Stowe are the slave children, whom she evidently viewed as part of the quaint furnishings below the Mason-Dixon line. If we take *Uncle Tom's Cabin* literally, "little negroes, all rolled together in the corners" could be found in slaves' quarters, big-house kitchens, and barrooms throughout the South.[6] Most closely resembling wild, boisterous puppies bent on driving the adults to distraction, these black children generally appear in tumbling heaps and bundles rather than as individuals. The only one whom Stowe seriously attempts to characterize is "poor, diabolic, excellent Topsy," as George Sand called her; consequently, this figure embodies in particular detail the traits the author felt to be endemic to the undomesticated African.[7]

Stowe introduces Topsy as the stereotypical pickaninny, with teeth gleaming, hair in bristling braids, eyes round and sparkling. A quick-witted, hyperactive child of eight or nine, she acts entirely from impulse and perversely flouts the accepted rules of polite white society, particularly those championed by the chilly, puritanical New Englander, Miss Ophelia. Inured to whipping and recalcitrant in the extreme, Topsy claims no natural origin – or, to be more precise, she offers a now-famous explanation of her own conception in such outrageously "natural" terms that it approaches the atheistic absurd: "I spect I grow'd. Don't think nobody never made me." She also justifies her destructive prankishness with a despairing resignation that exasperates Ophelia no end: "Cause I's wicked, – I is. I's mighty wicked, any how. I can't help it." Despite her mistress's best efforts, Topsy's behavior remains quirkily schizoid. Assigned to clean Ophelia's room, she either does so flawlessly or else unleashes a "carnival of confusion"; she learns to read and write "as if by magic" but refuses to master sewing (Chap. 20).

Stowe also hints at an eerie, otherworldly side to the "goblin-like" Topsy. In one of the more memorable scenes, the child responds to her owner's whistle like a pet displaying a favorite trick:

> The black, glassy eyes glittered with a kind of wicked drollery, and the thing struck up, in a clear shrill voice, an odd negro melody, to which she kept time with her hands and feet, spinning round, clapping her hands, knocking her knees together, in a wild, fantastic sort of time, and producing in her throat all those odd guttural sounds which distinguish the native music of her race; and finally, turning a summerset or two, and giving a prolonged closing note, as odd and unearthly as that of a steam-whistle, she came suddenly down on the carpet, and stood with her hands folded, and a most sanctimonious expression of meekness and solemnity over her face,

only broken by the cunning glances which she shot askance from the corners of her eyes.

Although this incredible passage incidentally reveals the author's rather odd and yet, for many whites of the time, entirely typical conception of Afro-American folk music and dance, of paramount importance is the emphasis Stowe places on the grotesque freakishness of Topsy's strange performance, for she identifies this darkly magical and faintly sinister quality of the "sooty gnome" with her unredeemed African nature. With her irrepressible penchant for "turning a summerset" and the mesmerizing power "her wild diablerie" maintains over Eva St. Clare and the other youngsters, Topsy is the imp child whose undisciplined devilish spirit must be controlled (Chap. 20).

Her scenes with Eva bring Topsy's allegedly innate African traits into sharpest relief. If Eva is the "fair, high-bred child, with her golden head, her deep eyes, her spiritual, noble brow, and prince-like movements," Topsy is her "black, keen, subtle, cringing, yet acute neighbor." Eva, "the Saxon," and Topsy, "the Afric," are both "representative of their races," and the moral struggle that ensues between them constitutes an important motif in *Uncle Tom's Cabin* (Chap. 20). On one side stands the precocious, cherubic Eva, whom Stowe describes as "an impersonation in childish form of the love of Christ."[8] On the other is Topsy, who embodies an innocent but still dangerous lack of self-control and restraint. And although fascinated by Topsy "as a dove is sometimes charmed by a glittering serpent" (the religious symbolism here is obvious), Eva holds the key to the black child's conversion as she tries to touch her "wild, rude heart" with "the first word of kindness" (Chap. 20). Initially, Topsy resists, linking her hopeless spiritual condition with her race: "Couldn't never be nothin' but a nigger, if I was ever so good. . . . If I could be skinned, and come white, I'd try then. . . . There can't nobody love niggers, and niggers can't do nothin'! *I* don't care." However, Eva's response — "O, Topsy, poor child, *I* love you!" — pierces her defenses. Prostrated by the gentle force of selfless love, Topsy breaks down, with Eva bending over her like "some bright angel stooping to reclaim a sinner" (Chap. 25). In Stowe's world, to be born black is to be born a pagan, but paradoxically close to a state of grace; once a character's heathen African nature is controlled, redemption becomes a possibility.

Stowe's depiction of Legree's henchmen, Sambo and Quimbo, reiterates this same formulation. Although easily the most immoral black characters in the novel, the two slaves have, Stowe hastens to point out, no real predisposition to cruelty. Their mocking of Uncle Tom and their participation in Legree's satanic, drunken revels result directly from their infamous master's example and instruction, for he "had trained them in savageness and brutality as systematically as he had his bull-dogs" (Chap. 32). In a subsequent discussion of African psychology, Stowe claims that blacks "are possessed of a nervous organisation peculiarly susceptible and impressible."[9] Not only does this trait explain Sambo and Quimbo's degraded condition on the Legree plantation but, from a Christian perspective, it entails what we can term an infinite capacity for conversion. Like Topsy, Sambo and Quimbo simply need more positive influence in order to be saved. Thus, witnessing Tom's agony brings about an immediate change, and they shed tears of repentence and grief when exposed to the Holy Word. Because of the impressionability and the innate fascination with things spiritual that allegedly typify the African race, Stowe's blacks, when apparently evil, are but misguided and always receptive to Christian rehabilitation.

Throughout *Uncle Tom's Cabin*, Stowe draws crucial distinctions in personality and behavior between full-blood and mixed-blood blacks. In her portrayal of the former — Sam, Andy, Topsy, Sambo, and Quimbo — she emphasizes the racial gifts she saw as innately African. The traits of her mulatto figures, however, resemble those conventionally associated with whites. This is why, for example, Stowe stresses their physical attractiveness and why, in contrast to the dialect (or at least rough colloquialisms) of the full-blood blacks, the speech of the mulatto slaves is generally "correct." Nonetheless, the dash of African blood ensures that many of these mixed-blood characters will never be more than poor approximations of genteel bourgeois whites. That is, when we laugh at the dandified, spoiled slave Adolph St. Clare as he tosses his head, fingers his perfumed hair, and waves his scented handkerchief, we are laughing at a boy mimicking adult affectations. And in their obsession with showy displays of manner and finery, the servants Jane and Rosa are but two girls pretending to be grown ladies. In each case, the style is ill fitting and the "clothes" too large. The humor in these house slaves' futile attempt to be white gives way to pathos, however, when they are sold after their owner's death. Their helpless, hysterical reaction to the harsh realities of chattel enslavement pitifully dramatizes what Stowe contends is one of the greatest evils of the institution – the domestic insecurity of even the most pampered slaves. The dark-skinned St. Clare cook, Aunt Dinah, describes their true status with pithy directness: "Don't want none o' your light-colored balls . . . cuttin' round, makin' b'lieve you's white folks. Arter all, you's niggers, much as I am" (Chap. 18).

On the one hand, the tragic experiences of the two most important mixed-blood black characters, Eliza and George Harris, also derive from their status as relatively well-treated slaves who are suddenly confronted with unjust treatment. On the other hand, they have precious little else in common with Adolph, Jane, and Rosa. In particular, Eliza and George rival any white in the novel in nobility of character and fineness of sensibility. That in a sense they *are* white suggests that they represent not only Stowe's attempt to have her target audience identify personally with the plight of the slaves but also her inability to view certain types of heroism in any but "white" terms.

A literate, polite Christian woman, the quadroon Eliza embodies the mid-nineteenth-century ideal of bourgeois femininity. In an attempt to counter the claim that female slaves lack maternal instincts, Stowe especially emphasizes the obsessive strength of Eliza's love for her son, Harry. Indeed, it is only this motherly devotion that leads to her frenzied, desperate flight from slavery, for her sheltered life and religious upbringing have taught her to accept her lot: "I always thought that I must obey my master and mistress," she says early in the novel, "or I couldn't be a Christian" (Chap. 3). Unfortunately, her maternal dedication and un-

shaken piety constitute virtually the entire range of her characterization; we see little real psychological depth or intellectual
vigor.

In contrast, Eliza's husband, George, more fully engages Stowe's
imagination, and his personality is rendered in greater detail as she
dramatizes the fall into atheism that she feared would afflict the ill-
treated, thoughtful slave. George's rational questioning of his condition marks the first stage in this process. Here he argues that by
white society's own standards, he deserves freedom as much as, if
not more than, his owner:

> My master! and who made him my master? That's what I think of –
> what right has he to me? I'm a man as much as he is. I'm a better
> man than he is. I know more about business than he does; I am a
> better manager than he is; I can read better than he can; I can write
> a better hand, – and I've learned it all myself, and no thanks to him,
> – I've learned it in spite of him; and now what right has he to make
> a dray-horse of me? (Chap. 3)

George soon asserts his independence without qualification: "I've
said Mas'r for the last time to any man. *I'm free!*" (Chap. 11). This
defiance, however, begins to undercut his belief in God. At one
point, he confesses to his wife, "I an't a Christian like you, Eliza;
my heart's full of bitterness; I can't trust in God. Why does he let
things be so?" (Chap. 3). Later, in rejecting the hackneyed religious sentiments of a white acquaintance named Wilson whom
he meets during his escape, George restates his doubts: "*Is* there a
God to trust in? . . . O, I've seen things all my life that have made
me feel that there can't be a God" (Chap. 11).

Stowe clearly appreciates George's position; nevertheless, she
cannot let his corrosive anger and potentially violent self-asser-
tiveness undercut her Christian conception of true heroism. Consequently, two chapters after his conversation with Wilson, he
finds refuge in a utopian Quaker settlement, where a mixture of
religious integrity, domestic security, and democratic egalitarian-
ism quickly assuages his spiritual malaise:

> This, indeed, was a home, – *home,* – a word that George had never
> yet known a meaning for; and a belief in God, and trust in his
> providence, began to encircle his heart, as, with a golden cloud of
> protection and confidence, dark, misanthropic, pining atheistic

doubts, and fierce despair, melted away before the light of a living
Gospel. (Chap. 13)

Although still determined to fight for his own freedom and that of
his wife, George now manifests a spirit softened, tranquilized by a
reborn religious faith; he promises Eliza, "I'll try to act worthy of a
free man. I'll try to feel like a Christian" (Chap. 17). His behavior
in a heated battle with some slave hunters exemplifies this new
attitude. After George shoots one of them, he, Eliza, and other
escaping slaves help the wounded man to a Quaker household,
where he is nursed back to physical and spiritual health.

Stowe's treatment of Harris reveals her deep reluctance to portray the pent-up rage of an intelligent, strong-willed male slave
without marbling it with a Christian restraint that entails the es-
chewing of violence. No such qualification is necessary in the case
of Uncle Tom, who stands in antithetical juxtaposition to the aggressive, embittered George. If Harris is the articulate mulatto,
correct in speech, rational, and initially impatient with religion,
Tom is the passive, full-blood black, simple in expression, solic-
itous of all around him, gentle, and rarely shaken in his Christian
faith. In fact, about the only traits the two slaves share are a
willingness to die for their beliefs and a disconcerting lack of a
sense of humor. Otherwise, they inhabit different worlds, parallel
dimensions that never intersect. A full-blood Clark Kent and a
mulatto Superman, they are never on stage at the same time. One
can imagine that, like matter and antimatter, if they were forced
into contact, the result would be an explosion of immeasurable
force that would leave only Tom, for he, not George, is Stowe's
real hero. It is Tom, not George, who so quickly entered the stock
of American cultural archetypes; it is Tom, to paraphrase Faulkner, who "endured."

We first hear of Uncle Tom when his master, Mr. Shelby, describes to a skeptical Haley how his most reliable slave elected not
to escape while conducting business for him in Cincinnati. This
steadfast refusal to violate a trust is one of Tom's most important
traits. Whereas George rejects his master's attempt to control his
life and runs away with a clear conscience, Tom cannot do so.
Despite the urging of his wife after his sale, he still maintains,

"Mas'r always found me on the spot – he always will. I never have broke trust, nor used my pass no ways contrary to my word, and I never will" (Chap. 5). In fact, Tom mentions that he wants to be free just three times in the novel. In the first case, Augustine St. Clare has already made plans to manumit him. Even then, after exclaiming that "bein' a *free man*" is "what I'm joyin' for," Tom vows that he will remain by his owner until "Mas'r St. Clare's a Christian" – an eventuality on which one would certainly not stake one's life (Chap. 28). During Tom's trials on the Legree plantation, the issue is raised again, this time by Cassy, who asks, "Tom, wouldn't you like your liberty?" He replies, "I shall have it, Misse, in God's time" (Chap. 38). The only occasion when he himself broaches the subject is after St. Clare's tragic death. With the utmost tact and humility, Tom approaches Ophelia and asks that she intervene for him with his master's widow, who feels no compunction whatsoever at reneging on her husband's promise to free him. Unfortunately, Stowe chooses not to present the scene in which Ophelia reports back to Tom, so we can only imagine the prayers he no doubt mutters under his breath when given the bad news.

Grounded in neither fear of recapture and subsequent punishment nor any explicit satisfaction with his enslaved condition, Tom's principled refusal to strike out aggressively for his freedom grows out of his unimpeachable personal integrity and his staunch faith in Providence. In her attempt to make Tom the ideal Christian, however, Stowe deprives him of most of his imperfect human nature; he becomes, as St. Clare observes, "a moral miracle" (Chap. 18). Not only does he exhort his fellow blacks to refrain from hating slave traders, but he also finds it in himself to bless "Mas'r George" after Shelby has sold him. Even the indulgent, resolutely cynical St. Clare is subject to Tom's tearful, teetotaling ministrations. Consequently, by the time he falls into Legree's clutches, Tom has become more of a saint than a man. His religious study having been "confined entirely to the New Testament," Tom approaches the Christlike in his passivity, piety, and resigned refusal to challenge the apparent will of God (Chap. 12). When he helps two old slave women, he does so in the spirit of Christian kindness, not from any sense of racial solidarity. And when he defies Legree, it is because the man is attacking his religion, not because the villain holds no rightful claim to him: "Mas'r Legree, as ye bought me," Tom pledges, "I'll be a true and faithful servant to ye. I'll give ye all the work of my hands, all my time, all my strength; but my soul I won't give up to mortal man. I will hold on to the Lord" (Chap. 36). Even his brief struggle with religious doubt and fear during his epic battle with Legree resembles Christ's momentary questioning of his fate shortly before his crucifixion more than it does Job's all-too-human response to his overwhelming misery.

Tom's relationship with Cassy, Legree's erstwhile mistress, best exemplifies his effect on other blacks. A proud, willful, mixed-blood woman who has been driven to infanticide by broken promises, sexual exploitation, and horrible suffering, Cassy resists her enslavement more fiercely and actively than any black character besides George Harris. It is Cassy who openly defies and steals money from Legree, and it is Cassy who plans her and Emmeline's elaborate escape. However, as he does with almost every lost soul he encounters, Tom soothes her intense bitterness and rights her unbalanced mind. In the face of Cassy's despair, Tom reminds her, "The Lord han't forgot us, – I'm sartin' o' that ar'. If we suffer with him, we shall also reign, Scripture says; but, if we deny Him, he also will deny us" (Chap. 34). Later, after refusing to help her murder Legree, Tom urges Cassy to give herself not to hatred and vengeance, but to love. Her furious contention that love for *"such* enemies . . . isn't in flesh and blood" receives a predictably earnest response from Tom: "No, Misse, it isn't . . . but *He* gives it to us, and that's the victory" (Chap. 38). At this point, Stowe apostrophizes the African race in the explicitly redemptive terms of sacrificial martyrdom: "And this, O Africa! latest called of nations, – called to the crown of thorns, the scourge, the bloody sweat, the cross of agony, – this is to be *thy* victory" (Chap. 38). An echo of Christ's final words, Tom's prayer just before his death completes the image: "Into thy hands I commend my spirit!" (Chap. 40).

The debate between Tom and Cassy dramatizes an important issue in *Uncle Tom's Cabin*, the key, in fact, to Stowe's social vision. From the outset, Stowe outlines a conflict in human nature, of which slavery's lamentable effect upon the moral condition of the

United States was but the most immediately visible evidence: On the one hand is the "feminine" side of human personality; on the other, the "masculine." The former is loving, warm, maternal, usually passive, and often childlike in its free expression of feeling; the latter is hard, chilly, aggressive, skeptical, analytical, and sometimes violent. In religious terms, the first tends toward New Testament Christianity, the second toward worldly cynicism and even atheism.

Given Stowe's commitment to this scheme, it is not surprising that the most admirable figures among the whites are generally female. Notable exceptions include the Quaker males, who have consciously acquiesced in the supremacy of what Stowe would term the feminine side of their personality. Another is the sensitive, indulgent Augustine St. Clare, whose proximity to this saving femininity gives him the limited moral strength he possesses. Unfortunately, he cannot totally renounce the paralyzing skepticism that prevents him from following his instincts. In contrast, his wife, Marie, has betrayed her own feminine nature by abdicating her maternal responsibilities, an especially grievous sin for Stowe. One need only compare Marie's tepid reaction to Eva's return home to that of Mammy to discern who is the child's true mother (Chap. 15).

With Eliza and George, the conventional gender roles are righted as Eliza desperately attempts to mollify the destructive force of her husband's rational, violently male rejection of slavery. In her discussion of the popular conception of the bourgeois woman's place in nineteenth-century America, Barbara Welter argues that an indispensable component of the "cult of true womanhood" was piety: "Religion belonged to woman by divine right, a gift of God and nature." Consequently, her moral duty was to bring "an erring man back to Christ" or, as Theodore Parker put it, "to correct man's tastes, mend his morals, excite his affections, inspire his religious faculties."[10] Stowe's endorsement of such ideas partially explains why George's embodiment of traditionally male traits precludes her unqualified approval of his behavior, no matter how apparently heroic and manly it is.

With Uncle Tom, the gender inversion occurs once again, for it is Tom, first with Aunt Chloe and then with Cassy, who provides the religious forbearance, indiscriminate love, and intuitive faith conventionally associated with women. Indeed, as Elizabeth Ammons has pointed out, "Stowe makes him a heroine instead of a hero." In addition to displaying the feminine qualities that Stowe feels the African innately possessed, Tom also exemplifies another important racial trait: a child's innocence and purity of spirit. Thus, with "the soft, impressible nature of his kindly race, ever yearning toward the simple and childlike," Tom can relate to Eva as a virtual peer (Chap. 14). In *The Key to Uncle Tom's Cabin,* Stowe presents this idea more explicitly, conflating concepts of race, gender, age, and religion into the extraordinary redemptive amalgam that is Uncle Tom: "The negro race is confessedly more simple, docile, childlike, and affectionate, than other races; and hence the divine graces of love and faith, when in-breathed by the Holy Spirit, find in their natural temperament a more congenial atmosphere." Together, Tom and Eva form the moral center of the novel, and their deaths reflect Stowe's sad belief that the slave South cannot endure those who approximate overmuch the divine.[11]

Northern readers embraced *Uncle Tom's Cabin* with such fervor that proslavery advocates could no longer dismiss abolitionist sentiment as a phenomenon restricted to New England negrophiles. Accordingly, the South and its allies reacted fiercely and immediately, and Stowe's novel became, as Langston Hughes put it, "the most cussed and discussed book of its time." James D. Hart reports that a Mobile, Alabama, bookseller was run out of town for stocking it. Stowe herself received countless threats and even an ear cut from a slave's head. In the course of a review of *The Key to Uncle Tom's Cabin,* William Gilmore Simms took time to attack Stowe personally, noting that her "daguerreotype . . . is such as to damage the reputation of any female writer under the sun." This ungentlemanly thrust typifies the condemnation of many disapproving commentators who argue that Stowe had compromised her femininity by producing such a work. Other writers decided to reply to Stowe's fiction in kind; Sterling Brown notes, "In the three years following the appearance of *Uncle Tom's Cabin* (1852), there were at least fourteen proslavery novels published." One such fictive response was *Aunt Phyllis' Cabin; or Southern Life as It Is* (1852), in which the Mammy figure holds center stage. In the case of John W. Page's *Uncle Robin in His Cabin in Virginia and Tom Without One in Boston* (1853), the title accurately summarizes the novelist's message.[12]

Some critics attacked Stowe for her treatment of southern whites and for her depiction of the quotidian workings of the slave system. The more perceptive of them, however, saw *Uncle Tom's Cabin* as an attempt to posit a conception of the Afro-American that would undercut the basic assumptions upon which proslavery defenses were built. Desperately desiring to counter this particularly pernicious threat to southern interests, several commentators found two major chinks in Stowe's abolitionist armor.

The first is her treatment of the mixed-blood blacks. In a review of *Uncle Tom's Cabin*, the southern critic Louisa S. C. McCord identifies the problem:

> Look again at the wonderful accumulation of instances she offers of *quadroons* and *mulattoes*, so fair as to be almost mistaken – frequently, quite mistaken – for white; with glossy brown curls, fair soft hands, &c., &c. Indeed, seeming to forget that her principal task is the defence of the negro, decidedly the majority of the persecuted individuals brought forward for our sympathy, are represented as whites, of slightly negro descent, not negroes.

She continues:

> The real unfortunate being throughout her work is the mulatto . . . and we confess that, in fact, although far below her horrible imaginings, his position is a painful one. . . . Raised in intellect and capacity above the black, yet incapable of ranking with the white, he is of no class and no caste.[13]

McCord here exposes the roots of Stowe's treatment of near-white slaves in the tradition of the tragic mulatto, a motif based on the assumption that mixed-blood blacks are somehow more self-aware, more sensitive to their oppressed condition than full-blood blacks. To concede the existence of major racial or genetic (and not merely environmentally determined) distinctions between mixed-blood and full-blood blacks does little, McCord contends, to support claims that Afro-Americans are equal to whites and thus deserving of equal treatment.

In *The Key to Uncle Tom's Cabin*, Stowe explicitly reveals her adherence to contemporary concepts of race: "It must be remembered that the half-breeds often inherit, to a great degree, the traits of their white ancestors." She refers here specifically to George Harris, and it is upon her characterization of this mixed-blood figure that Simms bases an attack not dissimilar to that leveled by his compatriot, McCord. Sarcastically terming Harris "the genius, the mulatto Apollo," Simms rather pruriently suggests that, as evidenced by Stowe's "most voluptuous portrait," the slave's "good looks and locks seem to have worked very happily upon her imagination." Disputing the attribution of great intelligence to Harris, Simms argues, with a somewhat suspect logical flourish, that once one establishes

> that the negro intellect is fully equal to that of the white race, . . . you not only take away the best argument for keeping him in subjection, but you take away the possibility of doing so. *Prima facie*, however, the fact that he *is* slave, is conclusive against the argument for his freedom, as it is against his equality of claim, in respect of intellect. . . . Whenever the negro shall be fully fit for freedom, he will make himself free, and no power on earth can prevent him.

Simms then lands a more telling blow by questioning Stowe's conception of racial heredity and black intelligence: "The genius of George is Caucasian, not Ethiopian; and the argument for intellectual equality falls prone, headlong to the ground." Stowe sets herself up for this attack when she describes George's ability to pass as white in the following terms:

> George was, by his father's side, of white descent. . . . From one of the proudest families in Kentucky he had inherited a set of fine European features, and a high, indomitable spirit. From his mother he had received only a slight mulatto tinge, amply compensated by its accompanying rich, dark eye. (Chap. 11)

It is also evident that when Stowe comments upon the childlike qualities of blacks or upon their grotesque music and passionate religious services, she is hardly referring to Eliza or George. We can no more envision these two slaves singing a spiritual or turning a "summerset" than we can Stowe herself.[14]

The second crucial weakness in Stowe's argument involves Uncle Tom, and here she found herself in a most precarious position. As Simms points out, southerners could accept her portrait of Tom easily:

> That such a negro should grow up under the institution of slavery, is perhaps sufficiently conclusive in behalf of the institution. The North has no such characters. We shall not deny Uncle Tom. He is a Southron all over. He could not have been other than a Southron. We have many Uncle Tom's.

The northern, proslavery novelist Nehemiah Adams puts it this way:

> SLAVERY MADE UNCLE TOM. Had it not been for slavery, he would have been a savage in Africa, a brutish slave to his fetishes, living in a jungle, perhaps; and had you stumbled upon him he would very likely have roasted you and picked your bones.

Thus, conceding the accuracy of her depiction of Tom, Stowe's critics proceed to offer him as proof that slavery, in Adams's words, "is not an unmixed evil."[15]

That one can view Tom as a positive product of slavery raises some troubling questions regarding the extent of Stowe's condemnation of the institution: Would Eliza have run away if Shelby had not sold her son, Harry? And would George Harris have fled if his owner had not jealously removed him from his position in the factory? Put more generally, can blacks ever be truly satisfied in their enslaved condition and slavery therefore condoned? Given that the expressed desire for freedom on the part of Stowe's black characters results exclusively from harsh or inhumane treatment, her answer to this last question must be a qualified "yes" – if one could regulate the disposition of slaves through sale and thereby guarantee the security of the family unit. Stowe contends that the slaveholders could never meet this condition; her southern critics vehemently disagree.

In other words, although *Uncle Tom's Cabin* is a powerful attack on the evil effects of the chattel slave system, Stowe does not consistently argue the immorality of all social institutions based on the presumption of one group's innate superiority over another. In rejecting what one scholar calls "the domestic metaphor of proslavery thought," Stowe endorses in its place a benevolent Christian maternalism best exemplified by the arrangement young George Shelby works out with his slaves at the end of the novel, an arrangement Harold Beaver aptly describes as the transformation of "a slave plantation to a mid-Victorian landed estate." Further, Stowe's desire that "the white race shall regard their superiority over the coloured one only as a talent intrusted for the advantage of their weaker brother" bears an uncomfortable resemblance to Louisa McCord's characterization of slavery as "a Godlike dispensation, a providential caring for the weak, and a refuge for the portionless." The basic assumptions about race underlying the two statements are, for all practical purposes, identical, and they buttressed not only proslavery arguments but also countless justifications of U.S. imperialism from the mid-nineteenth century to the present.[16]

Although most white northerners fell hopelessly and uncritically in love with *Uncle Tom's Cabin*, there were a number of dissenting voices. Like their southern counterparts, some northern critics noticed the distinctions Stowe draws between mixed-blood and full-blood slaves. Others questioned the consistency of Stowe's commitment to nonviolence, especially given her relatively sympathetic treatment of the more rebellious mulattoes. For example, after praising the novel as "eminently serviceable in the tremendous conflict now waged for the immediate and entire suppression of slavery," William Lloyd Garrison wondered whether Stowe was "a believer in the duty of non-resistance for the white man, under all possible outrage and peril, as well as for the black man." In contrast to Garrison, who ultimately saw Stowe's hero as an embodiment of "real moral grandeur of character and the spirit of unconquerable goodness," the abolitionist Charles Whipple had more difficulty approving of Tom's response to his enslavement. In a general discussion of violence as an antislavery weapon, Whipple sets forth "the laws which are to regulate our action against evil-doers":

LOVE YOUR NEIGHBOR AS YOURSELF!

LOVE EVEN YOUR ENEMIES!

OVERCOME EVIL *WITH GOOD!*

With particular regard to the slaves, he explains that "the wrong-

METHODIST COLLEGE LIBRARY
Fayetteville, N.C.

doing of the master to the slave does not in the slightest degree release the slave from *his* duties to God, and his obligation to obey God's law of love." Nonetheless, Whipple does not endorse passive resignation:

> His [the slave's] first duty of good-will to the slaveholder is utterly to refuse any longer to be a slave! to put a stop . . . to a relation in which the slaveholder was sinking himself deeper and deeper in sin and in manifold evil. . . .
>
> Quiet, continuous submission to enslavement is complicity with the slaveholder. . . . It is the duty of a man and a Christian not only to protest against this, but, if he is able, acting in the right way, to put a stop to it. . . . And circumstances must decide whether this duty shall be performed in the most satisfactory manner, by a firm, manly, open declaration made to the face of the slaveholder, or by the attempt to escape.

As a result, Whipple concludes, "I do not consider 'Uncle Tom' to be *the highest* type, either of the manly character or the Christian character, in the relation he bore to various slaveholders."[17]

Not only did the abolitionist Henry C. Wright agree with this judgment of Tom, but he further suspected that the public outpouring of sympathy represented an attempt to escape difficult moral questions, not to grapple with them. "I wonder not at the unprecedented popularity of Uncle Tom's Cabin," he wrote in 1852. "The conscience of this nation is lashed to madness by uncompromising Anti-Slavery. Uncle Tom's Cabin comes as a quietus, to some extent. Thousands will be satisfied by reading and praising it." Wright could easily have added, "and by crying over it," because among the most telling testimonials to the novel's power were the frequent accounts of its bringing grown men to their emotional knees. Indeed, any attempt to understand Stowe's strategy must begin with the recognition that from the outset she was aiming more for the heart than for the head. Her explicit goal was, in her words, "to awaken sympathy and feeling for the African race, as they exist among us; [and] to show their wrongs and sorrows, under a system so necessarily cruel and unjust as to defeat and do away the good effects of all that can be attempted for them by their best friends." Thus, her utilization of the sentimental novel – a literary mode of expression grounded in the presumption that emotion is superior to reason, sensibility to logical ratiocination, and feminine to masculine – represents an entirely appropriate conjunction of fictive form and ideological function.[18] Unfortunately, the debt *Uncle Tom's Cabin* owes to both the novel of sentiment and that of sensibility also limited the degree to which it could effect radical political change. Characterized chiefly by "emotional exaggeration" and "the implicit argument that persistent purity eventually overcomes vigorous vice," the early nineteenth-century sentimental novel soon spawned a closely related form – the novel of sensibility, which at its most indulgent "allowed one to feel deeply about any situation without having compunctions that something must be done to rectify it." Including aspects of both forms, *Uncle Tom's Cabin* elicited a series of public responses that tend to justify Henry Wright's cynicism. Not only was a children's version of *Uncle Tom's Cabin* issued in 1853 called *A Peep into Uncle Tom's Cabin,* but within a year there also appeared "Uncle Tom and Little Eva," a parlor game "played with pawns that represented 'the continual separation and reunion of families.' " In fact, Stowe's best-seller inspired a veritable flood of Uncle Tom poems, songs, dioramas, plates, busts, embossed spoons, painted scarves, engravings, and other miscellaneous memorabilia, leading one wry commentator to observe, "[Uncle Tom] became, in his various forms, the most frequently sold slave in American history." Finally, the more maudlin and broadly humorous strains in Stowe's novel lent themselves particularly well to the influential dramatic treatments of *Uncle Tom's Cabin* that were soon produced. It apparently bothered audiences not at all that these "Tom Shows" presented greatly adulterated versions of the novel – for example, adding bloodhounds to the scene of Eliza's escape over the ice where originally there were none, incorporating entirely irrelevant comic and musical minstrel interludes, and depicting Uncle Tom as a weak, white-haired, old darky despite the fact that in the book he is a "large, broad-chested, powerfully-made man" in, or at most just past, the prime of life (Chap. 4).[19]

Stowe's appeal to sentiment had another serious flaw. Just after the publication of *Uncle Tom's Cabin,* Frederick Douglass confidently predicted that "the touching portraiture she has given of *'poor Uncle Tom,'* will, of itself, enlist the kindly sympathies, of numbers, in behalf of the oppressed African race, and will raise up a host of enemies against the fearful system of slavery." The direct correlation Douglass assumes between arousing the "kindly sympathies" of the readers and successfully mobilizing that audience into an antislavery force also underlies the answer Stowe provides for the most important question raised by her novel – "But, what can any individual do [about slavery]?":

> There is one thing that every individual can do – they can see to it that *they feel right*. An atmosphere of sympathetic influence encircles every human being; and the man or woman who *feels* strongly, healthily and justly, on the great interests of humanity, is a constant benefactor to the human race. See, then, to your sympathies in this matter! (Chap. 45)

Apparently, Stowe did not foresee that the sympathies of many of her critics could lead them to disagree with her. As a "southern lady" put it in an open letter to British women who supported the abolition effort:

> We can think as women, and feel as women, and act as women, without waiting for the promptings of your appeals, or of Mrs. Stowe's imaginative horrors. It seems to us, that you should receive it as a strong proof of how much you have mistaken our system, that so many millions of women . . . have contentedly lived in the midst of it [slavery], and yet the common woman-heart among us has not risen up to call it *cursed*.

"Our system," she asserts, "abhorrent as it seems to your ladyships, has the sanction of our hearts and heads." That this writer could so easily share Stowe's language and assumptions about the female sensibility without reaching Stowe's conclusions regarding slavery demonstrates the danger of any attempt to tie moral judgment to emotional response.[20]

Stowe's adherence to what George Fredrickson terms the "romantic racialist" view of the Afro-American weakened her argument as well. This conception of the African personality held that the black was a "natural Christian" whose soft emotionalism and gentle passivity were destined to temper the harshness of Anglo-Saxon culture. Behind this apparently positive depiction of the Afro-American, however, was what Fredrickson describes as "the inability of the abolitionists to ground their case for the black man on a forthright and intellectually convincing argument for the basic identity in the moral and intellectual aptitudes of all races." Like most white writers of her day, Harriet Beecher Stowe was not especially committed to (or equipped to present) a complex, realistic depiction of blacks. For example, she describes Africans as "an exotic race, whose ancestors, born beneath a tropic sun, brought with them, and perpetuated to their descendants, a character so essentially unlike the hard and dominant Anglo-Saxon race, as for many years to have won from it only misunderstanding and contempt." Rather than reject such stereotypes directly, Stowe tries to effect, in Jean Fagan Yellin's terms, a "Christian transvaluation" of "what the world sees as the curse of racial inferiority and cultural deprivation." Unfortunately, to offer such a radical reconceptualization does not at all guarantee that it will be shared, especially in a society in which hardness and dominance were increasingly perceived to be prerequisites for success. Further, Stowe's tragic failure of imagination prevented her from envisioning blacks (free or slave, mulatto or full-blood) as viable members of American society, so she deports the most aggressive, intelligent, "acceptable" ones to Africa to fill the same role there that she assigns to women in the United States. Thus, the outrage of many black abolitionists at her apparent endorsement of colonization resulted less from a disagreement over tactics than from an accurate recognition of the limitations of Stowe's utopian social vision: Heavenly salvation might indeed be possible for blacks, but a truly just interracial society was inconceivable.[21]

Finally, a close reading of *Uncle Tom's Cabin* suggests that Stowe's fiercest critique was not directed at the patriarchal slave system at all, but rather at male domination in American society generally. Storming the fortress of masculine privilege under the cover of a Trojan horse named Uncle Tom worked against her most subversive agenda, however, for Tom's melodramatic story proved so captivating and her exposé of the abuses of slavery so moving that her wholesale attack on male hegemony went largely unnoticed. Moreover, regardless of her approach, positing the spiritual superiority of women and blacks was hardly likely to disrupt the status quo, for despite lip service to the contrary, many

Americans – especially males – simply did not share Stowe's pietistic, eschatalogical priorities. In examining Stowe's "gospel of womanhood," Gayle Kimball argues that she "wanted spiritual power for women rather than political power" and that "the legacy of this praise [of the moral superiority] of women was disastrous . . . [because] women had made the mistake of asking for their civil rights, not on the grounds of equal adulthood, but on the basis of moral superiority." Kimball's analysis applies with equal force to Afro-Americans as well. That is, both blacks and women were tolerated if they kept out of the white male sphere of direct political action. Ultimately, Stowe's challenge to the racial and gender hierarchies in American society was bounded by the same assumptions that helped support the superstructure she strove to topple.[22]

> Who has not wept as he has stood at the deathbed of poor old Uncle Tom, who, though a slave in body, was a philosopher in mind, a saint at heart, and a martyr in death.
> —Mary Church Terrell[23]

> Blest be the hand that dared be strong to save,
>   And blest be she who in our weakness came –
> Prophet and priestess! At one stroke she gave
> A race to freedom and herself to fame.
>   —"Harriet Beecher Stowe," Paul Laurence Dunbar[24]

> *Uncle Tom's Cabin* grappled in the mire of Southern slavery and lifted a despised and helpless race into living sympathy with the white race at the North.
> —Sutton E. Griggs[25]

The controversy over *Uncle Tom's Cabin* did not die out with the emancipation of the slaves and the military defeat of the South. Not only did late-nineteenth-century southern writers like Thomas Nelson Page and Thomas Dixon feel obliged to respond to Stowe's novel in their own fiction, but also "it was still possible at the beginning of this century," Edmund Wilson reports, "for a South Carolina teacher to make his pupils hold up their right hands and swear that they would never read *Uncle Tom*." Most southern critics in Stowe's day would have applauded the novelist

Margaret Mitchell when she wrote in 1938, "It makes me very happy to know that 'Gone with the Wind' is helping refute the impression of the South which people abroad gained from Mrs. Stowe's book." And they would have fully understood the hostility underlying William Faulkner's contention that "*Uncle Tom's Cabin* was written out of violent and misdirected compassion and ignorance of the author toward a situation which she knew only by hearsay."[26]

Likewise, Afro-Americans have struggled with the implications of Stowe's work well into the twentieth century. In 1946, for example, *Negro Digest* asked groups of blacks and whites, "Is 'Uncle Tom's Cabin' Anti-Negro?" Although it was a controversial stage production that occasioned the poll, that the vast majority of whites said "no" in contrast to the three out of every five blacks who responded "yes" suggests the degree to which the characters Stowe set loose in the American imagination still appealed to whites and, at the same time, elicited a troubled, divided response from blacks. Several years earlier, Richard Wright had entitled his first collection of stories *Uncle Tom's Children,* as if to stress the generational gap between Stowe's protest fiction and his own, while simultaneously acknowledging a familial relationship. In describing the genesis of his next book, however, he repudiates all connection with Stowe and, most importantly, with her sentimental appeal for white sympathy:

> I had written a book of short stories which was published under the title of *Uncle Tom's Children.* When the reviews of that book began to appear, I realized that I had made an awfully naive mistake. I found that I had written a book which even bankers' daughters could read and weep over and feel good about. I swore to myself that if I ever wrote another book, no one would weep over it; that it would be so hard and deep that they would have to face it without the consolation of tears.

Wright's transformation of Uncle Tom into Bigger Thomas marks a watershed in the relations between black authors and the most popular American novel on the race question ever written. Nonetheless, James Baldwin's subsequent critique, "Everybody's Protest Novel" (1949), and Ishmael Reed's satiric jousting with

Stowe's ghost in *Flight to Canada* (1976) suggest that the dialogue will continue as Afro-American writers strive to distance themselves from all that *Uncle Tom's Cabin* represents.[27]

Most free northern blacks in the 1850s, however, saw *Uncle Tom's Cabin* as a godsend destined to mobilize white sentiment against slavery just when resistance to the southern forces was urgently needed. Hailing Stowe's novel as the greatest weapon ever brought to bear in the abolitionist battle, blacks memorialized its author in print and from pulpits and convention platforms. William Wells Brown, the first Afro-American novelist, celebrated the publication of Stowe's book in a letter to *The Liberator:* "Uncle Tom's Cabin has come down upon the dark abodes of slavery like a morning's sunlight, unfolding to view its enormities in a manner which has fastened all eyes upon the 'peculiar institution,' and awakening sympathy in hearts that never before felt for the slave." The poet and future novelist Frances Ellen Watkins [Harper] was inspired to compose a poem about Eliza's escape, and the participants of the Colored National Convention in Rochester in 1853 resolved that *Uncle Tom's Cabin* was "a work plainly marked by the finger of God, lifting the veil of separation which has too long divided the sympathies of one class of the American people from another."[28]

With this sanguine view of the practical role *Uncle Tom's Cabin* could play in their struggle for justice, understandably few blacks publicly quarreled with her depiction of the slave experience. Nonetheless, several Afro-American readers did express serious reservations with regard to Tom's passivity. The son of a slave who died trying to escape, Reverend J. B. Smith seconded the sentiments of Whipple in his belief that "resistance to tyrants was obedience to God, and hence, to his mind, the only drawback to the matchless Uncle Tom of Mrs. Stowe was his virtue of submission to tyranny – an exhibition of grace which he . . . did not covet." William G. Allen, a free black teacher, also raised the issue:

> Uncle Tom was a good old soul, thoroughly and perfectly pious. Indeed, if any man had too much piety, Uncle Tom was that man. I confess to more of "total depravity." More shame to me, possibly, but nevertheless, such is the fact. My non-resistance is of the Doug-

lass, Parker, and Phillip's [sic] school. I believe . . . that it is not light the slaveholder wants, but *fire,* and he ought to have it. I do not advocate revenge, but simply, resistance to tyrants, if it need be, to the death.

The eagerness with which Afro-American leaders greeted the opportunity for blacks to prove their courage in the time-honored arena of warfare a decade later suggests that despite their support for Stowe's best-seller, they in no way rejected traditional measures of male worth, measures by which Uncle Tom fell considerably short of the mark.[29]

The most controversial aspect of Stowe's book and the one that many blacks felt they could not afford to let pass uncriticized was her apparent endorsement of emigration when she depicts George Harris relocating his family to Liberia in search of "an African nationality" (Chap. 33). (The reformed Topsy also ends up in Africa, where she is reportedly teaching in a missionary station.) To blacks like Allen and George T. Downing, Harris is "the only one that really betrays any other than the subservient, submissive, Uncle Tom spirit, which has been the cause of much of the disrespect felt for the colored man." For Stowe to have him despair of ever attaining his rights in the United States seemed to undermine the already precarious position of many free blacks who had opted to stay in this country and fight. One writer in an Afro-American newspaper vehemently protested, "Uncle Tom must be killed, George Harris exiled! Heaven for dead Negroes! Liberia for living mulattoes. Neither can live on the American continent. Death or banishment is our doom, say the Slaveocrats, the Colonizationists, and, save the mark – Mrs. Stowe!!" Stowe reportedly regretted her decision, explaining that she would end the novel differently if given the opportunity to write it over again. However, her popularity and increasing influence as a world-famous abolitionist probably did most to quell the protests.[30]

Describing a pilgrimage he made to Stowe's home, Frederick Douglass reported, without a shred of irony, how her Andover residence had come to be known locally as "Uncle Tom's Cabin." In addition to reflecting the nature of fads in American culture,

Douglass's observation hints at the power to shape reality that Stowe's fiction quickly attained, a power that blacks could not help but acknowledge. Some were more than willing to play along: The ex-slaves Lewis Clarke and Josiah Henson, for example, promoted themselves as the prototypes of George Harris and Uncle Tom, respectively. Henson, in fact, drove the black critic Benjamin Brawley to complain that "any student of [his] career is likely to be exasperated by his tendency to exploit himself." Stowe's prefaces to the 1858 edition of Henson's slave narrative and to Frank J. Webb's novel, *The Garies and Their Friends* (1857), further suggest the weight her imprimatur carried in establishing the credibility of black writers. Inevitably, other Afro-Americans responded to Stowe and the immense power she wielded as an interpreter of black life with frustration and resentment. We find the most dramatic evidence of such hostility in a public exchange of letters between Frederick Douglass and Martin R. Delany.[31]

In March 1853, Douglass explained in his newspaper that he had recently visited Stowe in order "to consult with the authoress, as to some method which should contribute successfully, and permanently, to the improvement and elevation of the free people of color." Delany's angry response to this admission comes within a month: "I beg leave to say, that she *knows nothing about us*[;] . . . neither does any other white person." Douglass's bristling retort reflects the heated nature of this debate: "The assertion that Mrs. Stowe 'knows nothing about us,' shows that Bro. Delany knows nothing about Mrs. Stowe; for he certainly would not so violate his moral, or common sense if he did." Predictably, the discussion soon encompasses Stowe's major contribution to the Afro-American cause. In a letter entitled "Uncle Tom," Delany sarcastically argues that because Stowe and her publishers were profiting so substantially from the book, it would be only right for Josiah Henson, the "real *Uncle Tom*," to receive compensation. Proceeding then to link some of Stowe's characters with their real-life counterparts, Delany delivers an impassioned, scathing attack upon the passivity embodied by Tom:

> I have always thought that George and Eliza were Mr. Henry Bibb
> and his first wife, with the character of Mr. Lewis Hayden, his wife

Harriet and little son, who also effected their escape from Kentucky. . . . I say the *person* of Bibb with the *character* of Hayden; because, in personal appearance of stature and color, as well as circumstances, Bibb answers precisely to George; while he stood quietly by, as he tells us in his own great narrative[,] . . . with a hoe in his hand, begging his master to desist, while he *stripped his wife's clothing off (!!!)* and lacerated her flesh, until the blood flowed in pools at her feet! To the contrary, had this been Hayden – who, by the way, is not like Bibb nearly *white*, but *black* – he would have bured the hoe deep in the master's skull, laying him lifeless at his feet.

Delany closes with the rather unconvincing claim that his familiarity with *Uncle Tom's Cabin* is due solely to *"my wife* having *told* me the most I know about it."[32]

Delany's skirmish with Douglass, whom he terms Stowe's "attorney," continues the following week, with the two black leaders bickering over Stowe's view of Haiti, the apparent endorsement of colonization in *Uncle Tom's Cabin,* and the proposed use of white instructors in the industrial school that Stowe and Douglass were discussing. By this point, however, it is clear that the debate between these two dedicated black men involves not just emigration, educational policy, or even the nature of Uncle Tom's heroism. Rather, the differences between them are both ideological and deeply personal. At the time, Delany was looking outside of the United States and, indeed, outside of white society's sphere of influence for a solution to the dilemma confronting Afro-Americans; Douglass endorsed an integrationist position and saw no reason to "find fault with well-meant efforts for our benefit." These stances necessarily entailed antithetical attitudes toward cooperation with sympathetic whites in general and especially with Stowe, considering her preeminent role as a literary and inevitably ideological authenticator of the black experience. When Delany tautly declares, "[N]o enterprize, institution, or anything else, should be commenced *for us,* or our general benefit, without *first consulting us,"* he is demanding the right of self-determination, a right that he felt Stowe was violating and one that blacks, in Douglass's mind, were too "disunited and scattered" to exercise effectively. In a broad sense, their argument is an early manifesta-

71

tion of a disagreement among Afro-American thinkers over tactics
– both literary and political – that still persists.[33]

Regardless of their feelings toward Stowe herself or toward her
creation, early Afro-American fiction writers inevitably wrote in
her wake. This is not to suggest that most black authors consciously modeled their work upon *Uncle Tom's Cabin*. To do so
would be to give the book, as great an impact as it had, more credit
than it deserves. Rather, Stowe's best-seller embodied a whole
constellation of preexisting, often conflicting ideas regarding race,
powerfully dramatized them in a sentimental fashion, presented
them with an unabashedly didactic reformist message, and, finally,
proceeded to sell like the dickens. Black writers could not help but
be convinced that if enough of the right ingredients were combined in the right proportions under the right conditions, they too
could concoct deeply political novels that might tap the same mass
audience that Stowe did and thereby shape the attitudes of whites
toward the black minority in the United States.

In bequeathing to Afro-American protest novelists writing after
her a literary form and stance as well as a white audience with
certain strong expectations, Stowe also helped to establish a range
of character types that served to bind and restrict black authors for
decades. As a result, *Uncle Tom's Cabin* was an abiding, at times
daunting, paradigmatic influence for most early Afro-American
fiction writers, casting its shadow over their diverse attempts to
define realistically the black capacity for heroic action while not
alienating the white audience that they felt they absolutely had to
hold in order to bring about political change. William Stanley
Braithwaite puts it this way: "The moral gain and historical effect
of Uncle Tom have been an artistic loss and setback. The treatment
of Negro life and character, overlaid with these forceful stereotypes, could not develop into artistically satisfactory portraiture."[34] For instance, many Afro-American writers tacitly endorsed the incipient class and color hierarchies underlying Stowe's
treatment of mixed-blood and full-blood black characters in her
fiction. It is, in fact, a short step from Stowe's depiction of full-
blood field hands as "low," often comic figures to the emphasis in
many Afro-American novels on the alleged distinctions in behav-

ior, education, speech, and appearance between generally light-skinned, bourgeois characters and dark-skinned, lower-class blacks.

Thus, although James H. W. Howard's *Bond and Free: A True Tale of Slave Times* (1886) is ultimately as much an antidote to Stowe's oversentimentalized depiction of slavery as it is to the work of the racist plantation tradition writers, it is also marred by the use of stereotypical black characterizations. For example, his portrayal of the slave Eloise reveals her to be kin to Topsy:

> Eloise was very fat, very round, and very ugly, with a face like a butter ball, and eyes that sat in her head like two holes burnt into a blanket. Her hair stood out straight from her head like the quills upon a porcupine. In addition to this, she was black, sly, . . . had an insatiable desire for mischief, and was as near being uncivilized as a human being can be without being actually so.

Even more grotesque is his treatment of a servant named Alanthe. The only acrobatic, cartoonish, black imp figure in the novel, she "might have been taken for a boy from the scarcity of hair on her head, and the coat-like garment she wore reaching down to her knees, exposing a pair of very black and very thin legs, [and] very large feet whose toes stood apart with perfect individuality." In a bit of gratuitous darky humor, Howard explains how, when sent on an errand, Alanthe "bounded from the room, turning a somersault through the window, and landing on the portico."[35]

Less crude but equally revealing endorsements of class and color distinctions are evident in the often ambivalent attitudes of nineteenth-century Afro-American writers toward black folk culture, something that, if not entirely foreign to their own experience, many of them would just as soon leave behind. In *Iola Leroy, or Shadows Uplifted* (1892), for example, Frances Ellen Watkins Harper undercuts the tragic mulatto motif by presenting light-skinned blacks who, although able to pass for whites, refuse to do so. Further, like George and Eliza Harris, these figures meet or surpass every white criterion for beauty, intelligence, respectability, and training. To depict such characters who are above white reproach on any count does indeed serve to prove that hostile portraits of Afro-Americans are neither fair nor completely valid. However, their unrelenting, high-minded propriety often subverts the verisimilitude Harper is struggling to establish, and the accompanying implied condemnation of black folkways does little to counter the suggestion that Afro-Americans need not be treated as equals until they become "white." Harper merely argues that such a cultural, if not racial, transmogrification is possible. Although both *Bond and Free* and *Iola Leroy* generally succeed as revisionist blows against the appalling array of antiblack novels, histories, and pseudoscientific studies that flooded the literary marketplace in the post-Reconstruction period, they also serve to perpetuate limited patterns of characterization that first received widespread currency in fiction through *Uncle Tom's Cabin.*

The most crucial aspect of the "artistic loss and setback" Braithwaite mentions involves Stowe's depiction of the appropriate black response to oppression. It is not merely that she makes Uncle Tom the major heroic figure in the text. Rather, it is that her contrasting portraits of Tom and George Harris posit a specific ethical basis for acceptable black behavior. If, as Richard Wright contends, "oppression spawned among them [blacks] a myriad variety of reactions, reaching from outright blind rebellion to sweet, other-worldly submissiveness," then Stowe obviously places a greater moral value on the latter, on a willing victimization that receives its reward in the hereafter. Struck by the forthright militance of George Harris, the modern reader might be tempted to conclude that Stowe sees this character as embodying a brand of heroism at least as attractive as Uncle Tom's. However, to interpret her location of George within an American patriotic tradition as a blanket endorsement of his stance is, I would argue, to misread her position. Many commentators have noted how adherents to the philosophy of nonresistance expressed ambivalence toward and occasionally even condemnation of the violent means used by American colonists to win their independence. In a speech in 1837, for example, William Lloyd Garrison declared, "This nation is destined to perish, because in wading through blood and carnage to independence, *it at the outset discarded the Prince of Peace, and elected George Washington to be its Saviour.*" Although Stowe is hardly so doctrinaire in her pacifism that she cannot find Harris's behavior appealing, her staunch New Testament Christianity forces her to view his urge toward rebellion as of questionable morality, for it can entail disobedience and, more importantly, a willingness to use violence.[36]

Stowe renders a similar judgment in her depiction of Cassy, whose militance must also be diluted. Unlike Harris, however, whose vehement resistance to slavery struck many readers (and, at some level, even Stowe herself) as manly, Cassy is a far more dangerous figure, for there was no readily available paradigm for acceptable female heroism that would safely permit her insurgence to stand unqualified by her apparent emotional derangement. That is, it is Eliza and not Cassy who meets the criteria of the mid-nineteenth century sentimental heroine; and given the extraordinarily dehumanizing racist image of the black slave woman held by most whites at the time, Eliza does indeed represent a step forward. Nonetheless, although Cassy's successful exploitation of Legree's guilt and fear exemplifies an indirect form of resistance through which slave women ensured their own survival and that of their families, Stowe provides no validation of the more direct, aggressive rebellion of the numerous female slaves who struck back and even killed rather than endure their oppression any longer. Clearly, Afro-American writers who sought to depict nonsentimental heroic female figures had to challenge not just racial stereotypes but gender stereotypes as well.

The novella *Aunt Lindy, A Story Founded on Real Life* (1892) by the black journalist and community worker Victoria Earle [Matthews] reveals in stark, disconcerting images the psychological cost of this Uncle-Tomish abjuration of violence on the part of the female protagonist. In this short melodrama, an ex-slave named Aunt Lindy takes in a white victim of a disastrous fire. While nursing him back to health, she discovers that he is her old master who had sold away her children. Before her urge for revenge can explode into action, however, she hears the sound of an "olden-time melody" from a prayer meeting located conveniently nearby, and she relents. The totally incredible resolution comes when we learn that the new black preacher in the neighborhood is Lindy's long-lost firstborn.[37]

Although *Aunt Lindy* superficially resembles the mawkish plantation tradition tale of the ex-slave who saves the life of his or her former white owner, Earle's characterization of Lindy differs radi-

cally from the black images in the works of writers like Thomas
Nelson Page and Joel Chandler Harris. It also represents an important motif in the developing of the black fictive protagonist: the
struggle to incorporate the human emotion of anger into a figure
whom the author wishes the white audience to view favorably.
Here Earle's description of Aunt Lindy's rage is undeniably powerful, albeit overwritten:

> Demoniac gleams of exultation and bitter hatred settled upon her
> now grim features; a pitiless smile wreathed her set lips, as she
> gazed with glaring eyeballs at this helpless, homeless "victim of the
> great fire," as though surrounded by demons; a dozen wicked im-
> pulses rushed through her mind – a life for a life. . . . Her blood was
> afire, her tall form swayed, her long, bony hands trembled like an
> animal at bay.[38]

This moment soon passes, however, for in Earle's world (as in
Stowe's), religion proves a palliative for such a near loss of control.
In a real sense, Lindy is "saved" from herself.

When black fiction writers more ambitious and technically ade-
pt than Earle turn away from the relative moral straightfor-
wardness of the slavery issue and try to confront ethically complex
contemporary racial problems, they encounter even greater difficulties in their characterizations. In particular, the majority of
them fall prey to the most pernicious and yet indispensable of
Stowe's tactics: the use of black victimization as an emotional
lever to move white readers to pity and even a sense of guilt.
Although such an approach ensures the moral superiority of the
Afro-American figure, in approximating the Christlike, the black
martyr leaves the realm of the human.

Two black Detroit journalists, Walter H. Stowers and William H.
Anderson, adopt this strategy in *Appointed* (1894). Late in the
novel, John Saunders, a fair-skinned, college-trained Afro-American, accidentally collides with a white man in a southern city. In
the resultant scuffle, the northern-bred Saunders instinctively de-
fends himself against his white assailant and is arrested. The authors' depiction of this middle-class young black man as he moves
from violent rage through a determination to hide his fear of the
gathering lynch mob to final grief is quite effectively rendered.
Unfortunately, before Saunders dies at the hands of that mob, he

finds enough breath to exclaim melodramatically, "Oh, my country! What scenes of carnage and strife, of woe and sorrow, will take place if these unworthy ideas and wild passions are allowed to hold such full sway." He then gives Seth Stanley, his white friend and the true protagonist of the novel, the message that Stowers and Anderson are doubtless directing to their white audience as well: "Stir up and create a public opinion and cease not, until it is so aroused that justice, waking from her long sleep, will demand equal protection and liberty, for all citizens of the Republic. God will be with you."[39] In *Appointed,* the authors present the literal annihilation of the black hero in the hope that his martyrdom will inspire in the receptive white reader a new understanding of and sympathy for the plight of the Afro-American. That Stowers and Anderson never convincingly endorse a Christian view of Saunders's fate indicates the desperate nature of the attempt to elicit a favorable white response. Unlike Uncle Tom's death, which, to Stowe, represents in itself the real victory – the entry into a heavenly afterlife – the significance of Saunders's martyrdom depends upon the subsequent actions of Stanley and, the authors hope, of the white reader.

The Afro-American writer most sensitive to the ethical dilemma raised by the attempt to depict blacks both as victims and as heroes is Charles W. Chesnutt. In *The Marrow of Tradition* (1901), he details the painful, inevitable conflict between antithetical strategies for coping with the virulent racism that made life so treacherous for Afro-Americans at the turn of the century. On one side stands William Miller, the bourgeois mulatto physician, whose response to prejudice is patience, rationalization, and a desperate hope that justice will win out. On the other stands Josh Green, the violent black laborer whose fierce pride and belief in his own self-worth motivate his suicidal posture of militant resistance. By the end of the book, Josh Green is dead, having given his life to defend the property of blacks from a destructive white mob; Miller's son has been killed by a stray bullet during the riot; and Major Carteret, the white editor responsible for instigating the tragedy, has come to beg Miller to save his own sick child. Like George Harris, Cassy, Aunt Lindy, and John Saunders, Miller initially responds to his predicament with an explosive, righteous anger seen all too rarely in early Afro-American fiction. He quickly yields, however, to the pleas of Mrs. Carteret and allows Janet, his wife and Mrs. Carteret's half-sister, to make the final decision. Predictably, she agrees to send him, and the book ends as he rushes out of the door on his errand of mercy.

Here, in the last scene of this powerful novel, Chesnutt gallantly attempts to recapitulate in a post-Reconstruction context the entire moral thrust of *Uncle Tom's Cabin*. Unlike Stowe and the authors of *Appointed*, however, Chesnutt does not sacrifice his main black character. Instead, he offers up the Millers' child – and a great deal of their credibility as characters – on the altar of racial conciliation. As we see in a number of nineteenth-century Afro-American novels, rage, bitterness, and a desire for revenge on the part of positively portrayed black figures must be curbed in order to establish them as self-controlled, all-forgiving, and eminently acceptable candidates for membership in the American mainstream. However, Chesnutt was not so blind to the realities of his time that he could show his characters' repudiation of their anger as the result of any genuine, unqualified acceptance by whites. That is, Mrs. Carteret's plea to the Millers is a far cry from the Quakers' bringing George and his family into the charmed circle of their loving household. Nor is Chesnutt so committed to an explicitly Christian view of social change that he can, like Stowe, justify the behavior of his characters in solely religious terms. Thus, the moral superiority of the Millers is important for primarily extraliterary reasons: It becomes a weapon Chesnutt uses to hammer away at the hard hearts and iron-clad consciences of white readers, who, he knows, are not thoroughly convinced that Afro-Americans are really human. It is both ironic and understandable that Chesnutt hoped that *Marrow* would "become lodged in the popular mind as the legitimate successor of Uncle Tom's Cabin."[40]

Underlying much of the fiction produced by Afro-Americans before World War I is not a desire to render black life as accurately and honestly as possible but rather a willingness to dissemble, to overemphasize, even to misrepresent – that is, to write with the aim of eliciting sympathy from the white reader. And evoking the appropriate response from that reader was no easy task, for unlike many black writers during the 1840s and 1850s, Afro-American novelists after Reconstruction could not count at all on the existence of a supportive white audience. As a result, in reading these texts today, one is sometimes struck in the course of a paragraph, a page, a chapter, or indeed an entire novel by the realization that the particular work of literature is not primarily about black people but rather designed to guide stock, inadequately developed characters through the motions of an empty ritual that had long since lost significance and to which the artists themselves, their protests to the contrary notwithstanding, could not wholeheartedly commit themselves.

In terms of genre, many nineteenth-century Afro-American writers simply could not effectively reconcile their urge toward realism with their antithetical desire to appropriate the emotional appeal of the sentimental novel, a genre grounded in a Christian conception of social redemption and, as a tool of political protest, best exemplified by *Uncle Tom's Cabin*. Stowe fortuitously tapped both a religious and a secular millennial ideology that would view the Civil War as divine retribution, Appomatox as the brave new world reborn, and Lincoln as the Christlike sacrificial lamb. Unfortunately for many of the writers who followed Stowe, although her images maintained their power – indeed, became more vivid and persistent as time passed – abolitionism may have been the last successful reform movement in the United States fueled largely by a progressive Christianity. If the salvation of the Union did not sufficiently release the tensions Stowe's novel had helped to screw tighter, then the accelerating secularization of American culture that accompanied the industrial and commercial explosion of the Gilded Age served to make moral appeals for change nearly irrelevant. The rise of Social Darwinism reinforced this trend by providing not only the terms racist theorists needed to justify the oppression of blacks but also the Sumnerian laissez-faire social policy that saw almost any reform at all as a futile violation of the inexorable evolutionary sorting of the fit from the unfit. Even some of the staunchest friends of the freed slaves manifested this tough new pragmatism; for example, Booker T. Washington's famous mentor, General Samuel C. Armstrong, once observed drily, "The whole darky business has been in the hands of women and sentimentalists." In the final analysis, post-Reconstruction Afro-American writers who desired to duplicate Stowe's success found themselves addressing an audience that could no longer be made to feel guilty and for whom a quasi-Christian appeal had lost much of its moral force. Few, if any, realized that, as the black poet Albery A. Whitman put it in 1885, "all 'Uncle Toms' and 'Topsies' ought to die. *Goody goodness* is a sort of man worship: ignorance is its inspiration, fear its ministering spirit, and beggary its inheritance." Few, if any, seemed to realize that they were courageously but futilely assailing what the turn-of-the-century black author James D. Corrothers called "the closed gate of justice" with weapons dulled by time and rendered obsolete by inevitable social change.[41]

NOTES

1 *The Uncle Tom's Cabin Almanack, or Abolitionist Memento* (London: John Cassell, 1853), p. 59.

2 George Eliot, review of *Dred; A Tale of the Great Dismal Swamp*, by Harriet Beecher Stowe, in *Critical Essays on Harriet Beecher Stowe*, ed. Elizabeth Ammons (Boston: G. K. Hall, 1980), p. 43.

3 [Frederick Douglass], "Literary Notices," *Frederick Douglass' Paper*, April 8, 1852, p. 2; "A Year's Work," *Frederick Douglass' Paper*, April 22, 1853, p. 2.

4 William Stanley Braithwaite, "The Negro in American Literature," in *The New Negro*, ed. Alain Locke (1925; rpt. New York: Atheneum, 1975), p. 30; Benjamin Quarles, *Black Abolitionists* (New York: Oxford University Press, 1969), p. 67; Leslie A. Fiedler, *The Inadvertent Epic: From "Uncle Tom's Cabin" to "Roots"* (New York: Simon & Schuster, 1979), p. 26. My essay was written before the publication of Thomas F. Gossett's *Uncle Tom's Cabin and American Culture* (Dallas, Texas: Southern Methodist University Press, 1985). In discussing Stowe's racial attitudes and the public responses to her novel, we draw upon some of the same sources.

5 Thomas Graham, "Harriet Beecher Stowe and the Question of Race," *New England Quarterly* 46 (December 1973):616. For discussions of how the minstrel show shaped white conceptions of the Afro-American, see William L. Van Deburg, *Slavery and Race in American Popular*

Culture (Madison: University of Wisconsin Press, 1984), pp. 39–49; Robert C. Toll, *Blacking Up: The Minstrel Show in Nineteenth-Century America* (New York: Oxford University Press, 1974).

6 Harriet Beecher Stowe, *Uncle Tom's Cabin; or, Life among the Lowly*, ed. Kenneth Lynn (1852; rpt. Cambridge, Mass.: Harvard University Press, 1962), chap. 11. Subsequent references to this edition of *Uncle Tom's Cabin* will be indicated parenthetically in the text by the chapter number.

7 George Sand, review of *Uncle Tom's Cabin*, by Harriet Beecher Stowe, in Ammons, ed., *Critical Essays*, p. 5.

8 Harriet Beecher Stowe, *The Key to Uncle Tom's Cabin* (1853; rpt. New York: Arno, 1968), p. 51.

9 Ibid., p. 45. The following remark, made by F. W. Boreham over a century after the publication of *Uncle Tom's Cabin*, attests to the persistence of this idea: "Shipped as savages from Africa, the coloured people brought virgin minds and vacant hearts to the new world" (F. W. Boreham, *The Gospel of Uncle Tom's Cabin* [London: Epworth Press, 1956], p. 15).

10 Barbara Welter, "The Cult of True Womanhood," *American Quarterly* 18 (September 1966):152, 153; Welter, "The Merchant's Daughter: A Tale from Life," *New England Quarterly* 42 (March 1969):11.

11 Elizabeth Ammons, "Heroines in *Uncle Tom's Cabin*," *American Literature* 49 (May 1977):162; Stowe, *Key*, p. 41.

12 Langston Hughes, Introduction to *Uncle Tom's Cabin*, in Ammons, ed., *Critical Essays*, p. 102; James D. Hart, *The Popular Book: A History of America's Literary Taste* (1950; rpt. Berkeley: University of California Press, 1963), p. 111; [William Gilmore Simms], review of *The Key to Uncle Tom's Cabin*, by Harriet Beecher Stowe, *Southern Quarterly Review* 24 (July 1853):221; Sterling Brown, *The Negro in American Fiction* (1937; rpt. New York: Atheneum, 1969), p. 21.

13 L. S. M. [Louisa S. C. McCord], review of *Uncle Tom's Cabin*, by Harriet Beecher Stowe, *Southern Quarterly Review* 23 (January 1853): 113, 117.

14 Stowe, *Key*, p. 117; [Simms], review of *Key*, pp. 232, 221–2, 223.

15 [Simms], review of *Key*, p. 234; Nehemiah Adams, *The Sable Cloud: A Southern Tale, with Northern Comments* (Boston: Ticknor and Fields, 1861), p. 135.

16 Severn Duvall, "*Uncle Tom's Cabin*: The Sinister Side of the Patriarchy," *New England Quarterly* 36 (March 1963):3–22; Harold Beaver, "Time on the Cross: White Fiction and Black Messiahs,"

Yearbook of English Studies 8 (1978):45; Stowe, *Key*, p. 56; [McCord], review of *Uncle Tom's Cabin*, p. 118.

17 [William Lloyd Garrison], review of *Uncle Tom's Cabin*, by Harriet Beecher Stowe, *The Liberator*, March 26, 1852, p. 50; [Garrison], "Letter from Rev. J. W. Loguen, *The Liberator*, May 5, 1854, p. 71; Charles K. Whipple, *The Non-Resistance Principle: With Particular Application to the Help of Slaves by Abolitionists* (Boston: R. F. Wallcut, 1860), pp. 6, 20, 21–2, 21.

18 Henry C. Wright, "Uncle Tom's Cabin – Objectionable Characteristics," *The Liberator*, July 9, 1852, p. 111; Harriet Beecher Stowe, Preface to *Uncle Tom's Cabin; or, Life among the Lowly* (1852; rpt. New York: New American Library, 1966), pp. v–vi.

19 Hart, *Popular Book*, pp. 57, 60, 112; Stephen A. Hirsch, "Uncle Tomitudes: The Popular Reaction to *Uncle Tom's Cabin*," *Studies in the American Renaissance* (1978):311. Stowe's conclusion to the serialized version of *Uncle Tom's Cabin* reveals the degree to which she aimed the novel at young readers: "Dear children, you will soon be men and women, and I hope that you will learn from this story always to remember and pity the poor and oppressed. When you grow up, show your pity by doing all you can for them. . . . Farewell, dear children, until we meet again" (Harriet Beecher Stowe, *The Annotated Uncle Tom's Cabin*, ed. Philip Van Doren Stern [New York: Paul S. Eriksson, 1964], p. 564).

20 [Douglass], "Literary Notices," p. 2; A Southern Lady, "British Philanthropy and American Slavery," *DeBow's Review* 14 (March 1853):260, 279.

21 George M. Fredrickson, *The Black Image in the White Mind: The Debate on Afro-American Character and Destiny, 1817–1914* (New York: Harper Torchbooks, 1971), pp. 103, 127; Stowe, Preface, p. v; Jean Fagan Yellin, *The Intricate Knot: Black Figures in American Literature, 1776–1863* (New York: New York University Press, 1972), p. 136.

22 Gayle Kimball, *The Religious Ideas of Harriet Beecher Stowe* (New York: Edwin Mullen Press, 1982), pp. 1, 71, 177. Perhaps Constance Rourke was the first to suggest that "it was Uncle Tom . . . with whom Mrs. Stowe most identified herself, covering him with a pity akin to self-pity, endowing him with a mild faith which she had struggled so long to attain" (Constance Mayfield Rourke, *Trumpets of Jubilee* [New York: Harcourt, Brace, 1927], p. 108).

23 Mary Church Terrell, *Harriet Beecher Stowe: An Appreciation* (Washington, D.C.: Murray Brothers, 1911), p. 12.

24 Paul Laurence Dunbar, "Harriet Beecher Stowe," in *Lyrics of the Hearthside* (New York: Dodd, Mead, 1899), p. 97.

25 Sutton E. Griggs, *The Hindered Hand; or, The Reign of the Repressionist* (1905; rpt. Miami: Mnemosyne, 1969), p. 207.

26 Edmund Wilson, *Patriotic Gore: Studies in the Literature of the American Civil War* (New York: Oxford University Press, 1962), p. 4; Margaret Mitchell to Alexander L. May, July 22, 1938, *Margaret Mitchell's "Gone with the Wind" Letters, 1936–1949*, ed. Richard Harwell (New York: Macmillan, 1976), p. 217; Joseph L. Fant III and Robert Ashley, ed., *Faulkner at West Point* (New York: Random House, 1964), p. 104.

27 Wallace Lee, "Is 'Uncle Tom's Cabin' Anti-Negro?", *Negro Digest* 4 (January 1946):68; Richard Wright, "How 'Bigger' Was Born," in *Native Son* (1940; rpt. New York: Harper & Row, Perennial Classics, 1966), p. xxvii; James Baldwin, "Everybody's Protest Novel," *Partisan Review* 16 (June 1949):578–85; Ishmael Reed, *Flight to Canada* (New York: Random House, 1976).

28 William Wells Brown, Letter, *The Liberator*, June 3, 1853, p. 87; Frances E. Watkins, "Eliza Harris," *Frederick Douglass' Paper*, December 23, 1853, p. 4; "Proceedings of the Colored National Convention, Held in Rochester, July 6th, 7th and 8th, 1853," in *Minutes of the Proceedings of the National Negro Conventions, 1830–1864*, ed. Howard Holman Bell (New York: Arno, 1969), p. 40.

29 William C. Nell, "The Colored Citizens of Boston," *The Liberator*, December 10, 1852, p. 199; William G. Allen, Letter, *Frederick Douglass' Paper*, May 20, 1852, p. 3.

30 George T. Downing, Letter, *Frederick Douglass' Paper*, December 22, 1854, p. 3; Quarles, *Black Abolitionists*, p. 220. George Downing alludes to Stowe's change of heart in his letter. In addition, the white abolitionist Louis Tappan claimed that he "wrote to have it [the reference to emigration in *Uncle Tom's Cabin*] omitted; but it was too late; otherwise she would have done so" ("American and Foreign Anti-Slavery Society," *Frederick Douglass' Paper*, May 27, 1852, p. 2). Thomas Graham points out, however, that "in her next antislavery novel *Dred*, she again wrote favorably of colonization" (Graham, "Harriet Beecher Stowe," p. 621).

31 [Frederick Douglass], "A Day and a Night in 'Uncle Tom's Cabin,'" *Frederick Douglass' Paper*, March 4, 1853, p. 2; Benjamin Brawley, *The Negro Genius* (New York: Dodd, Mead, 1937), p. 66. In a discussion of the authenticating strategies of ex-slave writers, Robert Stepto points out that in dedicating his narrative to Stowe, Solomon Northup calls it

This essay explores the ways in which *Uncle Tom's Cabin*, written three years after the meeting at Seneca Falls where feminists had spelled out their demands for full participation in American life, dramatizes women's roles in the fight against chattel slavery in America.

In 1836, public debate over the place of women in the life of the young republic was transformed when Angelina E. Grimké, youngest daughter of an aristocratic slaveholding Charleston family, identified herself with the Garrisonian abolitionists and published *An Appeal to the Christian Women of the South*.[3] Almost immediately, her effort to assume the leadership of American women was challenged by the northern educator Catharine Beecher. In *An Essay on Slavery and Abolitionism, with Reference to the Duty of American Females, Addressed to A. E. Grimké,* Beecher presented the basic tenets of an ideology that she developed to counter Grimké, an ideology historian Kathryn Sklar has dubbed "domestic feminism."[4] The Garrisonian abolitionists Angelina Grimké and her sister and co-worker Sarah responded with three polemics spelling out the basic tenets of nineteenth-century American feminism. By the time Stowe wrote her novel, the ideas on both sides had been elaborated. In her *Treatise on Domestic Economy* and elsewhere, Beecher had developed the notion of the moral superiority of females and the argument that by dominating domestic life, women could redeem American culture. Followers of the Grimkés' doctrine of sexual equality had organized the woman's rights movement, implementing their belief that women should reform American life by acting within the public sphere as well as within the home.[5]

The polemics by the Grimké sisters and Catharine Beecher agree on a number of points. All concur that slavery is a sin, that America is in danger, that Christian women have the power to end slavery and save the nation, and that they have a duty to act in this crisis. They clash, however, when they discuss how and where women should act. Their dispute is grounded not only in differing ideas about race and abolitionism but also in their divergent ideas about women and American democracy.

In her *Appeal to the Christian Women of the South,* Grimké had suggested that free white southern women oppose slavery by performing a series of unexceptional private acts within the domestic circle – reading, praying, being kind, convincing the males in their families that slavery is wrong, and persuading the slaves to remain submissive. But she had also urged these southern women to perform exceptional acts – to break state laws and emancipate their slaves, pay them wages, and teach them to read and write. She had proposed that these women flaunt the statutes forbidding emancipation and literacy in obedience to a Higher Law, and counseled that, if apprehended, they should practice the doctrine of Christian resignation: "If a law commands me to *sin I will break it;* if it calls me to *suffer,* I will let it take its course *unresistingly.*"⁶ Suggesting that southern women pattern themselves on the biblical Queen Esther and on the members of contemporary British Ladies' Anti-Slavery Societies, Grimké urged them specifically to risk engaging in political action and appealing to their legislators to end chattel slavery.

Catharine Beecher, asked to circulate the *Appeal* and learning of Grimké's plans to organize northern women in the abolitionist cause, responded by challenging Grimké directly. Postulating an aristocratic order in which "Heaven has appointed to one sex the superior, and to the other the subordinate station," and asserting that "woman holds a subordinate relation in society to the other sex," in a pamphlet framed as a letter to Grimké, Beecher defines the appropriate behavior for women:

> A man may act on society by the collision of intellect, in public debate; he may urge his measures by a sense of shame, by fear and by personal interest; he may coerce by the combination of public sentiment; he may drive by physical force, and he does not outstep the boundaries of his sphere. But all the power, and all the conquests that are lawful to women, are those only which appeal to the kindly, generous, peaceful and benevolent principles.
>
> Woman is to win every thing by peace and love. . . . But this is to all be accomplished in the domestic and social sphere.

Accordingly, Beecher asserts that women should limit the expression of their oppression to slavery to the domestic circle, where they should use their influence to mediate between opponents and advocates of slavery. Predictably, she is "entirely opposed to the plan of arraying females in any Abolition movement."[7]

As for Grimké's proposal that southern women petition their legislators to end slavery, Beecher asserts that "in this country, petitions to Congress . . . seem IN ALL CASES, to fall entirely without the sphere of female duty." Arguing that the crucial need is not for women to exert political power but to use their female force to promote a national "spirit of candour, forbearance, charity, and peace," Beecher urges Christian women to recognize their true calling as the guardians of American morals and American youth. By assuming this role, she argues, they can "exert a wise and appropriate influence, and one which will most certainly tend to bring an end, not only of slavery, but unnumbered other evils and wrongs."[8]

The Grimkés responded in three polemics setting forth the basic ideas of nineteenth-century American feminism. Grounding their arguments in the philosophy of natural rights and in a radical reading of the Bible, they assert woman's equal role with man as God's reasonable creature and as citizen of the Republic.

The cover of *An Appeal to the Women of the Nominally Free States,* their first pamphlet, suggests both its connections to and its quarrels with Beecher's polemic. Her call for women to respond to the current crisis is quoted, but her conclusions are countered by a text urging women to become abolitionist partisans within the political arena; an antislavery quatrain by the black poet Sarah Forten signals that instead of ignoring the role of black women, as Beecher had, this polemic pleads for unity among women of all races. It proposes that white women end their prejudice and urges black women to "mingle with us *whilst* we have the prejudice, because it is only by associating with you that we shall ever be able to overcome it."[9]

Angelina Grimké's fullest answer to Beecher, however, is *Letters to Catherine E. Beecher, in Reply to An Essay on Slavery and Abolitionism, Addressed to A. E. Grimké.* Written as Grimké was traveling on her historic lecture tour during the summer of 1837, this polemic radiates the energy sparked by her controversy with Beecher and fueled by her encounters with "promiscuous" audiences of men and women throughout New England. Grimké concludes with three essays on woman's role in the national struggle against chattel slavery and white racism. Presenting a natural rights argument that "woman's rights are . . . an integral part of her moral being" and asserting that "the mere circumstance of sex does not give to man higher rights and responsibilities than to women," she reasons that "whatever it is morally right for a man to do, it is morally right for a woman to do." It follows that women, like men, have a duty to end the sin of slavery by acting within both the domestic and public spheres. Similarly, women, like men, can appropriately engage in sharp argument, and they most certainly should join the abolitionists' petition campaigns:

> The right of petition is the only political right that women have. . . . Surely, we ought to be permitted at least to remonstrate against every political measure that may tend to injure or oppress our sex.

Attacking Beecher's *Letters* as an effort "to quench the flame of sympathy in the hearts of their fathers, husbands, brothers and sons," Grimké accuses her of lacking "deep sympathy for thy sister in bonds." "Where, oh where," she asks — exposing the raw nerve joining feminist politics and female culture — "are the outpourings of a soul overwhelmed with a sense of the heinous crimes of our nation, and the necessity of immediate repentance?"[10]

This polemic inspired two others. Sarah Grimké expanded its discussion of women into a comprehensive argument in *Letters on the Equality of the Sexes and the Condition of Woman*, the fullest statement of American feminism to precede the Declaration of Sentiments adopted at Seneca Falls in 1848. In addition, the Grimké sisters, working with Angelina's husband, Theodore Weld, apparently used its inclusion of southerners' descriptions of slavery as a model for *American Slavery As It Is: Testimony of a Thousand Witnesses*.[11] Composed of clippings from southern newspapers and statements from observers of southern slavery, this best-selling abolitionist fact book became an effective weapon in the abolitionist campaign for signatures on anti-slavery petitions to Congress.

American Slavery As It Is fulfilled an additional function: Harriet Beecher Stowe later wrote that she kept it "in her work basket by day, and slept with it under her pillow by night, till its facts crystallized into Uncle Tom."[12]

The women Stowe portrays in *Uncle Tom's Cabin* do not merely exist within the system of chattel slavery; they are largely defined by their various relationships to this system. Repeatedly – inevitably – they make choices and engage in actions that relate to the slavery question. In the beginning, these dramas of moral choice are acted out by Emily Shelby and Marie St. Clare, free white "Christian women of the South"; they are later reenacted by Mary Bird and Rachel Halliday, white women of the "nominally free states." Although Stowe includes among her characters female slaves – mulatto women like Eliza Harris and Cassy and black females like Aunt Chloe and Topsy – she does not present them with similar moral seriousness.

Because slavery determines the texture of their home life, Stowe's white southern ladies need not stray beyond their own walls to engage in this drama of moral choice. Mrs. Shelby is seated at her dressing table when she learns, from her husband's sale of Eliza's little Harry and Uncle Tom, the lesson she could have learned by reading Angelina Grimké's *Appeal to the Christian Women of the South*. She learns that slavery is

"A bitter, bitter, most accursed thing! – a curse to the master and a curse to the slave! I was a fool to think I could make anything good out of such a deadly evil. It is a sin. . . . but I thought I could gild it over, – I thought, by kindness, and care, and instruction, I could make the condition of mine better than freedom, – fool that I was!" (Chap. 5)

Watching her efforts to oppose these slave sales, we see an equivocal dramatization of Catharine Beecher's program. As if following Beecher's restrictions, Emily Shelby temperately asks permission to intercede for the slaves within her own home. But she is unsuccessful (and, in her distress, sounds the harsh tones of abolitionist reprovers, as her husband notes). Mrs. Shelby, although a member of the slaveholding class, as a married woman is powerless to prevent these sales. Forbidden by her husband from using her "practical mind" to right their financial affairs and to buy Tom back, only after Mr. Shelby's death is she able to settle the debts and try to redeem the old slave. It is Mrs. Shelby's son, young Mas'r George (whom she has raised to be a Christian), who then plays the role of the earthly emancipator of the Shelby slaves, but he has learned his part from his Christian mother. Although Mrs. Shelby fails to influence her husband − thus setting into motion the events of the novel − she persists in following Beecher's instructions and succeeds at last by influencing her son, who completes the action.

It has been pointed out that *Uncle Tom's Cabin* develops according to a typological pattern. Stowe presents a series of free white Christian mothers (including St. Clare's and Legree's) who, in accordance with Beecher's restrictions, attempt to influence their sons' actions in regard to slavery. What is striking is not that this pattern is repeated but that their influence is sometimes effective and sometimes not. This fact, centrally dramatized in the uncertainty of Mrs. Shelby's influence on her husband and son, resonates with significance. Is the problem of slavery in *Uncle Tom's Cabin* finally inseparable from the problem of women's political impotence? Is a hidden issue in the novel the feminist issue of political power for women?

The example of Marie St. Clare suggests that the problem of slavery in *Uncle Tom's Cabin* cannot be resolved by a simple shift of power to women because − unlike Emily Shelby, who has always felt that slavery is wrong − Marie St. Clare has always felt it to be right (Chaps. 5 and 16.) In the world of *Uncle Tom's Cabin*, although Christianity and sin are shown in active and deadly opposition, although most women appear to be morally superior to most men, and although women bear the responsibility of instilling Christian values in their sons, husbands, and slaves, Christian sympathy is not gender specific. Both women and men are capable of Christian feeling and its opposite. Marie's false religion and callousness toward her female slaves echo Angelina and Sarah Grimké's testimony about female slaveholders in *American Slavery As It Is;* she would whip a whole plantation of slaves if her husband did not prevent her. Although it is true that the idyllic center of Stowe's novel is the Quaker matriarchate of Rachel Halliday's kitchen, it is not only some men (like the reformed slave catcher

Tom Loker) who fail to develop the morality essential for participation in such a society; Marie St. Clare dramatizes that women, too, can be immoral.[13]

Marie St. Clare and Emily Shelby are not, however, the only female members of the slaveholding class in *Uncle Tom's Cabin*. Little Eva, whose drama fundamentally addresses the issue of spiritual salvation rather than earthly emancipation, is another – perhaps surprising – member of this group. (Stowe implicitly admits this kinship when she makes Little Eva assert her preference for the southern way of life over that of New England: "it makes so many more round you to love, you know" [Chap. 16].) The uniqueness of Evangeline's character as a member of this class is underscored by the fact that she lacks the guidance of a Christian mother. The St. Clare ménage, like the Legree plantation, is an antihome. Until the advent of Miss Ophelia, it had contained no woman who organized its kitchen and ordered its morals; Marie's refusal to do the former is directly related to her inability to do the latter. Although the "shiftless" chaos of Aunt Dinah's kitchen is countered by Mammy's warmth and "respectability" – and although Mammy is a Christian – neither of these women of color functions as a center in this mistressless house. Uncle Tom, who remains uncorrupted by slavery, is not the only "moral miracle" in Stowe's book. As her father states, Little Eva, who rises above her domestic environment and who remains uncorrupted by mastery, is another.

Although it is perhaps difficult to conceive of any development in Little Eva's character, she is not a completely static figure. We first see her acting out Grimké's suggestions to Christian female slaveholders, going among the slaves on the riverboat "with her hands full of candy, nuts, and oranges, which she would distribute joyfully to them" (Chap. 14). Two years later, a slightly more mature Eva responds differently to the evils of slavery. Learning to read, she comes to love the Bible, and she develops her antislavery sympathies into antislavery proposals. Eva voices her belief that slaves should be taught to read Scripture; then she wishes she had money to "buy a place in the free states, and take all our people there, and hire teachers, to teach them to read and write" (Chap. 22). Powerless to effect this modest program for emancipation and literacy, she nonetheless teaches Mammy her letters. When exposed to her cousin's tyrannical actions toward his slave, she confronts Henrique and condemns him: "How could you be so cruel and wicked to poor Dodo?" "I don't want you to call me dear Eva, when you do so" (Chap. 23). Later, physically ill but spiritually ecstatic, Eva "had vague longings to do something for . . . [the slaves], to bless and save not only them, but all in their condition."

Addressing Uncle Tom, the child speaks in the classic phrases of a martyr: "I would be glad to die, if my dying could stop all this misery. I *would die* for them, Tom, if I could" (Chap. 24). Talking with her father, however, Eva outlines a more prudential plan to end slavery in America. Explaining that she is sad "for our poor people" and wishes "they were all *free*," Eva proposes that St. Clare become an antislavery leader (one who does not, like William Lloyd Garrison, denounce his opponents):

"Papa, you are such a good man, and so noble, and kind, and you always have a way of saying things that is so pleasant, couldn't you go all round and try to persuade people to do right about this? When I am dead, papa, then you will think of me, and do it for my sake."

She then announces,

"I would do it, if I could." (Chap. 24)

Eva's distressed reactions to the slave culture in which she lives recall the agonies of Angelina Grimké's South Carolina childhood – which she and other abolitionists had publicized widely. In *American Slavery As It Is*, Grimké had written that she had "fainted away" at the age of thirteen, after seeing a boy whose head had been shaved and who had been "dreadfully whipped," and that a slave woman's accounts of whippings at the work house "smote me with such horror that my limbs could hardly sustain me." She wrote she had prayed that she might be permitted to be sacrificed to end slavery, and she believed it "the Lord's doing" that she "did not become totally hardened, under the daily operation of the system." Passionately, she recounted "the recollections of my childhood, and the effaceless imprint upon my riper years, with the breaking of my heart-strings," and recorded her misery when finally she recognized herself "powerless to shield the victims" of slavery.[14]

Like the juvenile Angelina, Stowe's little Evangeline − whose given name suggests Grimké's − is mentally and emotionally tortured by the violence of slavery that surrounds her. Are we to read her announcement that "I would do it, if I could" to mean that she would become an antislavery lecturer if she were an adult male like her father? Or does Stowe here more radically imply that if Eva were to grow into womanhood, she herself would become an antislavery lecturer − like Angelina Grimké, that other young Christian girl who, although a member of the slaveholding aristocracy, was also physically and mentally sickened by slavery?

Stowe's characterization invites such conjecture. Eva is (as her mother laments) hopelessly democratic. Always seeming "somehow to put herself on an equality with every creature that comes near her," she embodies an egalitarian Christian love. Her vision undermines the authoritarian religiosity endorsed by Marie's proslavery minister, who preaches that "all the orders and distinctions in society came from God; and that it was so appropriate, you know, and beautiful, that some should be high and some low, and that some were born to rule and some to serve, and all that, you know" (Chap. 16). Although addressing the issues of race and slavery and not the condition of women, this celebration of aristocracy recalls the hierarchical postulates of Catharine Beecher. If Little Eva's radically egalitarian Christianity encompasses issues of sex and gender as well as race and class − if in her eyes, as in Angelina Grimké's, social "orders and distinctions" concerning women are as ungodly as those concerning nonwhites and slaves − then, perhaps, had she lived, Eva might have assumed the role she proposes to St. Clare. She might, like Angelina Grimké, "go all around and try to persuade people to do right about this" (Chap. 24).

Stowe's illustrators implied the connections between Eva and the antislavery activists by rendering her conversion of Topsy in terms of an emblem the abolitionists had popularized showing a standing neoclassical figure of Justice as a white-skinned, white-gowned female rescuing a black female supplicant (Chap. 25). But Little Eva's importance rests elsewhere. She lives and dies a divine child. Powerless on earth, powerful in heaven, Stowe's female exemplar is less an advocate of mundane emancipation than a model of heavenly salvation. As her conversion of Topsy demonstrates, she is a spiritual, not a political, liberator.

Uncle Tom is Stowe's martyr. His tortured figure does not – like Eva's – recall the sacrificial aristocratic white Christian female Angelina Grimké had evoked in her first *Appeal*. Tom's passion echoes instead Sarah Grimké's testimony in *American Slavery As It Is*. She reported that a male black South Carolina slave had refused to deny Christ when ordered by his master as a test of his religious sincerity. Although "terribly whipped, the fortitude of the sufferer was not to be shaken; he nobly rejected the offer of exemption from further punishment at the expense of destroying his soul, and this blessed martyr *died*."[15]

Raised in what the Grimkés called a "nominally free state," Miss Ophelia seems a more likely candidate than Little Eva for the role of female abolitionist. But as the action unfolds, it becomes clear that Ophelia St. Clare is not representative of the northern women the Grimkés had recruited into female antislavery societies, much less of those who had joined the "promiscuous" abolitionist organizations composed of both men and women, and who had recently endorsed the feminist convention at Seneca Falls.

Although she deplored slavery, in Vermont Miss Ophelia had not been a member of the local abolitionist society. As a guest in the St. Clare household, she initially follows Beecher's advice by restricting her activities to the domestic sphere and attempting to moderate the inflammatory opinions around her. But her discussions parody the dialogues Beecher had projected. Ophelia's mildest comments enflame Marie's advocacy of slavery, and her debate with St. Clare becomes an occasion for him to echo the denunciatory testimonials of antislavery southerners in *American Slavery As It Is*. In *Uncle Tom's Cabin*, slavery is condemned by a southern male, not a northern female; when Miss Ophelia attempts to soften St. Clare's militant male rhetoric, she is vitiating a southerner's attack on slavery.

Her relationship with Topsy, however, recalls *An Appeal to the*

Women of the Nominally Free States; as the Grimkés' second polemic had argued, the northern woman's racism is a crucial problem. Indeed, the sign of Miss Ophelia's conversion after Eva's death is her eradication of this bias.

When Miss Ophelia gains legal title to Topsy, she is transformed from a representative "woman of the nominally free states" into a slaveholding "Christian woman of the South." In her role as slaveholder, Ophelia St. Clare appears to conform to the outlines Grimké had suggested in her first *Appeal:* She converts and educates her slave. Further, as a Christian slaveholding woman, Miss Ophelia shows that she has learned the lesson that Mrs. Shelby left unlearned until too late: that it is futile to educate and Christianize her slave unless she can also guarantee emancipation. Because Miss Ophelia has absorbed this lesson (and because, although a woman, she has control of her property), Topsy will never be persecuted like Emily Shelby's Eliza.

But because Ophelia takes Topsy with her to the free North, it becomes unnecessary for her to act out the more radical program Grimké had proposed to slaveholding women: to break the laws forbidding education and emancipation. Miss Ophelia succeeds in converting, educating, and emancipating Topsy without following either Grimké's radical proposal to southern women that they violate unjust laws or Grimké's radical proposal to northern women that they enter the political arena. In the world of Stowe's novel, the example of Miss Ophelia appears to validate Beecher's argument that women can work effectively against slavery within the domestic circle.

Although Ophelia St. Clare may serve as a model for southern women by Christianizing, educating, and emancipating her slave, and for northern women by overcoming her racism, perhaps Mary Bird is the most important model for Stowe's readers among women of "the nominally free states" whose involvement with slaves and slavery was less intimate. Stowe's dramatization of the invasion of Mrs. Bird's Ohio home by slavery's evil presence demonstrates that slavery shapes not only southern homes like the Shelbys' and the St. Clares' but also northern domestic life. In this scene, Stowe's narrator expresses surprise at Mrs. Bird's abrupt first words to her husband: "and what have they been doing in the

Senate?" In apparent approval of the housewife's characteristic lack of involvement with the political sphere, she comments:

> Now, it was a very unusual thing for gentle little Mrs. Bird ever to trouble her head with what was going on in the house of the state, very wisely considering that she had enough to do to mind her own. (Chap. 9)

Nevertheless, Mrs. Bird persists in questioning her husband about the passage of a new fugitive slave law, explaining, when he accuses her of "getting to be a politician, all at once," that her concern is not political, but spiritual:

> "I wouldn't give a fig for all your politics, generally, but I think this is something downright cruel and unchristian." (Chap. 9)

Although Senator Bird asserts that because the abolitionists have been harrassing Kentucky slaveholders, the fugitive slave law seemed "necessary . . . to quiet the excitement," his wife condemns the measure and – defying Beecher's warning – attacks her husband's political position in the clear accents of a "reprover": "You ought to be ashamed, John! . . . It's a shameful, wicked, abominable law."

Nor does she stop there. Mary Bird announces her intention to follow the radical path Angelina Grimké had urged:

> "I'll break it, for one, the first time I get a chance; and I hope I *shall* have a chance, I do!" (Chap. 9)

Refusing to take seriously her husband's arguments and explanations, Mrs. Bird rests her case like Grimké solely on Holy Scriptures, asserting, "Now, John, I don't know anything about politics, but I can read my Bible; and there I see that I must feed the hungry, clothe the naked, and comfort the desolate; and that Bible I mean to follow" (Chap. 9). Not satisfied with proclaiming her defiance, she attacks her husband's position until an interruption signals the appearance of the runaway Eliza and her son. It is only after the female fugitive has successfully appealed to the northern woman for protection, only after the free woman and the female fugitive slave have established their sisterhood as bereaved mothers, that the senator suggests a plan for Eliza's escape. Although Stowe's treatment of Mrs. Bird follows Catharine Beecher's strictures that women should act within the domestic sphere, Mary Bird's condemnations of the attempts by her husband (and the rest of the Senate) to mediate between the proslavery and antislavery forces, her proclamation of her defiance of unjust laws, and her actual defiance of them are contrary to Beecher's instructions.

But the world of *Uncle Tom's Cabin* is a fortunate world for northern white women who oppose chattel slavery within the domestic sphere. Mrs. Bird's husband, swayed by her argument, her actions, or Eliza's desperate situation, does not oppose his wife. Neither slave catchers nor United States marshals arrive at her door. Mrs. Bird is not forced to take the next step Grimké had outlined; she is not judged a criminal. Like the women of the slaveholding states, this northern woman encounters slavery in her home. Stowe shows her remaining there, permits her to take a moral antislavery position and – despite the immorality of this world – to avoid suffering any adverse consequences whatever.

Catharine Beecher's pamphlet had ignored the presence of women of color in the struggle against slavery. Although in her first *Appeal* Angelina Grimké had simply counseled both male and female slaves to be patient, in the second she had urged free Afro-American women to participate in the abolitionist movement despite its racism. Stowe's *Uncle Tom's Cabin* includes a number of nonwhite female characters – slave, fugitive, and free – but although it follows their physical actions with some attention, it expresses little interest in their moral choices. Indeed, in *Uncle Tom's Cabin* neither male nor female nonwhite characters are seriously treated as rational creatures engaged in the human activity of making moral choices, but instead are seen as natural creatures reacting to events. Like all of Stowe's characters, however, they have the duty to be Christians and to help others follow Christ.

Accordingly, Eliza Harris is shown as a Christian wife and mother who influences the spiritual salvation of her husband and children. In relation to the issue of earthly emancipation, her role is less clear. While a slave, Eliza first echoes Grimké's advice by counseling her outraged husband to be patient; when her little son Harry is threatened, she automatically obeys the voice of nature and attempts his rescue; finally free and safe, after converting her husband to Christianity, she happily follows him to Africa in an effort to save the pagans. In the process, we are presented with a detailed description of her efforts to elude her catchers. But we are not shown Eliza agonizing over her decisions; these are presented as simple reactions, not reasoned moral choices. Even Cassy, the prototypical "tragic mulatto" on the Legree place who, maddened by sexual abuse, once killed her baby to save him from a life of slavery, receives similar treatment. Although it is this dark female who tempts Tom to abandon his faith, her abrupt conversion occurs within the space of a single sentence (Chap. 41).[16]

Stowe consistently presents her blacker female figures with even less complexity. Although Topsy and Aunt Chloe, the most important ones, are first seen as comic and then shown as Christians, the moral choices inevitably involved in their transformations are scanted. Stowe's serious concern with the morality of free white aristocratic "Christian women of the South" and free white "women of the nominally free states" – women like Emily Shelby, Marie St. Clare, Ophelia St. Clare, Mary Bird and Rachael Halliday – contrasts dramatically with her summary treatment of the moral conflicts of black and mulatto female characters like the hardworking Chloe, the battered child Topsy, the heroic slave mother Eliza, and even the sexually abused Cassy.

> There is one thing that every individual can do, – they can see to it that *they feel right.*
>
> –*UTC,* Chap. 25

Uncle Tom's Cabin, it has been pointed out, is a jeremiad.[17] Harriet Beecher Stowe's narrator does not assume "the office of a mediator," presenting herself as "the advocate of charity and peace," as one who takes "every possible means to soothe exasperated feelings, and . . . [avoids] all those offensive peculiarities that in their nature tend to inflame and offend," as Beecher said females should.[18] Instead (although she is not, as her enemies charged, a "reprover" of the South), Stowe's narrator certainly is a reprover; she exacerbates the slavery issue – as Beecher charged the abolitionists did, and as she asserted women must not do.

Further, although writing in a literary form traditional to women and addressing a female audience (who surely read her words within the domestic sphere), Stowe echoed the Grimkés and other abolitionist-feminists by raising her woman's voice on the most volatile political issue of the day; and she compounded this brazenness by serializing her novel in the pages of an antislavery newspaper. Clearly, her intention was to politicize a female audience. But in this, she echoed not only the feminist Grimkés; she also repeated a contradiction at the heart of her sister's *Letters.* Immediately after their appearance, the Grimkés' defenders had pointed out that Beecher violated her own strictures on female behavior by engaging in public debate on a political issue.[19]

In *Uncle Tom's Cabin,* none of the characters – black, mulatto or white, male or female – becomes involved in the public struggle against slavery, as Grimké had urged. Although both Miss Ophelia and Mrs. Bird refuse to obey unjust laws, the New Englander simply takes her slave north, where slavery is illegal and education available, and proceeds to conform to the enlightened local statutes. Although the Ohioan does indeed run a risk by violating the new fugitive slave law, she fortunately escapes apprehension and punishment, as do Rachel and the other members of the Quaker community. If there are any legal consequences for the Kentuckian Mrs. Shelby caused by the actions of her son George, who plays the role of southern emancipator Grimké had urged on her female audience, we never hear of them. In contrast to the fugitive, emancipated, and freeborn Afro-American participants in the Convention of American Women Against Slavery whom Grimké had addressed in her second *Appeal,* Stowe's free black and mulatto women – Eliza Harris, Cassy, even Topsy – embrace colonization and become expatriates.

The narrator's announcement that her objective is "to awaken sympathy and feeling for the African race, as they exist among us," suggests that sympathy is a force essentially destructive of human injustice.[20] Despite the negative example of Marie St. Clare (who is incapable of sympathizing with anyone), both the action and the narration of the novel demonstrate that women have easy access to this revolutionary power. Yet none of Stowe's female characters uses it, as had the Grimkés and their followers, collectively to challenge institutionalized injustice in the public sphere. Instead,

Uncle Tom's Cabin shows individual women using the power of sympathy to enable them to act effectively in private against slavery when the servile institution threatens the domestic sphere. Stowe's female Christians act successfully against slavery without walking out of their own front doors.

To the extent that, within the process of defending Christian domestic values, Stowe's emphasis on individual sympathy and on the doctrine of Higher Laws functions not only as a critique of chattel slavery but also as a critique of racist patriarchal capitalist culture in America, and to the extent that it suggests an alternative society grounded in egalitarian Christianity and proposes a loving maternal ethic in opposition to patriarchal values, *Uncle Tom's Cabin* endorses nineteenth-century radical ideas.

In this regard, the crucial connections between sex and race in *Uncle Tom's Cabin* demand examination. The primary distinctions in Stowe's book are between non-Christians and Christians. Stowe assigns intellectual superiority and worldly power to the first group and spiritual superiority and otherworldly power – seen as infinitely more important – to the second. In the process, she conflates race and sex. Her first group consists primarily of white males. Her second group includes essentially white females and all nonwhites.

The connections between Uncle Tom, the cultural type of the True Woman, and Stowe's view of Jesus Christ have been repeatedly noted. But these connections involve more than Stowe's black martyr; in her book, nonwhites as a group, like women as a group, possess special religious attributes. In *Letters to Catharine E. Beecher*, Grimké had articulated her awareness of parallels between the oppression of slaves and the oppression of women, announcing that "the investigation of the rights of the slave has led to a better understanding of my own." Stowe's novel echoes other nineteenth-century analyses, however, in connecting "women and Negroes" not only in terms of their earthly powerlessness, but also as the reservoirs of a sympathy that signals their heavenly power and revolutionary potential.[21] To the extent that we take seriously the radical implications of Stowe's book, we can perhaps take seriously the connections between her divine child Evangeline and her feminist antiracist contemporary An-

101

gelina Grimké, and find in Stowe's heavenly child a budding social activist.

At issue here is not how forceful and revolutionary we judge the power of sympathy to be: Stowe echoes both Beecher and the Grimkés in dramatizing its regenerative force. At issue here is how Christians should use that power.

A dozen years ago, writing in the shadow of the modern freedom movement and examining *Uncle Tom's Cabin* as a response to the 1850 Fugitive Slave Law, I concluded that Stowe's "sentimentalized racialism" (the term is George Fredrickson's) opposed the active resistance of black and white abolitionists and insurrectionists.[22] Created in the context of radical abolitionist and insurrectionist responses to the 1850 Fugitive Slave Law, Stowe's book apotheosizes a black man who triumphs in heaven after practicing Christian resignation when tortured on earth (and pointing others toward eternal salvation) while celebrating more ordinary slaves who escape and expatriate themselves to Africa. Today, writing in the midst of the modern feminist movement and examining the treatment of female characters in *Uncle Tom's Cabin* as a response to the 1848 Seneca Falls Convention, I can only conclude that Stowe makes a similar move in relation to women. Created in the context of feminist demands for equal rights for women, Stowe's book apotheosizes a juvenile white female who triumphs in heaven after practicing Christian charity on earth, ameliorating the suffering of the slaves (and pointing them toward eternal salvation) while celebrating more ordinary women who practice not feminism and abolitionism but "domestic feminism" and colonization.

Although on a spiritual level Stowe's attack on the patriarchal institution challenges all oppressive earthly authority, ultimately both the spiritual and the mundane dramas in *Uncle Tom's Cabin* counter the practical measures urged by the black and white activists following the Grimkés' lead — women like Abby Kelley Foster and Sojourner Truth, who, for more than a decade, had been invading American public life, going "all around" trying "to persuade people to do right about this." Catharine Beecher must have been pleased.

NOTES

1 *An Essay on Slavery and Abolitionism, with Reference to the Duty of American Females, Addressed to A. E. Grimké,* (Philadelphia: Henry Perkins; Boston: Perkins & Marvin, 1837); quoted in [A. E. Grimké et. al.], *An Appeal to the Women of the Nominally Free States,* Issued by an Anti-Slavery Convention of American Women (New York: W. S. Dorr, 1837).

2 *Uncle Tom's Cabin* appeared as a serial in the *National Era,* June 3, 1851–April 2, 1852, and was published in book form in 1852. Parenthetical references in my text refer to the edition edited by Kenneth Lynn (Cambridge, Mass.: Harvard University Press, 1962); the passage quoted is in chap. 45.

3 Angelina Grimké, *Appeal to the Christian Women of the South, The Anti-Slavery Examiner* 1 (September 1836):[1]–35. For the Grimké sisters, see Gerda Lerner, *The Grimké Sisters from South Carolina* (1967; rpt. New York: Shocken Books, 1971); and Katharine Du Pre Lumpkin, *The Emancipation of Angelina Grimké* (Chapel Hill: University of North Carolina Press, 1974). For the situation of women, see, for example, Barbara Welter, "The Cult of True Womanhood," *American Quarterly* 18 (1966):151–74; Nancy Cott, *The Bonds of Womanhood* (New Haven, Conn.: Yale University Press, 1977); and Linda Kerber, *Women of the Republic* (Chapel Hill: University of North Carolina Press, 1980).

4 Kathryn Kish Sklar, *Catharine Beecher: A Study in American Domesticity* (New Haven, Conn.: Yale University Press, 1973).

5 See *An Appeal to the Women of the Nominally Free States,* which appeared as a statement of the 1837 Convention of American Women Against Slavery; A. E. Grimké, *Letters to Catharine E. Beecher, in Reply to An Essay on Slavery and Abolitionism, Addressed to A. E. Grimké* (Boston: Isaac Knapp, 1838); and Sarah Grimké's *Letters on the Equality of the Sexes and the Condition of Women, Addressed to Mary S. Parker, President of the Boston Female Anti-Slavery Society* (Boston: Isaac Knapp, 1838). Catharine Beecher's *Treatise on Domestic Economy for the Use of Young Ladies at Home and at School* (Boston: T. H. Webb, 1834), revised by Beecher and Stowe, appeared as *The American Woman's Home, or Principles of Domestic Science* (New York: J. B. Ford, 1869). For recent controversy concerning feminism and female culture in nineteenth-century America, see Ellen DuBois, M. J. Buhle, T. Kaplan, G. Lerner, and C. Smith-Rosenberg, "Politics and Culture in Women's History: A Symposium," *Feminist Studies* 6 (Spring 1980):26–64. Although sen-

sitive to the problems of terminology raised in these comments, in this essay I use "feminist" when referring both to supporters of the nineteenth-century women's rights movement who were essentially reformist and to those radicals who proposed an end to patriarchy. I do so because my purpose here is simply to differentiate between the Grimkés' "feminism" and Beecher's "domestic feminism," a crucial distinction inexplicably ignored in Ann Douglas's Introduction to a recent edition of *Uncle Tom's Cabin* (New York: Penguin Books, 1981).

6 Grimké, *Appeal to the Christian Women of the South,* p. 20.

7 Beecher, *An Essay on Slavery and Abolitionism,* pp. 99–100.

8 Ibid., pp. 104, 128, 145. Further, Beecher implicitly attacks Grimké's efforts to win northern women to abolitionism by attacking the proposal that women lecture in public. Her revulsion at Fanny Wright's public appearances was surely telling in a pamphlet addressed to Grimké, newest and most prominent of the female speakers: "If the female advocate chooses to come upon a stage, and expose her person . . . it is . . . right to express disgust at whatever is offenseive or indecorous" (p. 121).

9 [Grimké et al.,] *Appeal to the Women of the Nominally Free States,* p. 61.

10 Grimké, *Letters to Catharine E. Beecher,* pp. 108, 115, 112, 128–9.

11 For *Letters on the Equality of the Sexes,* see note 5. *American Slavery As It Is: Testimony of a Thousand Witnesses* (New York: American Anti-Slavery Society, 1839).

12 From an unpublished manuscript by Sarah Weld of reminiscences of her mother, Angelina Grimké Weld, quoted in Gilbert Hobbs Barnes, *The Antislavery Impulse, 1830–44* (1933; rpt. New York: Harcourt, Brace & World, 1964), p. 231.

13 See *Uncle Tom's Cabin,* chap. 19, and *American Slavery As It Is,* pp. 56, 24. For the matriarchal utopian impulse in *Uncle Tom's Cabin,* see Elizabeth Ammons, "Heroines in *Uncle Tom's Cabin,*" *American Literature* 49 (May 1977):161–79; also see Gillian Brown, "Getting in the Kitchen with Dinah: Domestic Politics in *Uncle Tom's Cabin,*" *American Quarterly* 36 (Fall 1984):503–23.

14 *American Slavery As It Is,* pp. 53, 55; also see Grimké's Letter to William Lloyd Garrison, August 30, 1835, published in the *Liberator* and widely reprinted, and the many press reports of Grimké's speeches describing her childhood suffering.

15 *American Slavery As It Is,* p. 24.

16 For a different view of Eliza, see Nina Baym, *Woman's Fiction* (Ithaca, N.Y.: Cornell University Press, 1978), p. 16; for Cassy as a quintessential figure in woman's fiction, see Sandra Gilbert and S. Gubar, *The*

Madwoman in the Attic (New Haven, Conn.: Yale University Press, 1979), pp. 533–5.

17 See Jane Tompkins, *Sensational Designs: The Cultural Work of American Fiction 1790–1860* (New York: Oxford University Press, 1985), pp. 122–46; cf. also Sacvan Bercovitch, *The American Jeremiad* (Madison: University of Wisconsin Press, 1978).

18 Beecher, *Essay on Slavery and Abolitionism*, pp. 128, 129, 138–9.

19 In 1837, Beecher had attacked editors of the antislavery press, singling out James Birney, who in Cincinnati had edited *The Philanthropist* with Gamaliel Bailey, the man who later serialized Stowe's novel in his *National Era; Essay on Slavery and Abolitionism*, pp. 32–3. [Richard Hildreth], *Brief Remarks on Miss Catharine E. Beecher's Essay on Slavery and Abolitionism* (Boston: Isaac Knapp, 1837).

20 Preface to *Uncle Tom's Cabin*, ed. Lynn.

21 Grimké, *Letters to Catharine E. Beecher*, p. 114. The issue of the commonality of the oppressed is complex. Grimké, for one, did not confuse the brutality of black slavery with the condition of free women like herself in noting that the former led her to examine the latter. For the complicated comment of another antislavery feminist, see L. Maria Child, "The African Race," *National Anti-Slavery Standard*, April 27, 1843, p. 187: "In comparison with the Caucasian race, I have often said that they [the Africans] are what woman is in comparison with man. The comparison between women and the colored race *as classes* is striking. Both are exceedingly adhesive in their attachments; both, comparatively speaking, have a tendency to submission; and hence, both have been kept in subjection by physical force, and considered rather in the light of property, than as individuals." For an interpretation asserting the radical character of sentiment that argues *Uncle Tom's Cabin* subverts the patriarchy, see Tompkins, *Sensational Designs*.

22 Jean Fagan Yellin, *The Intricate Knot* (New York: New York University Press, 1972), chap. 7; George Fredrickson, *The Black Image in the White Mind* (New York: Harper & Row, 1971).

4

Gothic Imagination and Social Reform: The Haunted Houses of Lyman Beecher, Henry Ward Beecher, and Harriet Beecher Stowe

KAREN HALTTUNEN

AS a child in Litchfield, Connecticut, Harriet Beecher feared that her house was haunted. There were rats in the garret over the room where she slept, and on the nights when winter winds arose, rumbling in the chimneys and making the beams of the old parsonage creak, the rats grew lively and "Harriet would dive under the bedclothes quaking with fear." She was terrified too of the parsonage smokehouse, a dark recess in the kitchen chimney from which rumblings and crackling sounds could be heard. Once she summoned her courage to open the door, and what she saw reminded her of the passage in *Pilgrim's Progress* where shepherds open a door in a hillside and discover a chimney to hell: "They looked in, therefore, and saw that within it was dark and smoky; they also thought that they heard a rumbling noise as of fire and a cry of some tormented, and they smelt the smell of brimstone." Harriet "closed the door and ran away trembling." "Thus," her son and grandson reported nearly a century later, "did the old parsonage exert its subtle influence, every day fashioning the sensitive, imaginative child."[1]

When Harriet Beecher Stowe decided, in 1851, to write a story that would describe slavery in "the most lifelife and graphic manner possible,"[2] she set its worst horrors in a haunted house, the moldering old mansion of a cotton plantation lying deep in the Louisiana swamps. On a "stormy, windy night, such as raises whole squadrons of nondescript noises in rickety old houses," the superstitious master of the house blusters, "Them noises was nothing but rats

The author expresses her gratitude to Robert Finlay and Sarah Maza for their critical readings of this essay.

and the wind." But when Simon Legree's half-crazed quadroon mistress jeeringly asks, *"What's the matter with that garret*, Simon, do you suppose?"*, Legree recalls the legend that the garret is haunted by a slave woman he had imprisoned there and slowly beaten to death.[3] And though Legree never actually sees that ghost, he does receive bedside visits from a veiled woman he believes to be his dead mother. As Edmund Wilson has said, "the nightmare plantation of Simon Legree" is "a prison and a place of torture."[4] But most of the torture takes place out of sight and hearing. Commanding the reader's attention in the Simon Legree sequence of *Uncle Tom's Cabin* is a haunted mansion.

Stowe's choice of the Gothic mode for her treatment of slavery at its worst had precedents in the writings of other prominent members of her reform-minded family. Her father, Lyman Beecher, had used the image of the haunted house to condemn the evils of drink in his *Six Sermons on Intemperance* (1826). And her brother, Henry Ward Beecher, had used the same device to represent the horrors of prostitution in his *Seven Lectures to Young Men* (1844). These three haunted houses offer new insight into the intergenerational religious development of the Beecher family, as well as a new perspective on the significance of the Simon Legree story in *Uncle Tom's Cabin*.

Lyman Beecher earned his place "at the center of the transformation of American Protestantism between 1790 and 1840"[5] by meeting the challenge of church disestablishment with a millennialist combination of religious revival and moral reform. In 1825, he unleashed his formidable powers as a preacher against the evils of intemperance, a social problem that was assuming alarming proportions in the early decades of the nineteenth century.[6] In a series of sermons on the subject, triggered by the discovery that a favorite convert was a confirmed drunkard, he preached "under such a power of feeling as never before or since." His graphic representations of the ravages of intemperance "took hold of the whole congregation" – though not of the particular drunkard who had prompted them – and the publication in 1826 of *Six Sermons on the Nature, Occasions, Signs, Evils, and Remedy of Intemperance* brought Lyman Beecher his first national recognition.[7]

One of the most powerful passages in the sermons is a Gothic representation of intemperance as a haunted house. Sermon 4, "The Remedy of Intemperance," opens with a text from the second chapter of Habakkuk: "Thou hast consulted shame to thy house by cutting off many people, and hast sinned against thy soul. For the stones shall cry out of the wall, and the beam out of the timber shall answer it. Wo unto him that giveth his neighbor drink."[8] Beecher seized upon this architectural image for his condemnation of the liquor traffic:

> If in every dwelling built by blood, the stone from the wall should utter all the cries which the bloody traffick extorts – and the beam out of the timber should echo them back – who would build such a house? – and who would dwell in it? (pp. 81–2)

The precise nature of this "house" of intemperance Beecher left unclear, but its Gothic characteristics are unmistakable:

> What if in every part of the dwelling, from the cellar upward, through all the halls and chambers – babblings, and contentions, and voices, and groans, and shrieks, and wailings, were heard, day and night! What if the cold blood oozed out, and stood in drops upon the walls; and, by preternatural art, all the ghastly skulls and bones of the victims destroyed by intemperance, should stand upon the walls, in horrid sculpture within and without the building! – who would rear such a building? (p. 82)

Beecher went on to describe the haunting of the distilleries, stores, and ships that engaged in the liquor traffic:

> What if at eventide, and at midnight, the airy forms of men destroyed by intemperance, were dimly seen haunting the distilleries and stores, where they received their bane – following the track of the ship engaged in the commerce – walking upon the waves – flitting athwart the deck – sitting upon the rigging – and sending up, from the hold within, and from the waves without, groans, and loud laments, and wailings! (p. 82)

Finally, Beecher asked, what if the sky itself whispered to us "all the lamentation and woe which intemperance creates" and the earth brought "up around us from beneath, the wailings of the damned, whom the commerce in ardent spirits had sent thither" (p. 82). If all these things were so, Beecher proclaimed, then "these tremendous realities, assailing our sense, would invigorate

109

our conscience, and give decision to our purpose of reformation'' (pp. 82–3). Then the preacher drove his point home: "But these evils are as real, as if, the stone did cry out of the wall . . . as real, as if day and night, wailings were heard in every part of the dwelling – and blood and skeletons were seen upon every wall'' (p. 83), and so he continued, summarizing his Gothic fantasy of intemperance.

By 1825, when Lyman Beecher was envisioning for his Litchfield parishioners the haunted house of intemperance, over half a century of Gothic literary tradition lay behind him. The haunted house – more precisely, the haunted castle – was "the entire stock-in-trade of horror-romanticism in its oldest and purest form,'' whose conventions had been fully set forth by a single work: *The Castle of Otranto,* written by Horace Walpole in 1764.[9] The popular "school of Walpole'' that emerged in the next several decades was dominated by this haunted castle with all its standard architectural appurtenances: heavy iron doors, trapdoors with metal rings, secret doors hidden behind tapestries, long galleys and winding staircases, underground vaults and labyrinthine passages, and neighboring convents, monasteries, and charnel houses. The central function of the haunted castle was to provide two sources of terror: the weird supernatural events that took place within the castle's gloomy walls and the inquisitional horrors of its deepest dungeons. This convention powerfully influenced Gothic writers – including in England Anne Radcliffe, Matthew Lewis, and Mary Shelley, and in America Charles Brockden Brown, Nathaniel Hawthorne, and Edgar Allan Poe, – though by the early nineteenth century the haunted castle was being replaced by a haunted house, especially in America, where castles were scarce. In 1825, of course, some of these writers' works were not yet available to Lyman Beecher, and most of those that were, this confirmed moralist would not read. But he and his children did voraciously consume the works of Sir Walter Scott and Lord Byron, and thus opened themselves to the influence of the Gothic genre.[10]

Lyman Beecher's Gothic representation of intemperance drew on the two sources of terror traditionally associated with the haunted castle. First, he used the convention of the weirdly supernatural – in his term, the "preternatural'' – depicting, for example, the ghosts of men destroyed by drink who haunt distilleries and liquor stores and stalk liquor-laden ships. His most powerful manipulation of the supernatural lay in his Gothic anthropomorphism — his portrayal of the house of intemperance as a living person that groans and wails, bleeds cold blood through the walls, and finally turns into skulls and bones. Lyman Beecher's haunted house represented the human body undergoing the physiological ravages of intemperance; this "ruin" was actually a human ruin. In his treatment of the haunted house as human, Beecher drew on a Gothic convention extending back to *The Castle of Otranto,* whose main character has been said to be the castle itself, and forward to the Hollywood horror film, in which the haunted house breathes and moans and drips blood. Moreover, by vividly imagining "all the ghostly skulls and bones of the victims destroyed by intemperance" standing "in horrid sculpture" on the walls of the house, Beecher revealed an affinity with the Gothic charnel-house tradition of Matthew Lewis before him (*The Monk,* 1795) and Edgar Allan Poe after him ("The Cask of Amontillado," 1846).

The second major source of terror in Lyman Beecher's Gothic treatment of intemperance lay in the "dungeons" he depicted. A recurrent theme throughout the passage is that true horror rises from below. Horrible "groans, and shrieks, and wailings" are heard "in every part of the [haunted house] from the cellar upward"; the "groans, and loud laments" of shipboard ghosts rise "up from the hold within," and "the wailings of the damned" are brought "up around us from beneath." For all his manipulation of the Gothic image of the dungeon, Lyman Beecher never lost sight of the ultimate horror below, which was hell. His haunted cellars and ship's holds were hypothetical places, and the cries that arose from them were imaginary; but for Lyman Beecher, hell remained an actual geographical location where the wailings of those souls damned by intemperance could really be heard. In an effort to save as many American souls as possible from this terrible fate, Beecher preached an "alleviated Calvinism" that tried to balance human ability with human dependency but ultimately stressed man's freedom to choose. All moral action, according to his simplified version of the New Haven theology, was voluntary. Sin lay not in a state of being but in the act of sinning, the active choice to violate moral law; thus every damned soul was "the voluntary cause of his own destruction."[11] In his *Six Sermons on Intemperance*, Beecher warned his parishioners that the intemperate are sinners doomed to hellfire unless they voluntarily chose to cease from sinning and be saved.

Why, then, did Beecher use the Gothic image of a haunted house to represent the evils of intemperance? The distinguishing characteristic of the Gothic mode is not its devices – the "crude claptrap" of secret panels, time-yellowed manuscripts, suddenly snuffed candles, or even the haunted castle itself – but its atmosphere of evil and brooding terror, whose purpose is to involve the reader by evoking an imaginative emotional response of fear.[12] In his fifth sermon on intemperance, Lyman Beecher was trying to hitch the power of the Gothic genre to the task of converting the American people to temperance. The haunted house sequence in "The Remedy of Intemperance" cast moral suasion – the "well-directed application of moral influence" (p. 86) – in Gothic form: By "assailing the senses" of his listeners with a Gothic representation of the true horrors of intemperance, he hoped to "invigorate their consciences" and "give decision to their purpose of reformation." He used the Gothic convention of the haunted house to frighten his audience into making the right liberal Calvinist choice: temperance.

As a thick-tongued, slow-witted boy, Henry Ward Beecher showed little promise of matching his father's powers as a preacher. But his diligent study of elocution was finally rewarded when the thirty-year-old minister preached up his first revival in Indianapolis. Emboldened by success, he delivered in the winter of 1843–4 a series of Sunday evening lectures addressed to the young men of that raw western town. Though he treated a wide range of moral concerns, the most powerful lecture of the seven was a diatribe against prostitution entitled "The Strange Woman." Opening with an attack on immoral literature – including the works of Chaucer, Shakespeare, Fielding, Dickens, and Balzac – Beecher moved on to describe the horrors of sexual vice. Though some parishioners found his subject matter too daring and refused to attend, the church was nevertheless packed that night. Published in 1844, Beecher's *Lectures to Young Men, on Various Important Subjects* brought the young minister the national recognition that led to his call from Plymouth Church in Brooklyn, New York, where his oratory established his reputation as the most popular preacher in nineteenth-century America.[13]

The central scene of "The Strange Woman" is a haunted house. Beecher's lecture offers a lurid guided tour through the prostitute's "house of death," where "all the vicissitudes of infernal misery" await the youth who enters.[14] The approach lies through a beautiful garden filled with lush plant growth and playing fountains. Yet the young man explores this garden at his peril, for its rich perfumes intoxicate him until, powerless to resist, he enters the strange woman's house, never to reemerge. Once inside, he passes through five chambers that reveal the deepening horrors of sexual vice. First is the luxurious Ward of Pleasure, where the visitors drink "amorous wine" while the strange woman "fans the flames of joy, scatters grateful odors, and urges on the fatal revelry" (p. 200). After the young men have fallen into a heavy sleep, they are taken to the Ward of Satiety, where they dream strange dreams in an atmosphere of "bewildering twilight" (p. 200). Only in the Ward of Discovery, where "sickly fumes" fill the air, "the naked walls drip filth," and the room "echoes with mirth concealing hideous misery" (p. 201), do they realize their true situation. The fourth room is the Ward of Disease, which is littered with the bodies of men afflicted with venereal disease. Finally, the strange woman "shovels" her victims into the Ward of Death, where they "fall headlong through the rotten floor" (p. 206). "Fiends laugh!" and "the cry of agony, the thunder of damnation, shake the very roof" (p. 206), as the walls run red with blood, and "fiery hands . . . pluck the wretches down" toward "the light of hell gleaming through" (p. 207).

Henry Ward Beecher's haunted house of prostitution drew on some of the same conventions as Lyman Beecher's haunted house of intemperance: the groans and shrieks of the victims, the blood running down the walls of the house, the supernatural presence, the notion that ultimate horror rises from the nether regions. Henry, like Lyman, used such conventions to create an atmosphere of evil and terror in an effort to frighten his listeners into moral reform. But the younger Beecher introduced some new elements into his Gothic fantasy. The rich interiors of his haunted house are clumsily evocative of William Beckford's overripe Oriental tale, *Vathek* (1786), or Edgar Allan Poe's "The Masque of the Red Death" (1842). In the Ward of Pleasure, Beecher wrote, "The eye is dazzled with the magnificence of its apparel – elastic velvet, glossy silks, burnished satin, crimson drapery, plushy carpets. Exquisite pictures glow upon the walls, carved marble adorns every niche" (p. 200). His Ward of Satiety resembles an opium den, where the strange woman's victims, drugged by her poisoned wine and enchanted fruit, lie stuporously on their couches: "They wake, to crave; they taste, to loathe; they sleep to dream; they wake again from unquiet visions" (p. 201). Henry Ward Beecher was fascinated by the altered mental states induced by drugs and dreams and the "midnight-madness" (p. 201) of sexual indulgence.

Henry Beecher also relied far more heavily than his father on the *Schauer-romantik*, the German school of horror-Gothic best exemplified in England by Matthew Lewis.[15] Whereas Lyman's haunted house of intemperance had walls mounted with the bones and skulls of its victims, Henry described the living corpses of the victims of prostitution as their flesh rotted. In the Ward of Disease, one "shuddering wretch is clawing at his breast, to tear away that worm which gnaws his heart"; near him lies another "whose limbs are dropping from his ghastly trunk"; yet a third has a "swoln tongue lolling from a blackened mouth" as his "yells of frantic agony appall every ear" (p. 203). In the tradition of Gothic fiction, Beecher invoked the tortures of the Inquisition as a parallel to the sufferings of venereal disease: "The wheel, the rack; the bed of knives, the roasting fire, the brazen room slowly heated, the slivers driven under the nails, the hot pincers, – what are these to the agonies of the last days of licentious vice?" (p. 204) Reveling in images of decay and corruption, Beecher wrote of the "stench" of this "lazar-room" (p. 203), of "its vomited blood, its sores and fiery blotches, its prurient sweat, its dissolving ichor and rotten bones!" (p. 205)

Clearly, Henry Ward Beecher's lurid "allegory" (p. 196) of prostitution was a powerful statement of sexual nausea. With prurient indirection, he repeatedly drew an analogy between the strange woman's house and the female body, which no man could enter without risking destruction. "Her HOUSE," he wrote, in arch capitals, "has been cunningly planned by an EVIL ARCHITECT to attract and please the attention" (p. 196). The house "stands in a vast garden full of enchanting objects" (p. 196) – fruits and fountains and, most significant, flowers (a euphemism, in the nineteenth-century Midwest, for female genitalia[16]). In his lengthy description of the grounds of the strange woman's house, Beecher drew abundantly on Christian mythological links between woman, sexuality, and the garden, as Nathaniel Hawthorne had in "Rappaccini's Daughter" (1844). The young man who moves deeper into this garden finds that the "flowers grow richer; their odors exhilarate" (p. 198) until he cannot hear the heavenly voice whose warning is weighted with anatomical significance: "COME NOT NIGH THE DOOR OF HER HOUSE. HER HOUSE IS THE WAY TO HELL, GOING DOWN TO THE CHAMBERS OF DEATH!" (p. 199) Those who do pass through that door eventually learn the true nature of the strange woman's "house" in the Ward of Discovery, where "The floors are bare; the naked walls drip filth," and "the air is poisonous with sickly fumes" (p. 201). In the final scene of this nightmarish portrayal of the female anatomy, the youth is forced into the innermost part of the house, where he sees blood oozing down the walls and feels fiery hands plucking him downward. "Will you sprinkle the wall with your blood?" Beecher pointedly asked his audience. "Will you feed those flames with your flesh?" (p. 207). In the Gothic tradition of *The Monk,* which graphically described an incestuous rape in a dungeon charnel house, Beecher was expressing a sexual nausea whose implicit focus was not the prostitute but female anatomy itself. With his treatment of the female body as outwardly alluring but inwardly foul and rotting, Beecher brought new meaning to the Gothic sense of horror at what lies below by representing the lower regions of woman's body as man's route to damnation.[17]

On one level, "The Strange Woman" represented a public exercise of private sexual anxiety, if not sexual pathology. Beecher's linking of sex with death might be traced to the death of his beloved mother, Roxana Foote Beecher, when he was three years old and to her rapid replacement by a cold and unapproachable stepmother, Harriet Porter Beecher, whose temperament was distinctly morbid. At the age of seventeen, Henry hastily courted a woman he scarcely knew, one Eunice Bullard; in 1837, after a four-year separation, they married, and Henry soon realized that he was yoked for life to a bitter, self-pitying woman. Not until 1874 was Beecher charged with adultery in the notorious Tilton affair, but as early as June 1844, six months after he lashed out at "The Strange Woman" from his Indianapolis pulpit, his sister Harriet had "a horrible presentiment" of a sexual fall by her favorite brother.[18] Whatever the foundation of Harriet's anxiety, Henry had felt compelled to place a ruined young minister in his house of the strange woman:

> Yonder is a youth, once a servant at God's altar. His hair hangs tangled and torn; his eyes are bloodshot; his face is livid; his fist is clenched. All the day, he wanders up and down, cursing sometimes himself, and sometimes the wretch that brought him hither; and when he sleeps, he dreams of Hell; and then he wakes to feel all he dreamed. (p. 202)

On another level, the Gothic sequence in Beecher's attack on prostitution expressed a larger cultural fantasy in its nightmarish inversion of the Victorian cult of domesticity. As the youth approaches the strange woman's house, "For a moment he recalls his home, his mother, his sister-circle; but they seem far-away, dim, powerless!" (p. 199). The house of the strange woman proves to be not a home but a passage to hell, and its central occupant is not a tender and pure representative of true womanhood — a loving mother or a gentle sister — but a terrifying monster who literally "shovels" her young male victims into the fiery pit. "Are angels singing?" the innocent youth asks after first entering her enchanted garden (p. 198). In fact, the house of the strange woman is inhabited by a woman who has been "baptized twice, — once to God, and once to the Devil" (p. 202). Beecher was drawing here on the central Victorial myth of woman as demon. The fallen woman was an "empowered outcast" whose freedom from the restricting bounds of domesticity endowed her with demonic magical powers, including the power to mesmerize and paralyze men. It was the pervasive fear of this unbounded woman that gave rise to the ideal of the domestically contained woman.[19] In "The Strange Woman," Beecher gave free play to his Gothic sense of "the horrors of the half-known life" of female sexuality[20] and used the image of the haunted house to invert one of the central pieties of American Victorian culture – the sacred cult of domesticity – to enlist his audience's sense of terror in the cause of moral reform.

Along with her brother Henry, Harriet Beecher Stowe was raised to believe that she would play a leading role in precipitating the millennium in America. But for years, the Cincinnati housewife found it difficult to take up her larger responsibilities as a Beecher, oppressed as she was by pregnancies, poverty, religious crisis, temporary blindness, nervous exhaustion, and the deaths of her brother George and her infant son.[21] With the passing of the Fugitive Slave Law in 1850, however, when Stowe was urged by her sister-in-law to "write something that will make this whole nation feel what an accursed thing slavery is," she accepted the challenge. To the editor of the *National Era,* an antislavery newspaper, she promised "a series of sketches" of slavery that would present both "the *best side* of the thing, and "something *faintly approaching the worst.*"[22] Though her serialized narrative began with the "best side of slavery" at the pastoral Shelby farm in Kentucky, Stowe's creative process actually began with "something faintly approaching the worst": Just after receiving communion one Sunday, she had a vision of a saintly slave being brutally beaten to death. After this first revelation, as she later reported, "the story can less be said to have been composed by her than imposed upon her. Scenes, incidents, conversations rushed upon her with a vividness and importunity that would not be denied."[23] Like a number of Gothic writers before her, including Horace Walpole, William Beckford, and Matthew Lewis, Harriet Beecher Stowe engaged in a kind of automatic writing,[24] producing at great speed under an inner compulsion a novel whose power drew unconsciously on her years of physical and spiritual suffering. When she sketched in the setting for Uncle Tom's death, she drew on the Gothic literary tradition to portray the full horrors of the slave system on the haunted plantation of Simon Legree.

More than Lyman or Henry before her, Stowe understood the uses of the Gothic landscape. Uncle Tom's approach to Legree's plantation begins with a journey on the "good steamer Pirate" up the Red River, whose "red, muddy, turbid current" and "steep, red-clay banks" suggest that Legree territory is soaked in blood (Chap. 31). After disembarking at a small town, the party of slaves begins a long trek through desolate wilderness toward their new master's house:

> It was a wild, forsaken road, now winding through dreary pine barrens, where the wind whispered mournfully, and now over log causeways, through long cypress swamps, the doleful trees rising out of the slimy, spongy ground, hung with long wreaths of funereal black moss, while ever and anon the loathsome form of the moccasin snake might be seen sliding among broken stumps and shattered branches that lay here and there, rotting in the water. (Chap. 32)

The remoteness of Legree's place, buried deep in the eerie Louisiana wilderness, drew on the Gothic convention of the "dream landscape," "a closed world separated from that of everyday,"[25] and the repeated images of darkness, death, and decay aimed at evoking a foreboding of unnameable evil. Stowe's treatment of the approach to Legree's plantation drew on that characteristically Gothic line, the serpentine – from the Red River's "tortuous windings" (Chap. 31) through the "winding" swamp road – to suggest the twisted nature of the man who led the way.[26] Like Lyman and Henry before her, Stowe chose the Gothic mode to represent the worst evils of the social sin she attacked because its characteristic atmosphere of evil and brooding terror provided her with an excellent device for engaging readers in her cause.

At length, "the inclosures of the plantation rose to view," and the figurative iron doors of Legree's dungeons swung shut. Uncle Tom and his companions find themselves on the grounds of a ruin whose "ragged, forlorn appearance" indicates "that the care of the former owner has been left to go to utter decay." The large house, with its wide, two-story verandah wrapping around all sides, lies in desolate disrepair: "some windows stopped up with boards, some with shattered panes, and shutters hanging by a single hinge, – all telling of coarse neglect and discomfort." The once well-tended lawn is littered with garbage; the garden is a patch of weeds where "here and there, some solitary exotic reared its forsaken head"; the conservatory contains dry flower pots planted with dead sticks. The condition of Legree's plantation, formerly owned by "a gentleman of opulence and taste" (Chap. 32), suggests what St. Clare's magnificent New Orleans establishment may one day become under the ruinous influence of the slave system. Stowe's description of St. Clare's exotic home, like her brother Henry's treatment of the Ward of Pleasure, reflected the debt of the Gothic genre to the eighteenth-century oriental tale[27]: Built in the Moorish style "to gratify a picturesque and voluptuous ideality," St. Clare's house surrounds an enclosed courtyard with arches and pillars, fountains filled with gold and silver fishes, mosaic walkways, and "marble vases of arabesque sculpture, containing the choicest flowering plants of the tropics" (Chap. 15). But just as the oriental sensuality of the Ward of Pleasure points the way to the Ward of Death, St. Clare's gorgeous home serves in Stowe's narrative as a kind of way station to the ruined mansion of Simon Legree.

Stowe's use of landscape and setting reflect her debt to the terror-Gothic school, the tradition of Anne Radcliffe. Terror, as Mrs. Radcliffe had explained, expands the soul and opens the mind to apprehension of the sublime, whereas horror contracts the soul and freezes the faculties, closing the mind with repugnance.[28] But Stowe was also influenced by the school of horror-Gothic in her treatment of physical torture on Legree's plantation. Like her brother Henry, she invoked the Inquisition as a parallel to the sufferings of slaves in the cotton fields, where Legree's drivers routinely kick and flog the workers and Sambo sadistically buries a pin up to its head in the flesh of a woman who has fainted. Worse incidents occur off stage: The slow beating to death of a slave woman by Legree in the attic of his house, and even the fatal flogging of Tom, are not witnessed by the reader. The greatest horrors of Legree's regime are only hinted at, as in Cassy's warning to Tom:

> Here you are, on a lone plantation, ten miles from any other, in the swamps; not a white person here, who could testify, if you were burned alive, – if you were scalded, cut into inch-pieces, set up for

119

the dogs to tear, or hung up and whipped to death. There's no law here, of God or man, that can do you, or any one of us, the least good; and, this man! there's no earthly thing that he's too good to do. I could make any one's hair rise, and their teeth chatter, if I should only tell what I've seen and been knowing to, here, – and it's no use resisting! (Chap. 34)

Cassy, Legree's quadroon mistress, tells Emmeline that Legree learned the "trade" of torture among the pirates in the West Indies, and hints that he once burned a slave alive (Chap. 36). Even in Stowe's manipulation of horror, her emphasis is on apprehension: "Explicitness runs counter to its effectiveness, for Gothic fear is not so much what is seen but what is sensed beyond sight."[29]

Stowe's Gothic parallel between the "inclosures" of Legree's plantation and the dungeons of the Inquisition suggested, as her father and brother had, that the greatest horrors lie in the nether regions. Simon Legree is the devil himself. As Cassy tells Tom, "You are in the devil's hands" (Chap. 34), and Legree confirms his identity by demanding that Tom cease to worship God and pay obeisance instead to his new master: "*I'm* your church now!" (Chap. 31) Physically, Legree is an early study in the southern grotesque, a hideous, short, bullet-headed man of gigantic strength, with immense, hairy hands "garnished with long nails, in a very foul condition" (Chap. 30), and a "glaring, greenish-gray eye" (Chap. 31) that can fascinate his victims. The evil of his nature is so powerful that Uncle Tom "felt an immediate and revolting horror at him" (Chap. 30), and for Emmeline, the newly purchased object of Legree's lust, "The expression of his eyes made her soul sick, and her flesh creep" (Chap. 32). It is Emmeline, too, who directly compares Legree with the snakes of the swamp, and thus implies his affinity with the ancient biblical serpent by saying, "I an't afraid of snakes! I'd rather have one near me than him" (Chap. 36). Legree is attended by two black henchmen, Sambo and Quimbo, who form "no unapt personification of the powers of darkness" (Chap. 33), and by a pack of ferocious dogs who serve as hell hounds. "Everything is pushing us into hell. Why shouldn't we go?" Cassy asks, and Tom is overcome by a sense that "all was darkness and horror" (Chap. 34).

But the hell that confines Cassy as Legree's mistress is not the torture cell of the slave quarters where she ministers to Tom after his first flogging. It is Legree's mansion. The interior of the house is as ruinous as the exterior, with its "sickening, unwholesome smell, compounded of mingled damp, dirt, and decay," its chilly atmosphere "like that of a vault" (Chap. 35), its empty, echoing hallways prowled by Legree's savage dogs. The damp walls of the sitting room, with their expensive paper torn and moldering, are stained with slops of liquor and defaced by chalked memoranda and sums that indicate what is really amiss with the house: Simon Legree uses it "merely as an implement for money-making" (Chap. 32). Thus, when he turns to Emmeline on the journey back from the New Orleans slave market to say, "Well, my little dear, we're almost home!" he lies (Chap. 32). This house is not a home, because Legree has violated the central tenet of the cult of domesticity: the separation of the home from the market.[30] His house, in fact, does not even appear to have a kitchen, a significant omission in a novel that consistently treats kitchens as the key to domestic polity, from the sacramental domesticity of the Quaker Hallidays ("holy days") in Ohio, whose kettle is a "sort of censer of hospitality and good cheer" (Chap. 13); through the orderly arrangements of the Shelby household, where black Chloe, "the first cook of the neighborhood," evicts her mistress from the kitchen and reigns alone (Chap. 4); to the "chaos and old night" of the St. Clare kitchen, which "generally looked as if it had been arranged by a hurricane," but was in fact presided over by that "self-taught genius," Dinah (Chap. 18).[31] Horrifying though Dinah's kitchen may be to the orderly New England soul of Miss Ophelia, more horrifying still is the house without a kitchen, whose "hearth was employed only to light Legree's cigars and heat his punch, not to warm the domestic circle."[32]

Legree's house is not a home partly because in place of a wife he has an enslaved mistress. Once a beautiful, cultivated woman raised in luxury by her white father and his slave mistress, Cassy was sold, after her father's death, as a concubine; after seeing her first two children sold, she killed a third with laudanum to spare it a life of slavery. She grew increasingly embittered as she passed from one man's hands to the next, until at last she was purchased by Simon Legree. Like Henry Ward Beecher's "strange woman," she exercises demonic powers: With a "glance like sheet-lightning" from her large black eyes, she cows a driver (Chap. 33); with a few soft words from her in French, "Legree's face became perfectly demoniacal" (Chap. 33); with her wild and supernatural laugh, she seems to Uncle Tom "an embodiment of the temptation with which he had been wrestling" (Chap. 34). "I've got the devil in me!" she warns her master, who believes her, calling her "she-devil," and because she sometimes lapses into "raving insanity," she becomes an "object of dread to Legree, who had that superstitious horror of insane persons, which is common to coarse and uninstructed minds" (Chap. 35). Cassy is an antitype of true womanhood: She is not pious, but blasphemous, even diabolical; not pure, but fallen; not domestic, but restless, maddened, a killer of her own child; not submissive, but defiant and dangerous.[33] In short, she is an example of the Victorian woman as demon, "an explosively mobile, magic woman," who is simultaneously victim and queen, defined by "a clash of extremes of powerlessness and power."[34]

If Harriet Beecher Stowe shared with Henry Ward Beecher a sense of the diabolical powers of the fallen woman, however, she moved beyond him in seeing the positive potential of that demonic energy. In the character of Cassy, Stowe explored "the possibility of women enacting their rage without being consumed by it" and depicted "a uniquely female mode of liberation.[35] Cassy does secure freedom for herself and Emmeline by manipulating Legree's superstitious fear of her, convincing him, with the assistance of some Gothic tricks, that his house is haunted, so that she and Emmeline can hide in the garret until they can safely slip away to Canada. But even as she courageously enacts the "familiar fiction" of "the madwoman in the attic,"[36] she is restored to true womanhood through domesticity and maternity. In a packing crate in the garret that she has furnished with mattresses and pillows, provisions, books, and a lamp hung on a nail, Cassy says to Emmeline, "This is to be our home for the present" (Chap. 39). In the light of that tiny domestic circle drawn in the darkness of Legree's great house, Cassy is magically transformed back into a mother. When Emmeline appeals to her for maternal love, "Cassy sat down by her, put her arms around her neck, stroked her soft, brown hair; and Emmeline then wondered at the beauty of her magnificent eyes, now soft with tears" (Chap. 40). In a sense, Cassy has atoned for the sin of infanticide by saving Emmeline from a fate worse than death, and her reward will be to have her first two children restored to her after she and Emmeline reach Canada. Stowe's demonic fallen woman, unlike her brother Henry's, was redeemable – not despite her demonic nature but through that uniquely female exercise of power, which liberates her from Legree. Cassy's female power clearly triumphs over his male power, for which she has nothing but contempt: When the terrified man boasts that he will take his pistols and go to the haunted chamber underneath the garret, Cassy jeers, "Do, sleep in that room. I'd like to see you doing it. Fire your pistols, do!" (Chap. 39). In the face of Cassy's scorn, Legree can only demonstrate his masculine impotence by stamping his foot and swearing.

Uncle Tom's Cabin has been faulted for the Gothic claptrap of Cassy's escape from Legree. To be sure, the episode does draw on the most hackneyed clichés of Gothic tradition. Cassy tells Legree that she hears groans coming from the garret at night and has seen a ghost in her own chamber; she inserts a bottle neck in a knot hole of the garret to make the wind wail and shriek; she ensures that a gust of wind from the garret will blow out Legree's candle one stormy night; and she plants a collection of Gothic tales where Legree will find and read "stories of bloody murders, ghostly legends, and supernatural visitations" (Chap. 30). But Stowe used this Gothic claptrap to satirize the tradition as Jane Austen had in *Northanger Abbey* (1818). Of the legendary garret ghost – the slave woman murdered by Legree – Stowe wrote:

> Authorities were somewhat divided, as to the outward form of the spirit, owing to a custom quite prevalent among negroes, – and, for aught we know, among whites, too, – of invariably shutting the eyes, and covering up heads under blankets, petticoats, or whatever else might come in use for a shelter, on these occasions. Of course, as everybody knows, when the bodily eyes are thus out of the lists, the spiritual eyes are uncommonly vivacious and perspicuous; and, therefore, there were abundance of full-length portraits of the ghost, abundantly sworn and testified to, which, as is often the case

with portraits, agreed with each other in no particular, except the common family peculiarity of the ghost tribe, – the wearing of a *white sheet*. (Chap. 42)

Stowe shared some of Austen's scorn for the literary effort to arouse terror with snuffed candles and things that go bump in the night.

Stowe's purpose in satirizing Gothic claptrap with this false haunting, however, was to highlight the true haunting of Simon Legree. For Legree is a haunted man even before Cassy begins her machinations against him. A divided self in the Gothic tradition of the tyrannical villain-hero,[37] he is torn between the evil of his desire for absolute dominion over others, the legacy of a brutal father, and his memory of the innocence that has been cherished in him by a pious mother. She had tried to win him from sin, and "His heart inly relented, – there was a conflict, – but sin got the victory, and he set all the force of his rough nature against the conviction of his conscience" (Chap. 35). But when word came of his mother's death and her forgiveness of him, a lock of her hair fell from the letter and entwined round his finger, and ever since, his nights have been haunted by a "pale mother rising by his bedside," a lock of hair twining round his fingers and throat, and whispering voices that fill him with horror (Chap. 35). "There is a dread, unhallowed necromancy of evil," wrote Stowe, "that turns things sweetest and holiest to phantoms of horror and affright" (Chap. 35). Simon Legree is not actually haunted by a super-natural presence, but by a sense of guilt rising from his mother's enduring grip on one side of his dual nature, assisted by Uncle Tom's success in awakening the "slumbering moral elements" (Chap. 39) in him. Finally, Legree is haunted by himself: "What a fool is he who locks his door to keep out spirits, who has in his own bosom a spirit he dares not meet alone" (Chap. 42).

In representing the true haunting of Simon Legree, Harriet drew both on her father's condemnation of strong drink and on her brother's diatribe against illicit sexuality. But whereas the haunted houses of Lyman and Henry had represented ruined bodies, the haunted house in *Uncle Tom's Cabin* represented a ruined mind. Far more than her father or her brother, Harriet Beecher Stowe explored the psychological potential of the Gothic genre, using the haunted house as an emblem of the tormented mind, as Simon Legree tries in vain to lock "the chambers of his brain" (Chap. 36) to keep out the ghost of his terrible guilt as slaveholder. For Stowe, as for many mid-Victorians, psychology was never entirely distinct from the supernatural. She agreed with her husband, Calvin, that it was not "absurd to suppose that some peculiarity in the nervous system, in the connecting link between soul and body, may bring some more than others into an almost abnormal contact with the spirit world."[38] Even so, the true haunting of Simon Legree is more psychological than supernatural; the horrors he confronts arise out of the depths of his own mind. Stowe had an implicit understanding of the close connection between "the dream and the underworld," between the unconscious of depth psychology and the hell of Christian theology.[39] She wrote of "the shadowy world of sleep" as "that land whose dim outlines lie so fearfully near to the mystic scene of retribution" (Chap. 36). When Simon Legree descends into that shadowy dream world, he seems to be entering hell:

> Then it seemed to him he was on the edge of a frightful abyss, holding on and struggling in mortal fear, while dark hands stretched up, and were pulling him over; and Cassy came behind him laughing, and pushed him. And then rose up that solemn veiled figure, and drew aside the veil. It was his mother; and she turned away from him, and he fell down, down, down, amid a confused noise of shrieks, and groans, and shouts of demon laughter, – and Legree awoke. (Chap. 36)

In this passage, Stowe used the major elements of her brother Henry's Gothic hell: the deep pit, the hands pulling the victim down, the woman pushing him in, the shouts of demon laughter. But Stowe's hell is different in one significant sense: Simon Legree sees the abyss, struggles at its brink, falls into its depths, – and then awakens. Legree descends nightly into the hell of his own mind and is punished for his sins as a slaveholder even before death claims him; in his soul, "the fire that never shall be quenched is already burning" (Chap. 40). And under the strain of his self-haunting, he succumbs to insanity, "that frightful disease that seems to throw the lurid shadows of a coming retribution back into the present life" (Chap. 42). In the orthodox religious imagination of Lyman Beecher, hell was an actual place below the surface of the earth. For Henry Ward Beecher, hell was an allegorical representation of the body of woman. But for Harriet Beecher Stowe, hell was the abyss of the haunted mind.

With the best of paternal intentions, Lyman Beecher attended to the spiritual lives of his children by painting vivid pictures of hell and then pointing to the ease of joining Christ. His fervent plea to his son Edward in 1821 was typical: "Oh, my dear son, *agonize* to enter in. You *must* go to heaven; you *must not* go to hell!"[40] With Henry and Harriet, as with all eleven of his children, Lyman was unsuccessful: Though he instilled in both a positive terror of hell, he could not lead them to the experience of saving grace. According to Lyman Beecher's liberal Calvinism, every person had the moral ability and the moral responsibility to repent of his or her own free will. Henry and Harriet strove mightily, but their adolescent "conversions" proved to be false hopes, and both subsequently plunged into a period of religious humiliation and distress. As a student at Amherst College, Henry underwent an anguished period of skepticism; Harriet, as a student and then as a teacher at her sister Catharine's female seminary in Hartford, spent many nights groaning and crying over her religious state.[41] To say that all the Beecher children found Lyman's God "intolerable"[42] may be to overstate the case, but it is clear that they seriously questioned his justice. Fully aware that Lyman's theology was liberal within the Calvinist fold, the Beecher children were nonetheless repelled and distressed by what they perceived to be the Calvinist double bind: Though depraved by nature, they were expected to exercise moral ability in conversion. As Harriet expressed it,

> The case seems to me exactly as if I had been brought into the world with such a thirst for ardent spirits that there was just a possibility, but no hope that I should resist, and then my eternal happiness made to depend on my being temperate.[43]

Guilt-ridden Henry was similarly oppressed by a sense of spiritual helplessness. Convinced of the horrors of hell, yet unable to achieve the conversion that alone could save them from eternal torment, brother and sister entered adulthood with a heavy psychological legacy, evidenced in Henry's migraine headaches and attacks of dizziness and in the nervous difficulties suffered by Harriet in her thirties.[44]

In their search for spiritual release, Henry and Harriet gradually moved away from Lyman Beecher's Calvinism toward a theology of Christocentric liberalism, which emphasized not the judgment of God but the love of Christ and the availability of salvation for all.[45] As a young minister, Henry quietly avoided such topics as eternal damnation and eventually abandoned them entirely. Of Jonathan Edwards's "Sinners in the Hands of an Angry God," he wrote, "I think a person of moral sensibility alone at midnight, reading that awful discourse, would well-nigh go crazy."[46] Harriet's journey out of Calvinism was more difficult than her brother's. Her entire life was to center on a "long and agonizing struggle with the religion of her fathers, and more particularly with the religion of her father."[47] Yet Harriet too increasingly embraced a Christ whose love surpassed his judgment and whose humanity was distinctly feminine. The Christocentric liberalism of Henry and Harriet was a sentimental religiosity, concentrating not on dogma but on the emotive experience, while affirming the close link between spirituality and domesticity; it "brought God down from heaven and installed him by the hearth."[48] By 1877, Henry had concluded that such a loving God would not condemn His children to eternal torment:

> To tell me that back of Christ is a God who for unnumbered centuries has gone on creating men and sweeping them like dead flies – nay, like living ones – into hell, is to ask me to worship a being . . . much worse than the conception of any medieval devil. . . . I will *not* worship cruelty, I *will* worship Love – that sacrifices itself for the good of those who err.[49]

Harriet was not quite so direct. When her son Charley asserted that he no longer believed in hell, she responded:

> When you say . . . you do not believe in any Hell I do not understand you for first you must see in this life that there is suffering mysterious and unalterable, awful, and fruitful of sin. There is before our eyes the hell of the drunkard, the murderer, the dishonest . . .[50]

In this evasive assertion of a this-worldly hell, Harriet did not deny hell as emphatically as her brother, but from as early as 1857, the year of her son Henry's death, she expressed her doubts about its place in a divine scheme overflowing with God's love.[51]

Before their Christocentric liberalism came to maturity in the 1850s and 1860s, however, Henry and Harriet both gave full expression to the Calvinist sense of horror that had been inculcated in them as children and had remained with them into their adult years. The Gothic nightmares of "The Strange Woman" and *Uncle Tom's Cabin* were not Christ centered but demon centered, depicting a claustrophobic world dominated by the devil himself. The nightmare was not liberal, for its focus was human depravity. Nor did that nightmare pay sentimental homage to the cult of domesticity. Instead, it envisioned a horrible perversion of the domestic ideal – in Henry's expression of sexual nausea and his portrayal of woman as monstrously demonic, and in Harriet's depiction of forced concubinage and sexual hatred. Most important, these nightmares revealed that both authors retained a lively sense of hell, although their hell assumed a new form, more Gothic than Calvinist.

Their expression of religious horror took on Gothic form because the haunted house was a powerful metaphor for their spiritual condition. First, the haunted house symbolizes "anxiety with no possibility of escape," "a neurosis" centered on "the dread of oppression and of the abyss."[52] The haunted house clearly symbolizes physical entrapment: the imprisonment of the young men who enter the strange woman's house never to return, the imprisonment of black slaves on the plantation of Simon Legree (though here dramatic interest is generated by the daring escape of the Gothic madwoman from her attic). But the power of the image derives from its statement of psychological entrapment, as with the youths, who cannot break away from lust, and Legree, who cannot escape from himself. For Henry and Harriet, the image of the haunted house captured their sense of spiritual anxiety with no possibility of escape. Second, the haunted castle of Gothic tradition symbolized the weight of patriarchal inheritance. For Henry and Harriet, that inheritance consisted of "the religion of their fathers, and more particularly of their father." The sense of a Calvinist inheritance weighed heavily on Harriet, as her New England novels demonstrate, but it was Henry who made explicit the analogy between ancestral mansion and Calvinist theology when he expressed the hope that the doctrines of foreordination and election might in time become beautiful, "like old castles when they are no longer inhabited, and when vines and ivy have grown all over them."[53] Both of these meanings of the Gothic haunted house – psychic anxiety and patriarchal inheritance – were captured by Henry's and Harriet's deeply troubled brother, Charles, writing of Jonathan Edwards:

> A man's theological system is like an old hereditary mansion; –
> taken as a whole it may be gloomy, ruinous, forbidding. Yet there
> may be a room or two of Southern aspect, in which the man lives.
> Into the ghostly walks, and corridors and haunted chambers, and
> appalling dungeons, he may never or seldom enter . . . a man does
> not build the Ancestral Castle which he inhabits . . .[54]

For all three of these Beechers, the haunted house symbolized their Calvinist inheritance, a gloomy and ghostly mansion none of them had built or wished to occupy, a place of anxiety and psychic confinement.

At the same time, the peculiar appeal of the Gothic genre to Henry and Harriet extended beyond these specific symbolic uses of the haunted house. As Joel Porte has argued, Gothic fiction was fundamentally a Calvinist expression of religious disquietude and terror, within "a religious drama, the dark rites of sin, guilt, and damnation."[55] As children of Calvinism, Henry and Harriet were drawn to the Gothic genre's central fable of inexpiable guilt and unremitting punishment. But as troubled apostates from their theological heritage, they were even more strongly drawn to Gothic fiction's sympathetic representation of "the tormented condition of a creature suspended between the extremes of faith and scepticism, beatitude and horror."[56] Harriet's particular interest in this "tormented condition" was revealed in her lifelong fascination with Byron, the heroic figure of dark romanticism, whose soul had been driven into war with itself, in Stowe's view, by his Calvinist upbringing.[57] Some years after the publication of *Uncle Tom's Cabin*, Harriet explored the Gothic legacy of Calvinism in her finest New England novel, *Oldtown Folks* (1869): The New England theology, she wrote, had the "power of lacerating the nerves of the soul, and producing strange states of morbid horror and repulsion."[58] Unwittingly, she was offering a compelling explanation of her own Gothic representation of slavery, as well as her brother Henry's Gothic portrayal of prostitution.

For these children of Lyman Beecher, then, the Gothic mode offered a way of expressing simultaneously their Calvinism and their revulsion from that theological system. It thus represented a midway point on their journey from the Calvinist orthodoxy of their past toward the Christocentric liberalism of their future, even while it captured their terror in making the journey.[59] Caught between the hope-filled Christocentric liberalism lying before them and the gloomy Calvinism that lay behind them, Henry Ward Beecher and Harriet Beecher Stowe expressed their spiritual anxiety in Gothic form. As Emily Dickinson, another child of New England Calvinism, wrote, "One need not be a Chamber – to be Haunted."[60]

NOTES

1 Charles Edward Stowe and Lyman Beecher Stowe, *Harriet Beecher Stowe: The Story of Her Life* (Boston: Houghton Mifflin, 1911), pp. 17, 14.

2 Quoted in E. Bruce Kirkham, *The Building of Uncle Tom's Cabin* (Knoxville: The University of Tennessee Press, 1977), p. 67.

3 Harriet Beecher Stowe, *Uncle Tom's Cabin; or, Life Among the Lowly*, ed. Kenneth S. Lynn (Cambridge, Mass.: Belknap Press of Harvard University Press, 1962), Chap. 39.

4 Edmund Wilson, *Patriotic Gore: Studies in the Literature of the American Civil War* (London: Oxford University Press, 1962), p. 10.

5 Barbara M. Cross, Introduction to *The Autobiography of Lyman Beecher*, vol. 1 (Cambridge, Mass.: Belknap Press of Harvard University Press, 1961), p. xxxvi.

6 See W. J. Rorabaugh, *The Alcoholic Republic: An American Tradition* (Oxford: Oxford University Press, 1979).

7 *Autobiography of Lyman Beecher*, vol. 2, pp. 22–3.

8 Lyman Beecher, *Six Sermons on the Nature, Occasions, Signs, Evils, and Remedy of Intemperance* (Boston: T. R. Marvin, 1829), p. 75.

9 Eino Railo, *The Haunted Castle: A Study of the Elements of English Roman-*

ticism (London: Routledge and sons, 1927), p.7. Also see K. Mehrota, *Horace Walpole and the English Novel: A Study of the Influence of 'The Castle of Otranto' 1764–1820* (Oxford: Blackwell, 1934); Devendra P. Varma, *The Gothic Flame* (London: Arthur Baker, 1957); Elizabeth MacAndrew, *The Gothic Tradition in Fiction* (New York: Columbia University Press, 1979); Donald A. Ringe, *American Gothic: Imagination and Reason in Nineteenth-century Fiction* (Lexington: University Press of Kentucky, 1982).

10 Marie Caskey, *Chariot of Fire: Religion and the Beecher Family* (New Haven, Conn.: Yale University Press, 1978), pp. 28–30.

11 Quoted in Stuart C. Henry, *Unvanquished Puritan: A Portrait of Lyman Beecher* (Grand Rapids, Mich.: William B. Eerdmans, 1973), p. 41. Also see Caskey, *Chariot of Fire*, chaps. 1 and 2; Cross, Introduction, *Autobiography of Lyman Beecher*.

12 Robert D. Hume, "Gothic vs. Romantic: A Revaluation of the Gothic Novel," *PMLA* 84 (March 1969):282–90. The phrase "crude claptrap" is from Lowry Nelson, "Night Thoughts on the Gothic Novel," *Yale Review* 52 (1962):248.

13 See Clifford E. Clark, Jr., *Henry Ward Beecher: Spokesman for a Middle-Class America* (Urbana: University of Illinois Press, 1978), chaps. 2 and 3; Jane Shaffer Elsmere, *Henry Ward Beecher: The Indiana Years, 1837–1847* (Indianapolis: Indiana Historical Society, 1973), pp. 192–4; Caskey, *Chariot of Fire*, chap. 8; Milton Rugoff, *The Beechers: An American Family in the Nineteenth Century* (New York: Harper & Row, 1981), chap. 14.

14 Henry Ward Beecher, *Lectures to Young Men, on Various Important Subjects* (Boston: John P. Jewett, 1850), p. 196.

15 See Varma, *Gothic Flame*, chap. 6.

16 John Mack Faragher, *Women and Men on the Overland Trail* (New Haven, Conn.: Yale University Press, 1979), p. 121.

17 For a feminist analysis of this image, see Sandra M. Gilbert and Susan Gubar, *The Madwoman in the Attic: The Woman Writer and the Nineteenth-century Literary Imagination* (New Haven, Conn.: Yale University Press, 1979), pp. 29–36. Henry Ward Beecher's sexual use of the haunted house placed him within that subcategory of the Gothic that Sigmund Freud identified as "the uncanny." According to Freud, "the uncanny is that class of the terrifying which leads back to something long known to us . . . a hidden, familiar thing that has undergone repression and then emerged from it." This psychic phenomenon accounts for the ambivalence of the German word *heimlich*, which means familiar, belonging to the home, as well as concealed, kept

from sight, *unheimlich.* One of Freud's examples of the uncanny is the feeling common among men that there is something both terrifying and familiar about female genital organs: "This *unheimlich* place, however, is the entrance to the former *heim* [home] of all human beings, to the place where everyone dwelt once upon a time and in the beginning . . . In this case, too, the *unheimlich* is what was once *heimlich,* home-like, familiar; the prefix "un" is the token of repression." From a Freudian perspective, then, Henry Ward Beecher's sense of dread and creeping horror about the female genitalia was an experience of the uncanny, the emergence from repression of something long known to him. And since "an *unheimliches* house" can only be rendered in English as "a *haunted* house," Beecher's allegorical representation of female anatomy may be especially telling. See Sigmund Freud, "The Uncanny," in *On Creativity and the Unconscious: Papers on the Psychology of Art, Literature, Love, Religion,* ed. Benjamin Nelson (New York: Harper Torchbooks, 1958), pp. 122–61. The quotation is from pp. 152–3.

18 Quoted in Wilson, *Patriotic Gore,* p. 21. Also see Rugoff, *Beechers,* p. 117; Caskey, *Chariot of Fire,* pp. 219, 233; Clark, *Henry Ward Beecher,* chap. 10.

19 Nina Auerbach, *Woman and the Demon: The Life of a Victorian Myth* (Cambridge, Mass.: Harvard University Press, 1982), pp. 160, 2, and passim.

20 The phrase was Herman Melville's, from chap. 58 of *Moby Dick.* It has been applied to nineteenth-century male attitudes towards women's sexuality by G. J. Barker-Benfield in *The Horrors of the Half-known Life: Male Attitudes Toward Women and Sexuality in Nineteenth-century America* (New York: Harper Colophon Books, 1976).

21 Elizabeth Ammons, Introduction to *Critical Essays on Harriet Beecher Stowe* (Boston: G. K. Hall, 1980), p. xiv; Charles H. Foster, *The Rungless Ladder: Harriet Beecher Stowe and New England Puritanism* (Durham, N.C.: Duke University Press, 1954), chap. 2.

22 Quoted in Forrest Wilson, *Crusader in Crinoline: The Life of Harriet Beecher Stowe* (Philadelphia: J. P. Lippincott, 1941), p. 252; and in Kirkham, *Building of Uncle Tom's Cabin,* p. 66.

23 Quoted in Foster, *Rungless Ladder,* p. 29.

24 For a discussion of the Gothic use of the unconscious, see Varma, *Gothic Flame,* chap. 3.

25 MacAndrew, *Gothic Tradition,* p. 47.

26 Linda Bayer-Berenbaum, *The Gothic Imagination: Expansion in Gothic*

Literature and Art (London and Toronto: Associated University Press, 1982), chap. 2.

27 See Martha Pike Conant, *The Oriental Tale in England in the Eighteenth Century* (New York: Columbia University Press, 1908).

28 See Hume, "Gothic vs. Romantic."

29 James M. Keech, "The Survival of the Gothic Response," *Studies in the Novel* 6 (Summer 1974):132.

30 See Nancy F. Cott, *The Bonds of Womanhood: "Woman's Sphere" in New England, 1780–1835* (New Haven, Conn.: Yale University Press, 1977), chap. 2.

31 See Ellen Moers, *Literary Women: The Great Writers* (New York: Oxford University Press, 1977), pp. 37–8.

32 Mary P. Ryan, *The Empire of the Mother: American Writing about Domesticity 1830–1860* (New York: Haworth Press, 1982), p. 135.

33 See Barbara Welter, "The Cult of True Womanhood, 1820–1860," *American Quarterly* 18 (Summer 1966):151–74.

34 Auerbach, *Woman and the Demon*, pp. 1, 4.

35 Gilbert and Gubar, *Madwoman in the Attic*, p. 533.

36 Ibid., p. 534.

37 See Railo, *Haunted Castle*, chaps. 4 and 6; Varma, *Gothic Flame*, pp. 117–20; MacAndrew, *Gothic Tradition*, chap. 1.

38 Quoted in Wilson, *Patriotic Gore*, p. 59.

39 See James Hillman, *The Dream and the Underworld* (New York: Harper & Row, 1979). Stowe's interest in spiritualism made her a pioneer of the first system of dynamic psychiatry; see Henri Ellenberger, *The Discovery of the Unconscious: The History and Evolution of Dynamic Psychiatry* (New York: Basic Books, 1970), chaps. 2 and 3.

40 *Autobiography of Lyman Beecher*, vol. 1, p. 341.

41 Harriet's childhood terror of hell was related by her son and grandson in their account of her life; see Stowe and Stowe, *Harriet Beecher Stowe*, pp. 13–14. For evidence of Henry's similar sense of terror, see Henry, *Unvanquished Puritan*, p. 229. On Henry's adolescent crisis of faith, see Caskey, *Chariot of Fire*, pp. 214–15; on Harriet's youthful spiritual crisis, see Stowe and Stowe, *Harriet Beecher Stowe*, pp. 53–62.

42 Cross, Introduction to *Autobiography of Lyman Beecher*, vol. 1, p. xiii.

43 Quoted in Stowe and Stowe, *Harriet Beecher Stowe*, p. 61.

44 See Cross, Introduction to *Autobiography of Lyman Beecher*, vol. 1, p. xiii; and Foster, *Rungless Ladder*, pp. 24–5.

45 See Caskey, *Chariot of Fire*, chaps. 7 and 8.

46 Quoted in ibid., p. 228.

47 Henry F. May, Introduction to Harriet Beecher Stowe, *Oldtown Folks* (Cambridge, Mass.: Belknap Press of Harvard University Press, 1966), p. 4.
48 Caskey, *Chariot of Fire*, p. 363.
49 Quoted in Rugoff, *Beechers*, p. 510.
50 Quoted in Edward Wagenknecht, *Harriet Beecher Stowe: The Known and the Unknown* (New York: Oxford University Press, 1965), p. 205.
51 See Gayle Kimball, *The Religious Ideas of Harriet Beecher Stowe: Her Gospel of Womanhood* (New York: Edward Mellen Press, 1982), p. 52; Foster, *Rungless Ladder*, p. 102.
52 Mario Praz, "Introductory Essay," *Three Gothic Novels* (Baltimore: Penguin Books, 1972), p. 20; J. M. S. Tompkins, Introduction to Varma, *Gothic Flame*, p. xiii.
53 Quoted in Rugoff, *Beechers*, p. 512.
54 Quoted in Caskey, *Chariot of Fire*, p. 332.
55 Joel Porte, "In the Hands of an Angry God: Religious Terror in Gothic Fiction," in G. R. Thompson, ed., *The Gothic Imagination: Essays in Dark Romanticism* (Pullman: Washington State University Press, 1974), p. 45.
56 G. R. Thompson, "Introduction: Romanticism and the Gothic Tradition," in Thompson, ed., *Gothic Imagination*, p. 3.
57 Kenneth S. Lynn, Introduction to Harriet Beecher Stowe, *Uncle Tom's Cabin*, p. xx. For a full discussion of Stowe's complex response to Byron, see Alice C. Crozier, *The Novels of Harriet Beecher Stowe* (New York: Oxford University Press, 1969), chap. 6.
58 Harriet Beecher Stowe, *Oldtown Folks*, p. 71.
59 G. R. Thompson has argued that Gothic literature expressed "an existential terror generated by schism between a triumphantly secularized philosophy of evolving good and an abiding obsession with the medieval conception of guilt-laden, sin-ridden man." See Introduction to *Gothic Imagination*, pp. 5–6.
60 Quoted in Foster, *Rungless Ladder*, p. 11. Gilbert and Gubar have pointed out the resemblance of Dickinson's haunted brain to the haunting of Simon Legree; see *Madwoman in the Attic*, p. 624.

5

Sharing the Thunder: The Literary Exchanges of Harriet Beecher Stowe, Henry Bibb, and Frederick Douglass

ROBERT B. STEPTO

IN an October 1852 number of *Frederick Douglass's Paper* appears a book notice entitled "Stolen Thunder." Briefly described therein is W. L. G. Smith's "Life at the South; or Uncle Tom's Cabin as it is," one of the many books that followed close upon Harriet Beecher Stowe's novel in an attempt to gain a corner of the market *Uncle Tom's Cabin* had singlehandedly created. In regard to Smith's book, "stolen thunder" has a double meaning, for, according to the reviewer, Smith is not just attempting to "make money out of the popularity of 'Uncle Tom's Cabin,'" but also seeking "withal a little capital for the 'patriarchal institution.'"[1]

"Stolen thunder" aptly describes most of these publishing ventures, particularly those that were shamelessly entrepreneurial and those pursued by white Americans, even when, like Stowe, they vilified slavery. But the phrase falls short of the complex relationship between Stowe's novel and the many Afro-American antislavery texts published in the late 1840s and early 1850s. Some of these appear to have followed the stolen thunder pattern: Solomon Northup's *Twelve Years A Slave* (1853), for example, was dedicated, with great flourish, to Stowe ("whose name, throughout the world, is identified with the GREAT REFORM") and was generally promoted – and received – as "another key to Uncle Tom's Cabin," or, as one newspaper put it, "Uncle Tom's Cabin – No. 2."[2] On the other hand, the relationship between *Uncle Tom's Cabin* and *Twelve Years A Slave* is not a simple one of promotion and sales or of two products vying for the same finite market. The two narratives share internal features that bind them together in literary history: When Northup divulges the existence of a thriving slave market in the nation's capital city, exposes the brutal forms

135

of slave life in the Red River region of Louisiana, or rehearses the figure of Stowe's George Shelby in his own "saviors" from the North (Henry B. Northup of New York, but also the Canadian, Samuel Bass), he is not so much stealing Stowe's thunder as substantiating the antislavery literary conventions established (if not exactly invented) by her – all the while telling his own story, of course. *Uncle Tom's Cabin* did not provide Northup with his tale or his stance against the "peculiar institution," but it may well have affected his autobiographical acts of remembering. In this regard especially, the relationship between Stowe's and Northup's works is both complex and literary; the textual conversation between the two narratives prompts the idea that Stowe and Northup shared the antislavery thunder of the 1850s: Despite the activities of his white editor and amanuensis, David Wilson, Northup cannot be said to have poached upon Stowe's success.

The relationship between *Uncle Tom's Cabin* and Frederick Douglass's novella, "The Heroic Slave" (1853), provides an even more interesting study of antislavery textual conversation, partly because Douglass, unlike Northup, was easily Stowe's equal as a prominent antislavery activist and partly because Douglass and Stowe knew each other and corresponded repeatedly during the period in which their antislavery fictions were being composed. Although dedicated alike to the task of eradicating slavery and to other causes such as the promotion of temperance, Stowe and Douglass differed profoundly on certain related issues – for instance, African colonization and the extent to which the American church community had succored slaveholders and hence abetted slaveholding. Although they debated these matters directly in their correspondence, and indirectly in public pronouncements, it can also be said that they conversed further in the pages of their antislavery fictions. The features of this exchange – of this sharing of the antislavery thunder – are explored in the rest of this essay.

In July 1851, a scant month after the Washington, D.C., *National Era* had begun its serialization of *Uncle Tom's Cabin*, Harriet Beecher Stowe wrote Frederick Douglass a rather spirited letter. She began politely with a request for Douglass's assistance in acquiring accurate information about the details of life and work on a southern cotton plantation, but soon thereafter shifted her subject and tone, taking Douglass to task for what she understood to be his critical view of the church and of African colonization. Both parts of this letter tell us something about the composition of *Uncle Tom's Cabin* and are suggestive as well about what may be termed the countercomposition of "The Heroic Slave."

Stowe's request of Douglass is expressed in this way:

> You may perhaps have noticed in your editorial readings a series of articles that I am furnishing for the Era under the title of "Uncle Tom's Cabin or Life among the lowly" – In the course of my story, the scene will fall upon a cotton plantation – I am very desirous to gain information from one who has been an actual labourer on one – &. it occurs to me that in the circle of your acquaintance there might be one who would be able to communicate to me some such information as I desire – I have before me an able paper written by a southern planter in which the details &. modus operandi are given from *his* point of sight – I am anxious to have some more from another standpoint – I wish to be able to make a picture that shall be graphic &. true to nature in its details – Such a person as *Henry Bibb*, if in this country might give me just the kind of information I desire you may possible know of some other person – I will subjoin to this letter a list of questions which in that case, you will do me a favor by enclosing to the individual – with a request that he will at earliest convenience answer them – [3]

Above and beyond what I sense to be a remarkable admixture of civility and imperiousness, two features of this statement warrant mention. One is that, although Stowe was undeniably an armchair sociologist of the South, here she appears to be rather assiduous in gathering southern testimony and in seeking the forms of black testimony that could both counter and corroborate the white testimony she already had in hand. The idea of weighing white and black testimony alike in order to gain a "picture" of plantation life that is "true to nature" was probably anathema to most white southerners of the late 1850s. But Stowe's practice here shows clearly that, contrary to the opinion of many southern whites (including Mary Boykin Chesnut), she did assay southern views, white and black, while composing *Uncle Tom's Cabin*.

The other signal feature is Stowe's reference to Henry Bibb. Bibb was a Kentucky slave, born probably in 1815, who escaped from bondage only to return repeatedly to Kentucky to rescue his family as well. None of his efforts met with success; indeed, at one point, Bibb was recaptured and sold "down river" with his family to slaveholders in the Red River region. Further attempts to escape as a family were also thwarted. Eventually, Bibb once again escaped on his own, arriving in Detroit, but only after additional trials of bondage, including a time in which he was the property of an Indian slaveholder, and after another brave effort to save Malinda, his wife, which ended when he discovered she had become her master's favorite concubine. Bibb's account of his story was published in 1849 under the title *Narrative of the Life and Adventures of Henry Bibb, An American Slave, Written By Himself;* it was undoubtedly one of the principal slave narratives discussed in antislavery circles during the period in which *Uncle Tom's Cabin* was being composed and first serialized.

Interest in Bibb's narrative continues today. Gilbert Osofsky included it among the narratives collected in *Puttin' On Ole Massa* (an anthology that, along with Arna Bontemps's *Great Slave Narratives,* introduced a generation of fledgling Afro-Americanists to slave narratives other than Douglass's of 1845), and I have elsewhere discussed its particular narrative strategies.[4] Among its enduring features is Bibb's story of his Indian captivity, an account that places the narrative in the popular tradition of captivity narratives and that, however obliquely, touches upon a key issue of Bibb's day – whether the practice of slaveholding should be allowed to expand into the Indian Territories, especially once they had become states of the Union. Another key feature is Bibb's love for and dedication to his still enslaved family, particularly as repeatedly expressed in his willingness to venture back across the Ohio River, deep into the bowels of danger, in order to attempt their rescue and release. His portrait of family unity against the odds (unity up to a point – since, as we know, Bibb was eventually compelled to abandon them) unquestionably struck a chord with the abolitionists of the 1850s, who brought it forth as further proof of slavery's sinful assault upon the slave's effort to maintain a semblance of Christian home life. Moreover, it is one of the accounts that has encouraged historians of our time, including Herbert Gutman and John Blassingame, to insist that the slave family

could and did, in Gutman's words, "develop and sustain meaningful domestic and kin arrangements."⁵

A third feature, as central to Bibb's narrative as the portrait of
family life, is his caustic view of the complicity between the church
and the institution of slaveholding. Although Bibb is presented by
his guarantors – abolitionists in Detroit – possibly out of necessity
as a member of a Sabbath school and a man of "Christian course,"
it is clear in the body of *his* text that he has been variously wounded by the conduct of American Christians, and that as a result he is
suspicious of them and "their" church. Fairly early in the *Narrative*, for example, Bibb makes his way back south in quest of his
family, but is captured by a mob of slaveholders and soon imprisoned in Louisville. Of the mob, he says:

> In searching my pockets, they found my certificate from the Meth-
> odist E. Church . . . testifying to my worthiness as a member of that
> church. And what made the matter look more disgraceful to me,
> many of this mob were members of the M. E. Church, and they
> were the persons who took away my church ticket, and then rob-
> bed me also of fourteen dollars in cash, a silver watch for which I
> paid ten dollars, a pocket knife for which I paid seventy-five cents,
> and a Bible for which I paid sixty-two and one half cents. All this
> they tyranically robbed me of, and yet my owner, Wm. Gatewood,
> was a regular member of the same church to which I belonged.⁶

Much later in the narrative, after Bibb and his family have been
sold into an abominable state of bondage in Louisiana, he records
the following about his new master, a church deacon:

> And while I was offering up my prayers to that God who never
> forsakes those in the hour of danger who trust in him, I thought of
> Deacon Whitfield; I thought of his profession, and doubted his piety.
> I thought of his handcuffs, of his whips, of his chains, of his stocks,
> of his thumb-screws, of his slave driver and overseer, and of his
> religion; I also thought of his opposition to prayer meetings, and of
> his five hundred lashes promised me for attending a prayer meeting.
> I thought of God, I thought of the devil, I thought of hell; and I
> thought of heaven, and wondered whether I should ever see the
> Deacon there. And I calculated that if heaven was made up of such
> Deacons, or such persons, it could not be filled with love to all
> mankind . . . as we know it is from the truth of the Bible.⁷

In light of these pronouncements, grounded as they were in the most bitter of experiences, it is not surprising that Bibb claims elsewhere in his story that "I never had religion enough to keep me from running away from slavery in my life."[8]

Finally, Bibb's *Narrative* endures as much for its figurative language as for its rhetoric and ideology. I refer here to Bibb's descriptions of the Ohio River (which separated freedom in Ohio from bondage in Kentucky) as a road to freedom and, for the bonded black, a river Jordan. The most remarkable passage in this vein begins:

> Sometimes standing on the Ohio River bluff, looking over on a free State, and as far north as my eyes could see, I have eagerly gazed upon the blue sky of the free North, which at times constrained me to cry out from the depths of my soul, Oh! Canada, sweet land of rest – Oh! when shall I get there?[9]

As the passage concludes, Bibb's language reminds us first of Frederick Douglass's earlier description of the images of freedom offered by Maryland's Chesapeake Bay, and then of more contemporary imaginings, such as those moments in John Edgar Wideman's *Brothers & Keepers* (1984) when he explores the irony of his brother's incarceration in a prison (called "Western") along the banks of the Ohio:

> I have stood upon the lofty banks of the river Ohio, gazing upon the splendid steamboats, wafted with all their magnificence up and down the river, and I thought of the fishes of the water, the fowls of the air, the wild beasts of the forest, all appeared to be free, to go just where they pleased, and I was an unhappy slave![10]

I have quoted at some length from Bibb's narrative principally to suggest that Mrs. Stowe's interest in it may not have been limited to Bibb's account of life on Red River cotton plantations (for which, see his chapters X–XII). At the very least, I would argue that her portrayal of Eliza Harris's escape to freedom across the ice patches of the Ohio River was prompted in part by Bibb's high symbolism of the Ohio as a pathway of freedom. It also seems clear that Bibb's allegiance to his family gave impetus to Stowe's portraits of the Harris family and of Tom's family as well. It also seems altogether possible that Stowe's George Harris is a fictive Bibb – in his light skin, which would have abetted his escape, and in his vociferous allegiance to family, his vivid dreams of freedom in Canada, and his occasional grave doubts about the social and moral efficacy of Christian practice.

In short, Stowe's story of George and Eliza Harris is roughly that of Henry and Malinda Bibb, once a happy outcome to the Bibbs's plight has been, as some nineteenth-century pundits liked to say, "bestowed." Altogether, Stowe's debt to Bibb's *Narrative* is as great as that she incurred while reading another 1849 narrative, *The Life of Josiah Henson, Formerly a Slave, Now an Inhabitant of Canada, as Narrated By Himself.* Much has been made over the decades, some by Stowe herself, of Tom's resemblance to Henson, and of how Henson's escape to Canada may have inspired Stowe's presentation of the Harrises' settlement there. But when we study the texts alone, it is clear that the parallels between George Harris and Bibb are as pronounced and that Bibb's experiences on a Red River cotton plantation probably had as much to do with the composition of *Uncle Tom's Cabin* as did Henson's escape to Canada. Indeed, Harris in Canada is something of a Henson and a Bibb, much as Tom in Louisiana is both a Bibb and a Henson.

If Stowe's novel favors Henson's text, the evidence is in her treatment of the two subjects that take up the balance of her 1851 letter to Douglass. Having made her request of him and referring to Bibb in the process, Stowe writes:

> – I have noticed with regret, your sentiments on two subjects, – the church – &. African Colonization – &. with the more regret, because I think you have a considerable share of reason for your feelings on both these subjects – but I would willingly if I could modify your views on both points.[11]

Nothing comes of her intention to debate Douglass's criticisms of African colonization. But in what remains of the letter, she is thoroughly impassioned in defending the church: She is, as she says, a minister's daughter, a minister's wife, the sister of six ministers, and she thereby chooses to take questions of the church's stand on slavery as in some measure charges against her own and her family's conduct. Having defended herself and her kin ("it has been the influence that we found *in the church* & by the altar that has made us do all this"), Stowe ends her letter in this way:

> After all my brother, the strength &. hope of your oppressed race does lie in the *church* – In hearts united to Him . . . Every thing is against you – but *Jesus Christ* is for you – &. He has not forgotten his church misguided &. erring though it be. . . . This movement must &. will become a purely religious one. . . . christians north &. south will give up all connection with [slavery] &. later up their testimony against it – &. thus the work will be done –[12]

Given these views, it is not surprising that in *Uncle Tom's Cabin* Stowe created both Tom and George Harris, and chose to present them, albeit in rough, nearly unrealized fashion, as a kind of bifurcated, black antislavery hero – one almost white, the other very black; one hot-tempered, the other stoic to the point of meekness; one impelled by circumstances farther and farther north, the other farther and farther south; one central to her narrative ideologically, as an emblem of African colonization, the other central spiritually, and hence the "better half" of Stowe's hero, since he is emblematic of exalted Christian faith. The curiosity of this construction is that, although Tom is the "better" and true hero of Stowe's novel, whose character and presence create strong ties between her own and Henson's text – ties that would endure well into the remainder of the century through the other publishing activities of Stowe and Henson alike – it is in George Harris, not Tom, that Stowe confronts what were for her and other white Americans the most troubling issues in the antislavery debate, and confronts as well the tone and argument of the more problematic (though doubtless inspiring) slave narratives of the late 1840s: those of Bibb, Douglass, and a few other miscegenated hotheads. In Tom, Stowe expresses her consuming respect for Henson. In George Harris, she creates a composite portrait of Bibb, Douglass, and the rest of their type; and although she honors them throughout the bulk of her long novel, judiciously imagining how they, had they been Harris, would have responded to a given crisis or turn of events, she also sends them packing, first to Canada and then to Liberia. In short, the paragraphs on African colonization missing from Stowe's letter to Douglass are to be found in the chapters of *Uncle Tom's Cabin* that she would write soon after. She revises the close of Bibb's *Narrative*, where it is evident that he resides not in Canada but (still) in the United States, and replies as well to Douglass's many criticisms of the church and colonization alike, suggesting that he might just consider, in light of his views, removing not merely from Boston to Rochester, as he had just done, but from the Afro-American's New World to his Old.

Much as Stowe completed her letter in the pages of *Uncle Tom's Cabin*, so Douglass responded in his written account of the slave revolt hero, Madison Washington, whose story he had offered many times in the 1840s, here and abroad, in oral tellings. Known as "The Heroic Slave," the novella shares certain features with Stowe's novel but also challenges her text, especially in its presentation of a black hero as dark-skinned as her Tom (apparently magnificently so) and yet as rebelliously violent and skeptical of the American church as her George Harris. In this regard, and in its hero's "self-extrication" from the United States to the Bahamas, Douglass's novella of 1853 converses with Stowe's novel and replies to her 1851 letter, written during the composition of *Uncle Tom's Cabin*.

"The Heroic Slave" was written as Douglass's contribution to *Autographs for Freedom*, a publication created by the Rochester (New York) Ladies' Anti-Slavery Society to subsidize *Frederick Douglass's Paper* (known prior to 1853 as *The North Star*). Stowe herself was a contributor: She submitted an "autograph" and also took part in certain editorial activities, as the following 1852 announcement of the society suggests:

> . . . we intend to publish an anti-slavery annual. . . . It was first designed to name the book, *"The Anti-Slavery Autograph;"* but the gifted authoress of *"Uncle Tom's Cabin"* has christened it *"Autographs for Freedom;"* and we willingly accept her baptism for the forthcoming volume.[13]

Douglass shared the society's regard for Stowe and her novel. In a March 1853 account of a visit to the Reverend and Mrs. Stowe at their Andover, Massachusetts, home, Douglass remarks upon what he perceives to be her modest demeanor and then writes:

> It is only when in conversation with the authoress of *"Uncle Tom's Cabin"* that she would be suspected of possessing that deep insight

into human character, that melting pathos, keen and quiet wit, powers of argumentation, exalted sense of justice, and enlightened and comprehensive philosophy, so eminently exemplified in the *master book* of the nineteenth century.[14]

Soon thereafter, Douglass developed a set piece of praise for *Uncle Tom's Cabin* and its commanding international influence, which he worked into many speeches, no matter what the occasion or topic. In one version of the piece, Douglass implores that a fugitive slave act be passed every day of the week, so that "fresh feelings and new editions of *Uncle Tom*" may be created.[15] In most other versions (of 1853 and 1854), he argues that the American abolitionist movement cannot be thwarted, either by silencing its speakers or by burning its books, including Stowe's novel:

> They might cut out my tongue, and the tongue of every abolitionist in the States north of Mason &. Dixon's line; they might disband every anti-slavery organization in the land; they might gather together all the tracts, pamphlets, and periodicals ever published against slavery; they might take "Uncle Tom's Cabin" out of the ten thousand dwellings of this country, and bring them all into their splendid capitol – in their magnificent metropolis, Washington – and there set fire to them, and send their flame against the sky, and scatter their ashes to the four winds of heaven; but still the slaveholder would have no peace.[16]

Douglass's praise of Stowe was, I think, variously motivated. For one thing, he truly respected her gift and accomplishment, perhaps especially so in 1852 and 1853, when he was wrestling with the written version of Madison Washington's story, a story he had told orally, but usually quite sketchily, many times. (The doubts of a beginning fiction writer are surely expressed when Douglass says of Stowe in 1853, "We are all looking for examples, and we look for them among the great ones; if we cannot imitate them in their great works we can, at least, imitate them in their manners and bearing."[17]) On the other hand, we should acknowledge that Douglass praised Stowe partly because he wanted something from her – her support, including that of a monetary nature, for one of his pet projects of the 1850s, an industrial college for black youth, preferably to be located in his newly adopted city of Rochester. Douglass never realized the project, as we know, though the dream was fulfilled decades later when Samuel C. Armstrong created Hampton Institute and Booker T. Washington later founded Tuskegee. But while the school was still a possibility, Douglass praised Stowe publicly and for the most part chose to debate their differences "in conference," or, if publicly, often circuitously. His most ingenious act of circuity was, as I have been suggesting, "The Heroic Slave."

In comparing *Uncle Tom's Cabin* and "The Heroic Slave," one sees immediately which antislavery literary conventions the works share. Unlike most novels of the 1850s, but clearly in anticipation of the work to come from Mark Twain and the local colorists, both works offer an almost formidable display of American vernaculars and dialects, issuing from white and black characters alike. Stowe and Douglass differ in their pursuit of this convention in the range of vernaculars attributed to blacks. In *Uncle Tom's Cabin*, the gamut runs from the standard English of George Harris (hardly the vernacular of a racial character) to the folksy, if not exactly broken, speech of, say, Aunt Chloe: "Missis let Sally try to make some cake, t'other day, jes to *larn* her, she said. 'O, go way, Missis,' said I; 'it really hurts my feelin's, now, to see good vittles spilt dat ar way! Cake ris all to one side – no shape at all; no more than my shoe; go way!' "[18] In Stowe, the various black vernaculars reinforce what she suggests in other ways about black stratification according to color, ambition, employment, geographical location, possibly gender, and, quite often, given name: The most degraded slaves in the novel, such as Simon Legree's black accomplices, Sambo and Quimbo, are in name, speech, and sensibility "African residuals," whereas Tom, Emmeline, and others are, by contrast, to be received as Afro-Europeans of some order, their names functioning as indicators of the plausibility of their high feelings, unswerving religiosity, and fierce moral convictions.

Douglass proceeds in another fashion, preferring the voice of a single slave hero to an exhibit of the sociolinguistic range of a race. On the other hand, his strategy is similar to Stowe's in that his black hero's name – Madison Washington – is as much a sign of his literacy as it is of his state of origin (Virginia), his credentials as a revolutionary, and his quintessential Americanness. One result is that Madison's speeches, not unlike some of George Harris's, are overwrought and hence not "true to nature," except perhaps in being much like some of Douglass's addresses and those of Virginia's other famous sons. Another result, much in keeping with Douglass's predilections and activist strategies, is that every serious discussion of slavery in the novella is conducted on a dignified level, each speech exhibiting grammatical correctness as well as social courtesy, especially when the exchanges are between blacks and whites. We turn to other, presumably lower, levels of American conversation only when whites discuss slavery amongst themselves. Here Douglass employs diacritical simulations of American speech, not to suggest the condition of the lowest blacks but to characterize the lowest whites – those who are, in effect, confreres of Stowe's Simon Legree and who speak his language, or worse.

Stowe and Douglass also shared an interest in American symbolic geography as seen from the slave's point of view. This leads, in both fictions, to a meticulous presentation of the geography of freedom, which focuses on Ohio as well as Canada. As suggested before, Stowe picks up where Bibb leaves off in depicting the significance and risk of a slave's managing to cross the Ohio River – recall here Eliza Harris's leaping from river ice patch to ice patch while grasping her child, in flight from her would-be captors. But whereas Bibb is altogether scant in portraying his north-of-the-Ohio benefactors, including Mr. D_____, perhaps because he fears compromising their service to other escaping slaves, Stowe works up an elaborate study of Senator and Mrs. Bird, who assist Eliza Harris, and of the many Quakers who eventually help the Harris family as a whole.

Unlike Stowe and Bibb, Douglass does not pause in "The Heroic Slave" to sketch the northern banks of the Ohio as freedom's green shore; eloquence of that sort and for that subject is reserved instead for the prospect of safety on British soil, in Canada and later the Bahamas. However, the state of Ohio is, for Douglass, unquestionably a portion of freedom's realm, less because of its famous southern river than because of the brave souls residing there who choose to aid fugitive slaves. In this regard, he proceeds quite differently than he does in his 1845 *Narrative*, where he is most circumspect about how he escaped and about who, if anyone, assisted him: He joins Stowe in offering what are probably thinly veiled protraits of active abolitionists and their families. Douglass's Ohio abolitionists, the Listwells, turn out to be an economical creation as well: They constitute a composite portrait of helpfulness, understanding, and antislavery zeal, not only because they probably represent many actual abolitionists but also because they perform all the tasks and express all the feelings that Stowe distributes among at least three groups – the Birds, the Shelbys, and the Quakers.

In their presentation of social spaces, Stowe and Douglass proceed rather uniformly. For both, the striking contrast between model domestic settings and the seamy affairs of tavern life, repeatedly and variously elaborated, is a principal means of clarifying phenomenologically the distinctions between good and evil, heaven and hell, family life and other coarser, possibly "unnatural," arrangements, and the right and wrong sides of the slavery issue. In "The Heroic Slave," Douglass's strategy is as simple as it is effective. At the heart of the novella, much is made of the contrast between the Listwells' Ohio home, where Madison Washington found comfort and aid, and the appointments inside and out of a Virginia tavern frequented by loafers and slave drivers. Quite to the point, the tavern had once been a house, complete with outbuildings and other physical features suggesting the honorable pursuit of animal husbandry and agriculture. But now the property bears the "ineffaceable marks" of "time and dissipation": "The gloomy mantle of ruin is, already, outspread to envelop it, and its remains . . . remind one of a human skull, after the flesh has mingled with the earth."[19] The fact that the tavern had been a home before it became a setting for knavery and intemperance allows Douglass to build his comparison in relentless detail. Barn is compared with barn, hearth with hearth, good housekeeping with its absence, nourishing food with debilitating drink. Even the dogs are made use of, Listwell's faithful Old Monte being an obviously better companion than the listless hounds that lie about the tavern. Douglass varies his strategy in the final section of the novella, where two Virginia sailors discuss the *Creole* revolt and the slavery question in general in a tavernlike setting. Although the scene rehearses to a degree the conversation between Listwell and the loafer in the earlier Virginia tavern – and is indebted particularly to the singular exchange between George Harris and his former employer, Mr. Wilson, in what is perhaps Stowe's most important tavern episode (Chap. 11) – it takes on its own ideological character in Douglass's insistence that the place is not a tavern but a coffee house. Possibly because of his temperance movement activities, Douglass refused to join Stowe in suggesting, even in fiction, that serious discussion could take place in the presence of alcohol.[20]

Stowe's tavern episodes – recall that she begins the novel with one – are as numerous as those of model domestic life, and the two settings pair up accordingly. We are thus led to compare the elder Mr. Shelby, in a "dining parlor" with the brandy-drinking Haley, with Shelby at home in the company of his virtuous wife. Likewise, the tavern scene depicting Haley and his henchmen is answered in the activities and serious, moral talk of the Bird household, and the tavern discussion of George Harris and Mr. Wilson is followed by the sequestering of the Harrises in the Quaker settlement, a place so domestically harmonious, according to Stowe, that "even the knives and forks had a social clatter as they went on to the table" (Chap. 13).

Stowe's most ingenious and ideological handling of these contrasts appears in the Simon Legree chapters – for example, Chapter 32, "Dark Places." The description makes clear that Legree's shabby house was once a handsome home, sheltering a family as opposed to the motley assembly of miscegenated women who variously and sullenly serve him. So, too, we are to understand that its rooms were once used for much loftier domestic purposes than the drinking bouts Legree now conducts in them. In short, a once proud home is now something of a brothel and much of a tavern; in this regard, it is fair to say that Legree's degraded domicile is the model for Douglass's Virginia tavern. Stowe's great touch involves not her descriptions of dissipation but her resolution of these affairs by the captive women. Weakness for drink delivers Legree into Cassy's hands and softens him for the strategems she works against him. Although Cassy's success does not fully restore domesticity to the Legree household, it does allow her and Emmeline to have a "home of their own" in the upper rooms that Legree dares not enter.

Despite such sharings, Stowe and Douglass created quite different fictions, the differences reflecting contrasting views on the church and colonization as well as the portrayal of black heroism. On the latter score, one may observe that the primary features of Bibb's *Narrative* that Stowe chose not to rehearse are, in fact, reproduced in Douglass's novella. For example, the heroic return from safety to danger in quest of captive kin is undertaken in *Uncle Tom's Cabin* only by white near kin, like young George Shelby, seeking Tom's release. In contrast, Douglass's hero, like Bibb's persona, undertakes this task himself, traveling south from Canada to a slave state, undergoing recapture and reenslavement, and suffering as well the loss of a wife when he regains his personal freedom. Tom is not reunited with Aunt Chloe any more than Bibb and Washington are reunited with their wives, but at least in their versions of the common tale of slave families torn apart, it is the black male family co-head, and not a white surrogate, who seeks reunification.

Moreover, whereas Stowe acknowledges black skepticism about the church's role in the fight against slavery but relegates all such concern to her secondary black hero, George Harris, Douglass, like Bibb, locates this skepticism in the character of his primary hero. That skepticism even touches Listwell, Douglass's primary white hero, who remarks of Washington:

> . . . to him those distant church bells have no grateful music. He shuns the church, the altar, and the great congregation of Christian worshippers, and wanders away to the gloomy forest, to utter in the vacant air complaints and griefs, which the religion of his times and his country can neither console nor relieve.[21]

Listwell obviously is an abolitionist of a different stripe than the Beechers and the Stowes. He is, in brief, a western abolitionist, not a New England one; at the very least, he completes Douglass's vision of such a figure.

Regarding African colonization, Stowe's views appear in the Harrises' successful escape to Canada, their removal thence to France — where George gains the university training he probably cannot receive elsewhere — and their eventual emigration to West Africa to help found a new black society. This is pure Stowe;

neither Bibb nor Henson was interested in any such final solution. Nor was Douglass, although in his fiction if not in fact he was keener on forsaking the United States than was Bibb. In "The Heroic Slave," Madison Washington escapes finally to the British Bahamas – that is, to a New World territory free of slavery with a large black population. Washington's presence there, rather than in Africa or Canada, is much in keeping with Douglass's view that, far from submitting to any removal schemes, American blacks should stick together in the New World. As he put it elsewhere, "Individuals emigrate – nations never."[22]

Although Stowe's and Douglass's differing portrayals of black heroism may be seen to arise from their differences about the church and colonization, their handling of the issue of color is also significant here. In *Uncle Tom's Cabin*, Tom is dark and George is fair, a time-hallowed arrangement supporting all the myths of black meekness and white aggression, myths that dictate the heroic qualities of each man. In "The Heroic Slave," Douglass squarely challenges such myths, refusing to bifurcate his hero as well as emphasizing his blackness and valor alike. In this respect, Douglass specifically revises Stowe's characterization of Tom. A comparison of the physical descriptions of Stowe's Tom and Douglass's Washington makes this clear. Here is Stowe's first "daguerrotype" of Tom:

> He was a large, broadchested, powerfully-made man, of a full glossy black, and a face whose truly African features were characterized by an expression of grave and steady good sense, united with much kindliness and benevolence. There was something about his whole air self-respecting and dignified, yet united with a confiding and humble simplicity. (Chap. 4)

Douglass revises this in his portrait of Washington:

> Madison was of manly form. Tall, symmetrical, round, and strong. In his movements he seemed to combine, with the strength of the lion, a lion's elasticity. His torn sleeves disclosed arms like polished iron. His face was "black but comely." His eye, lit with emotion, kept guard, under a brow as dark and as glossy as the raven's wing. His whole appearance betokened Herculean strength; yet there was nothing savage or forbidding in his aspect. A child might play in his arms, or dance on his shoulder. A giant's strength, but not a giant's

heart was in him. His broad mouth and nose spoke only of good nature and kindness. But his voice, that unfailing index of the soul, though full and melodious, had that in it which could terrify as well as charm. He was just the man you would choose when hardships were to be endured, or danger to be encountered – intelligent and brave. He had the head to conceive, and the hand to execute. In a word, he was one to be sought as a friend, but to be dreaded as an enemy.[23]

Tom and Madison are both kind, benevolent, good-natured, and steady, as well as big, handsome, and black. But Madison is also intelligent, brave, possessed of a body promising action and a voice promising speech. Obviously, Madison revises Tom, but the point is that the revision occurs by way of addition to Tom, or rather, to Stowe's portrait of him. Since it can be said that Tom is in his way brave, intelligent, and so forth, the issue is not that he lacks these qualities but that Stowe chooses not to see or remark upon them. It may be argued that Stowe in this way creates space for her other, "brighter" hero, George Harris. It may also be argued that Stowe had no such strategy and simply portrayed Tom in the truncated form she wished him to assume. From this latter point of view, she seems, like Garrison and other New Englanders Douglass grew to distrust, the very sort of "blind" abolitionist he sought to enlighten in "The Heroic Slave." Douglass's revision of Tom in Madison Washington not only renders Tom fully visible, it forces abolitionists of a certain, Yankee stripe to see him.

In his essay "Everybody's Protest Novel," James Baldwin argues that Afro-American protest fiction began with *Uncle Tom's Cabin*, and further, that protest fiction has never quite worked its way out of the "cage" Stowe created for it. One feature of that cage is the notion, among black and white protest writers alike, that when God created blacks, He did not do so in His image.[24] Baldwin's argument produces an impassioned assessment of Stowe and Richard Wright, but it does little justice to Douglass's "The Heroic Slave." Madison Washington suffers doubts, but not about his blackness: He never sees himself as one of God's lesser children. And it may be that Baldwin did not fully take in the complexity of Stowe either. Tom may conform to Baldwin's views, but Nat Turner does not, and it was Nat Turner and his insurrection that she took up in her next novel. In a sense, Douglass won his debate with Stowe, for he could claim some role in inducing her to write about a black revolutionary. But she won, too: When she wrote about a rebel, she wrote about one – from Virginia – who failed.

NOTES

1 "Stolen Thunder," *Frederick Douglass's Paper,* October 22, 1852, p. 2.
2 Sue Eakin and Joseph Logsdon, Introduction to Solomon Northup, *Twelve Years A Slave* (1853; rpt. Baton Rouge: Louisiana State University Press, 1968), p. xiv.
3 Harriet Beecher Stowe, Letter to Frederick Douglass, July 9, 1851, in Charles Edward Stowe, ed., *Life of Harriet Beecher Stowe* (Boston: Houghton Mifflin, 1890), pp. 149–53.
4 Gilbert Osofsky, ed., *Puttin' On Ole Massa* (New York: Harper & Row, 1969); Arna Bontemps, ed., *Great Slave Narratives* (Boston: Beacon, 1969); Robert B. Stepto, *From Behind the Veil: A Study of Afro-American Narrative* (Urbana: University of Illinois Press, 1979), pp. 6–11.
5 Herbert B. Gutman, *The Black Family in Slavery and Freedom, 1750–1925* (New York: Vintage, 1977), p. xxi.
6 Henry Bibb, *Narrative of the Life and Adventures of Henry Bibb, An American Slave, Written By Himself,* in Osofsky, ed., *Puttin' On Ole Massa,* p. 105.
7 Ibid., p. 127.
8 Ibid., p. 114.
9 Ibid., p. 72.
10 Ibid.
11 Stowe, Letter to Douglass, July 9, 1851; see note 3.
12 Ibid.
13 *Frederick Douglass's Paper,* November 19, 1852, p. 3. The announcement appears at least once again, on November 26, 1852.
14 Frederick Douglass, "A Day and Night in 'Uncle Tom's Cabin,'" in Philip S. Foner, ed., *The Life and Writings of Frederick Douglass,* vol. 2 (New York: International, 1950), p. 227.
15 Frederick Douglass, "Slavery the Life Issue: Addresses Delivered in Cincinnati, Ohio, on 11–13 April 1854," in John W. Blassingame, ed., *The Frederick Douglass Papers, Series One: Speeches, Debates, and Interviews,* vol. 2 (New Haven, Conn.: Yale University Press, 1982), p. 468.

16 Frederick Douglass, "Bound Together in a Grand League of Freedom: An Address Delivered in Toronto, Canada West, on 21 June 1854," in Blassingame, ed., *The Frederick Douglass Papers, Series One*, vol. 1, p. 495.

17 Douglass, "A Day and Night in 'Uncle Tom's Cabin,'" p. 227.

18 Harriet Beecher Stowe, *Uncle Tom's Cabin* ed. Kenneth Lynn Cambridge, Mass.: Harvard University Press, 1962),Chap. 4.

19 Frederick Douglass, "The Heroic Slave," in Abraham Chapman, ed., *Steal Away: Stories of the Runaway Slaves* (New York: Praeger, 1971), p. 169.

20 For additional remarks, see my "Storytelling in Early Afro-American Fiction: Frederick Douglass' 'The Heroic Slave,'" *Georgia Review* 36 (Summer 1982):355–68.

21 Douglass, "The Heroic Slave," p. 151.

22 Douglass, Letter to Harriet Beecher Stowe, March 8, 1853, in Foner, ed., *The Life and Writings of Frederick Douglass*, vol. 2, p. 233.

23 Douglass, "The Heroic Slave," p. 149.

24 James Baldwin, "Everybody's Protest Novel," in *Notes of a Native Son* (1955; rpt. New York: Bantam, 1964), pp. 9–17.

6

Stowe's Dream of the Mother-Savior: *Uncle Tom's Cabin* and American Women Writers Before the 1920s

ELIZABETH AMMONS

NO book matters more to the literary history of women in America than *Uncle Tom's Cabin*. Before Stowe there were important, groundbreaking writers: Anne Bradstreet in the seventeenth century; Phillis Wheatley in the eighteenth; Lydia Maria Child, Catharine Sedgwick, Mrs. E. D. E. N. Southworth, Caroline Lee Hentz in the nineteenth.[1] *Uncle Tom's Cabin* built on their accomplishments. It was not a matter of Stowe's bringing women's literature into the mainstream. It was already there. What Stowe did was to take on the major political issue of the day, slavery, and her novel riveted the nation, selling in the millions, keeping printing presses running night and day, making grown men weep and preachers rail. Emerson, Holmes, Whittier, and then in the next generation James and Howells (not to mention politicians such as Horace Greeley and President Lincoln) paid homage to the middle-aged mother who, in the words of Emerson, wrote the book that "encircled the globe."[2] The most widely praised, widely read, widely sold American novel of the nineteenth century, bar none, was the work of a woman.

The meaning of this event for subsequent American women writers is impossible to overemphasize. Internationally, the author of *Uncle Tom's Cabin* stood as a link to the great English and continental authors. George Eliot became a fond and cherished correspondent; George Sand wrote a review of the novel calling Stowe a saint.[3] In the United States, Stowe became a model for nineteenth-century female literary culture. Sarah Orne Jewett read and

For valuable suggestions on a draft of this essay, I am grateful to Dorothy Berkson, Judith Fetterley, and Deborah McDowell.

reread Stowe's New England fiction.[4] Annie Fields eulogized her as "a great spirit," saying that "the world's children have been blessed in her coming, and they who know and understand should praise God reverently in her going."[5] Frances Ellen Harper wrote poems memorializing characters created by Stowe.[6] Elizabeth Stuart Phelps publicly praised her for her gentle, wise criticism of early work.[7] The influence of Harriet Beecher Stowe on the women writers who succeeded her – the love they felt for her, the courage they took from her – comprises a major chapter in American literary history.

My purpose here is to contribute to that history by looking at one of the central lines of shared intellectual disposition and strategy running from Stowe's great antislavery novel in 1852 through the work of important writers such as Louisa May Alcott, Elizabeth Stuart Phelps, and Sarah Orne Jewett, on the one hand, and Harriet E. Wilson, Frances Ellen Harper, and Angelina Grimké, on the other. My separation of white and black writers in this way is artificial, since, as I will argue, all held in common the matrifocal values so brilliantly exploited by Stowe in *Uncle Tom's Cabin*. At the same time, however, the black writers' relation to Stowe's novel was distinct. It was more complex than that of the white writers (even if more direct in some ways) and therefore is best served by coherent, concentrated attention. Consequently, my discussion falls into three unequal parts. First, I discuss maternal ideology and *Uncle Tom's Cabin;* then I sketch the way Stowe's argument echoes and reverberates thematically in the work of later white women writers; finally, I discuss in detail the complicated connection between Stowe's novel and selected works by black women writers before the 1920s.

My thesis throughout is that Stowe's manipulation of maternal ideology is adapted and remodeled in illuminating ways in the work of American women writers before the 1920s and that, taken together, this body of fiction from Stowe forward constitutes a rich female tradition in American literature that challenges the dominant, twentieth-century, academic construction of the canon in terms of the adventure tale and the antisocial, which is to say antifeminine, escape narrative.[8] Stated simply: in the tradition that Stowe heads, if we look at it seriously and on its own terms, there exists an important and radical challenge to the emerging industrial-based definition of community in the nineteenth century as something organized by work, ruled by men, and measured by productivity (of things, ironically called "goods"). In place of that ideal there is posited by a number of women writers, black and white, an alternative and matrifocal concept: an ideal of community as something defined by family (rather than work), measured by relationships (rather than products), and ruled by women (rather than men). It is a vision of community at least as radical as the more frequently valorized indictment of American culture offered by nineteenth-century white male writers, who, one could argue, simply fled, taking to the sea, or a raft, or a shed by a pond — seeking in solitude, or at most couplehood (Huck and Jim, Ishmael and Queequeg), individual salvation. Women writers in the nineteenth century, in contrast, can more often be seen seeking group salvation. Characteristically, they do not look for escape *from* society, but escape *into* some recovered or reconstituted social system more humane and nonviolent than that of Victorian America. For women, already wealthy in intimate relationships, particularly same-sex ones (as Carroll Smith-Rosenberg's classic essay on female friendship explains[9]), the issue, quite logically, was not escape from the large, impersonal group into some loving community of two. Rather, the issue was escape for people as a group (and for society as a whole) into some large and more perfect corporate system, one modeled not on individualism but on motherhood.

1

Harriet Beecher Stowe's own experience of motherhood was difficult. She gave birth to twins within the first year of marriage, went on to have five more children, one of whom died as a baby despite everything she could do to save the child, and she found herself overwhelmed, to the point of prostration, by the endless bottles of soured milk and the countless interruptions that dragged her down as she struggled to become a writer in the mud-rutted outpost of Cincinnati in the years before *Uncle Tom's Cabin*.[10] To be sure, she was better off than her mother, who like other women of her generation bore a child every two to two and a half years until death or menopause, whichever came first, released her. Stowe, in contrast, had the birth control of abstinence available as a socially sanctioned choice.[11] Still, her life as a mother was not one to make a person idealize the experience. Yet she did. Moreover, she was said to have loved being a mother and appears to have been an unusually caring one.[12] This enthusiasm for motherhood does not seem either hypocritical or mysterious. Instead, it reflects her deep intellectual commitment to nineteenth-century maternal ideology, which was rooted, emotionally, in her yearning for the kind of mother love that she feared she had missed (her own mother died when she was five) – a yearning, in turn, everywhere reinforced by the pervasive ideal of angelic motherhood dominant in Victorian America.

It is essential to remember that motherhood – as idea, myth, institution, experience – is always a cultural variable. It changes depending on time, place, ethnic group, and class. Because we still live within a Victorian ideology (hence the conceptual longevity of Freud, for example), there is a tendency to assume that motherhood is a fixed concept, that what we assume and expect has always been assumed and expected. In fact, the maternal ideology that Stowe (and we) take for granted is a relatively new invention – the result of a shift in white Western thinking from parenting to mothering as the dominant ideal around the end of the eighteenth and the beginning of the nineteenth centuries.

As the historian Ruth H. Bloch explains, motherhood as a unique, idealized category did not exist in white preindustrial America. It was "assumed that parental obligation was either vested primarily in fathers or shared by both parents without sexual distinction."[13] With the Industrial Revolution, however, came significant change. In agrarian society both men and women worked in and around the home, which meant that work and domesticity were more or less integrated; husbands and wives shared duties and responsibilities of many kinds, including the management and instruction of children. But as men left this shared environment to work in mills and offices, a theory of feminized parenthood, of "motherhood," developed. It was from our point of view reactionary. The new concept of motherhood served to rationalize women's remaining in the home at a time when changes in the economy (industrialization, increasing urbanization) were for the first time raising the possibility of economic self-sufficiency for large numbers of women. That is, the promotion of motherhood as a full-time occupation for women conveniently emerged at just the time that a fundamental change in the traditional pattern of female dependence might have occurred. On the other hand, it is important to remember that for most people work outside the home during the nineteenth century offered very low pay, long hours, no financial security, and any number of physical dangers. Being assigned to the domestic realm may very well have looked not much different from, and even a little better than, work in the commercial sector. It is not, in short, a simple matter of the new ideology being either good or bad for women. Understood historically, it was both.

Harriet Beecher Stowe both accepted and confronted this new ideology. She heartily embraced the Victorian idealization of motherhood and channeled it into an argument for widespread social change. Like her famous sister Catharine Beecher, she concurred in the culture's insistence on the importance, even sacredness, of maternal values, and she argued from that premise that, rather than segregate maternal ethics into some private domestic realm, motherhood − the morality of women − should be made the ethical and structural model for all of American life. There were problems with this utopian appropriation of patriarchal motherhood. Stowe's idealism encouraged her − and generations after her − to embrace an ideology that emphasizes difference rather than equality between the sexes. Also, the Victorian ideal taught women to acquiesce in a realpolitik imbalance of power that, no matter how morally superior woman's domain was said to be, excluded a huge proportion of society from full and direct encounter with independent adult life. At the same time, however, Stowe's dream of matrifocal reorganization, her dream of reconstituting society in the image of maternal rather than paternal values, placed woman at the center of a radical script for social change. Intellectually, Stowe used the new conservative ideology to argue against the very premise on which it rested: father rule. Called the ideal of the "Moral Mother" by Bloch and the ideology of "qualitative motherhood" by Kathryn Kish Sklar, the new thinking found in feminine piety, patience, and emotional responsiveness the perfect qualities for raising productive, moral citizens for Victorian America. As Sklar explains, using Catharine Beecher as her representative ideologist, the relationship that emerged "between childhood and society was an essentially modern one." Motherhood began to be viewed

> as a qualitative rather than a quantitative activity, useful to society for the kind of child rather than the numbers of children it produced. . . . Rather than viewing society as a traditional set of established controls, she [Beecher] saw society as an uncontrolled growth, except as it was regulated by the internalized values of "character" developed during early childhood. Seeing it possible to exert in early childhood an influence of lifelong personal and social significance, Victorians were far more sensitive than their ancestors had been to the importance of the right kind of mothering.[14]

This "right kind of mothering" became woman's supreme calling in Stowe's America. To provide children with love and to teach them to internalize the values of hard work, integrity, and the avoidance of evil was the sacred, and extremely socially useful, job of Mother. The dominant culture preached that the very essence of society, its morality, depended upon such mothering. Rupture the maternal bond and society would stand at risk. Support the work of mothers and a moral society would emerge.

Given this ideology, Stowe's argument that women could change society through motherhood was far from naive; it grew out of and exploited the new but widely shared idealization of motherhood as a powerful moral force within the body politic. As the historian Mary Kelley points out, woman was not supposed to be merely the "central figure in the home." She was to be, in addition, and by virtue of that domestic position, "a reformer of and servant to an American society judged to be in dire need of regeneration."[15] Likewise, Nina Baym emphasizes that domesticity was "set forth as a value scheme for ordering all of life," with the goal being that "home and the world would become one."[16] Motherhood, in short, was already a highly politicized concept when Harriet Beecher Stowe wrote *Uncle Tom's Cabin*. She simply accepted that fact and set about defining whose politics it should serve.

As *Uncle Tom's Cabin* argues on practically every page, Stowe emphatically believed that motherhood should not continue to serve the politics of men. In Chapter 1, sarcastically titled "In Which the Reader is Introduced to a Man of Humanity," Stowe bluntly presents slavery as a transaction in human flesh designed and carried out by white men to the horror, as the next chapter – "The Mother" – declares, of women. The novel, in other words, opens quite self-consciously with men and women pitted against each other, and what we see in particular is white men destroying the family, the basic unit of community in Stowe's view. We meet Mr. Shelby in the act of selling two people: Tom, the man who rocked him in his arms as a baby, and little Harry, the only child of Eliza. True, this planter is squeamish about selling these particular slaves to the trader Haley – a man so hardened that he would sell his own mother, we are told; and certainly Shelby finds it distasteful to have to listen to the trader's discourse on the best way to extricate mothers from their children: "I've seen 'em as would pull a woman's child out of her arms, and set him up to sell, and she screechin' like mad all the time; – very bad policy – damages the article – makes 'em quite unfit for service" (Chap. 1).[17] Haley prefers to threaten slave mothers into submission or to sneak children off in the dead of night, a strategy that Shelby, who sneaks off to avoid seeing Tom led away in chains, has already mastered.

The response of Mrs. Shelby to this cruelty and cowardice is immediate and direct: "This is God's curse on slavery! – " she says; "a bitter, bitter, most accursed thing! – a curse to the master and a curse to the slave! I was a fool to think I could make anything good out of such a deadly evil. . . . I never thought that slavery was right – never felt willing to own slaves" (Chap. 5). She refuses to sneak away and hide while Tom is being bound and carried off: " 'No, no' said Mrs. Shelby; ' I'll be in no sense accomplice or help in this cruel business. I'll go and see poor old Tom, God help him, in his distress!' " (Chap. 5). This initial contrast establishes Stowe's paradigm. In her novel, white men, from ordinary Mr. Shelby to pathetic Augustine St. Clare (a man who knows what is right but lacks the courage to act) to grotesquely masculine Simon Legree, with his bullet head and iron knuckles, uphold and defend a system that Stowe defines as an abomination against motherhood and Christ. The two are synonymous in this novel, which dramatizes its author's argument not only in a series of mothers, black and white, but also in the two unusual, linked, maternal Saviors: the girl-child Eva and the black man Tom.

"This story is to show how Jesus Christ, who liveth and was dead, and now is alive and forevermore, has still a mother's love for the poor and lowly," Stowe declared of her novel a couple of years after its publication.[18] This feminized Christ should not be thought of as an idiosyncracy. As historian Barbara Welter explains, nineteenth-century America witnessed a major religious conversion not of nonbelievers into believers, but a conversion by believers, who increasingly were female, of belief itself into a more and more feminized faith. As America began changing from an agrarian to an industrial society and from colonial to national status, Christianity, formerly a major political tool and therefore carefully husbanded by powerful men, moved out of the masculine realm into the control of women. The result was that "it entered a process of change whereby it became more domesticated, more emotional, more soft and accommodating – in a word, more 'feminine.' "[19] This identification of women and religion made conceptual sense at a time when "women and the church were excluded from the pursuit of wealth just as much as they were kept out of the statehouse, and for the same rhetorical reasons. Both women and the church were to be above the counting house, she on her pedestal, the church in its sanctuary." As a result, "women . . . precisely because they were above and beyond politics and even beyond producing wealth, much less pursuing it, could maintain the values of an earlier age."[20] Stowe, like her sister Catharine, had no problem with this arrangement. The daughter, sister, and wife of ministers, and a born theologian and preacher herself, she obviously found the alliance between Christianity and women not only comfortable but advantageous. It gave her, as a woman in nineteenth-century America, a public forum.

Even more important, the coalition of values represented by the feminization of Christianity was one in which Stowe wholeheartedly believed. She lived in a world sharply divided into masculine and feminine spheres, the former commercial and competitive, the latter domestic and cooperative, and she had absolutely no doubt that the latter should serve as the model for society as a whole. She believed that maternal values should be the values of America. She has a character exclaim in exasperation in a novel published twenty years after *Uncle Tom's Cabin:* "Shall MOTHERHOOD ever be felt in the public administration of the affairs of state?"[21] The question might well serve as the epigraph of *Uncle Tom's Cabin.*

In practice, as Welter explains, the feminization of religion produced changes in outer forms, with women becoming visible as leaders in educational areas of church life (for example, Sunday schools and missionary societies), as well as changes in doctrine itself: the softening of the concept of infant damnation, for instance. Equally significant were the new sects founded by women – Shakers, Christian Scientists – in addition to other groups and experiments supportive of women's issues and concerns, such as the Oneida Community, Brook Farm, or even the Mormons.[22] But for women's fiction the most important change, it seems to me, was the feminization of Christ. As Welter points out, "the assignation to God of typically female virtues was nothing new. Presumably a God who was defined as perfect would have all known virtues, whether or not he had a beard." But the bold reassignment of gender and the political implications thereof – these were not ordinary. Welter explains:

> The female saviour is an interesting amalgam of nineteenth-century adventism, the need for a Protestant counterpart to the cult of the Virgin, and the elevation of pure womanhood to an almost supernatural level. If the world had failed its first test and was plunging into an era of godlessness and vice, as many were convinced, then a second coming seemed necessary. Since the failure of the world also represented a failure of male laws and male values, a second chance, in order to effect change, should produce a different and higher set of values.[23]

Precisely this desire for a different and higher set of values – for an opportunity to reconstitute the world along female rather than male lines, for, in short, the coming of the female Christ – animates *Uncle Tom's Cabin.* The idea appears in Stowe's idealization of mothers, white and black; in her remarkable characterization of the motherly black Christ, Tom, supreme heroine of the novel and literal victim unto death of the masculine social system Stowe attacks; and, most obvious perhaps, in her glorification of the "St. Clare" she names for the mother of the race, Christlike Eva.

The child is pure symbol. As Stowe tells us, Evangeline St. Clare has "an undulating and aerial grace such as one might dream of for some mythic and allegorical being" (Chap. 14). Her face has a "dreamy earnestness," her hair floats "like a cloud," her eyes shine with a "deep spiritual gravity"; clearly, she is marked "out from other children"(Chap. 14). Tom gazes on this ethereal child who glides, flies, floats, and wafts (but never walks), and he sees "something almost divine. . . . He half believed that he saw one of the angels stepped out of his New Testament" (Chap. 14). This child *is*, allegorically, the feminine Christ Welter describes. Even more particularly, she embodies Stowe's concept of the "mother's love" of Christ. Named for the mother of the race, this golden-haloed Eve-angel/Evangel, who always appears in white and re-mains too pure to survive in this world, embodies the essence both of motherhood and of Christianity as Stowe defines them in *Uncle Tom's Cabin*. The child's whole being focuses on self-sacrifice. She says of slavery: "I can understand why Jesus *wanted* to die for us. . . . I *would die* for them, Tom, if I could" (Chap. 24). She does. Second Eve – second and sinless mother of the race – this totally unrealistic character whose name and character yoke the Old and New Testaments, personifies for Stowe the spotless motherly Christ come to redeem the world from the sins of the fathers.[24] It is significant that the chapter introducing Eva arrested Stowe; she found herself unable to complete the installment and had to sub-mit it one month late.[25] The result of the delay was that Christlike Eva first appeared in the Christmas Day issue. In the angelic figure of an innocent child named for Eve, Stowe offered on Christmas Day the maternal Christ, the divine motherly love and light (en-coded in the child's last name), which she believed could lead America out of the night of slavery.

Progenitor and antithesis of this heavenly Eva is the worst mother in the novel, ironically named Marie (the most perfect of Christian mothers), a woman who is despicable precisely because she so utterly fails to live up to the Victorian ideal of the loving mother. Marie is vain rather than modest, selfish rather than self-less, indolent rather than industrious, worldly rather than spir-itual, and cruel rather than compassionate. The opposite of Christlike Eva, she represents in female flesh the double of satanic Simon Legree. She not only tortures and degrades her slaves, but she delights in doing so; like the devil, her pleasure comes from others' pain. Her Moorish plantation house, which she rules with an iron hand from her plush and tufted fainting couch (clearly this is no Christian home), stands out as one of the hells of Stowe's novel because it, like Legree's Red River inferno, has in effect no mother. To be sure, a mother, as we saw on the Shelby plantation, might actually be able to do very little to oppose slavery; but she can at least resist – she can at least protest, conspire, connive, comfort. These actions may not be much in and of themselves, Stowe's novel concedes; but they can help individuals (Eliza does escape) and lead to radical change (the Shelby son and heir, George, decides to follow in the footsteps of his mother, not his father); and they do reflect the superior morality that can, Stowe fervently proposes, offer an alternative to the dominant masculine American model of human relations typified by slavery. If Eva's father is admirable in direct proportion to the extent of his wom-anishness (his inclination to follow the dictates of his heart rather than his head), Eva's mother is abominable because she will not think and feel like a mother. She behaves instead, in the terms of this novel, like a man: ruthless, greedy, self-centered, cruel. And she is a monster.

St. Clare's parents – Eva's grandparents – perfectly illustrate the polarity Stowe anatomizes. His mother was "a direct embodiment and personification of the New Testament" (Chap. 19). A born democrat, she had "a voice more like an angel than a mortal woman" and, like her granddaughter and namesake, Eva, "she always wore white" (Chap. 19). Her son exclaims of this woman, who despised slavery with every atom of her being, *"she* was *divine!"* (Chap. 19). St. Clare's father, in contrast, "was a born aristocrat. . . . He could have divided Poland as easily as an or-ange, or trod on Ireland as quietly and systematically as any man living" (Chap. 19). For this man blacks are subhumans, the "intermediate link between man and animals" − a philosophical position that contributes nicely to his material success, which is considerable. Indeed, he epitomizes the white male success ethic in Stowe's eyes. Described as "an inflexible, driving, punctilious business man; everything was to move by system, − to be sustained with unfailing accuracy and precision" (Chap. 19), he chooses as his support and cohort a diabolical overseer from New England who foreshadows Simon Legree (and thus serves the double purpose for Stowe of contributing to her attack on masculine ethics while simultaneously identifying slavery as a problem with roots in the North as well as the South). The overseer is "a great, tall, slab-sided, two-fisted renegade son of Vermont . . . who had gone through a regular apprenticeship in hardness and brutality, and taken his degree to be admitted to practice. My mother never could endure him, nor I," Augustine explains, "but he obtained an entire ascendency over my father; and this man was the absolute despot of the estate" (Chap. 19).

Born to these elder St. Clares, who embody the profound schism between feminine and masculine values that Stowe deplores, are twins who inherit their parents' duality. One − his father's boy − is "proud, dominant, overbearing, to inferiors, and utterly unmerciful to whatever set itself up against him." The other, Eva's father, is his mother's child. He has "blue eyes, golden hair, a Greek outline, and a fair complexion" (Chap. 19). His mother's pet, this son was in childhood "remarkable for an extreme and marked sensitiveness of character, more akin to the softness of woman than the ordinary hardness of his own sex" (Chap. 19). Yet neither boy grows into an admirable man. Though Augustine St. Clare dies with the word *"Mother!"* on his lips (Chap. 28), he does not live with her on his conscience. He despises slavery, he describes its evils and decries its abuses, and he puts up with it. He is, in fact, the most unsettling portrait of masculinity in the novel. He knows that he should oppose slavery in deed as well as word, but he prevaricates, procrastinates, capitulates. For all his rhetoric, this white man is not Stowe's idea of the ideal man.

Indeed, no white man is. Rather, Stowe makes the living double and soul mate of ethereal motherly Eva the black man Tom. It is he who literally enacts with Eva in the muddy Mississippi Christ's injunction to be born again into the light. Tom's passivity, his piety, his gentleness, his inexhaustible generosity of spirit, his non-violence, his commitment to self-sacrifice: these are not, in Stowe's novel (as they have become in the national folklore), signs of weakness. These are the virtues of Christ, which are in Stowe's theology maternal. As she would state bluntly twenty-five years after the publication of *Uncle Tom's Cabin,* Christ and his mother were virtually one. "He was bone of her bone and flesh of her flesh – his life grew out of her immortal nature. . . . He had no mortal father. All that was human in him was her nature; it was the union of divine nature with the nature of pure woman. . . . There was in Jesus more of the pure feminine element than in any other man. It was the feminine element exalted and taken in union with di-vinity."[26] Tom, far from being the least admirable of Stowe's cre-ations, is the ultimate herione of *Uncle Tom's Cabin.*

Blessed with "a voice as tender as a woman's" (Chap. 10); "full [with] the gentle, domestic heart, which – woe for them! has been a peculiar characteristic of his unhappy race" (Chap. 10); selfless in his love for his fellow slaves and steadfast in his refusal to let vicious Simon Legree make him "hard" – that is, brutal, authoritarian, equipped to oversee the other slaves (Chap. 33) Stowe's Tom *is* soft. He personifies the motherly Christ. He, along with Eva and literal mothers of both races, articulates Stowe's deepest aversion to slav-ery, which she sees as an economic and ethical system grounded in hard, masculine, rational values that define human life as a com-modity, regard violence as an inevitability, and elevate might over right – power over love – as the correct, or again the inevitable, motive force in human life. That Tom is not classically masculine – that he does not fight for his life but instead puts the lives of others first, that he refuses to meet violence with violence, that he remains compassionate, giving, and emotional to the end – illustrates Stowe's political genius in *Uncle Tom's Cabin.* What better way to inflame the culture against slavery than by characterizing her hero as a stereotypical Victorian heroine: pious, home-centered, self-sacrificing, nonviolent? The characterization does rely on the ante-bellum stereotype of blacks as loyal, faithful retainers. At the same time, however, it contradicts the widespread racist categorization of blacks as brutes, subhuman creatures incapable of emotions and ideas. And it insinuates Tom, a black man, into the nineteenth-century idealization of motherhood. In making one of her motherly Christs a physically powerful black man (as opposed, for example, to a black woman), Stowe insists on the symbolic content of her argument. Implicitly *Uncle Tom's Cabin* asks, with its strong black protagonist as gentle as Mother and yet as morally irradiating as Christ, who, without forsaking reverence for motherhood and the sanctity of the Christian Home, could fail to champion Tom's right to liberty for himself and his family and, by extension, for all slaves?

Stowe provides a glimpse of the maternal paradise America might be in the Quaker community that harbors Eliza, Henry, and George Harris on their flight to Canada. The community is agrarian, nonviolent, egalitarian, and, above all, matrifocal. At its center is "the ample, motherly form" of Rachel Halliday (Chap. 13), active opponent of slavery and nonracist in deed as well as word. This woman dominates Stowe's utopian settlement. The center of the community is the home; the center of the home is the kitchen – "large, roomy, neatly-painted" (Chap. 13); the center of the kitchen is Rachel's well-worn rocking chair: "a larger sized one, motherly and old, whose arms breathed hospitable invitation" (Chap. 13). This big homey throne symbolizes Rachel's power and centrality. Therefore it is telling that at the beginning of Chapter 13, we meet in this rocker "gently swaying back and forward, her eyes bent on some fine sewing . . . our old friend Eliza" (Chap. 13). In the bosom of Rachel rocks the abused young slave mother. The image suggests rest and joy, but also motion: motion that stays in place, that is nonlinear, nonmasculine, circular: motion that does not seek variety and change but instead repeats the old, healing, maternal rhythms over and over. Stowe gives these maternal values prime importance by using the image to open her chapter on "The Quaker Settlement," which sets up the heroic interpretation of motherhood that controls the whole novel. Rachel, of whom one of her children remarks with wonder, "Mother can do almost everything" (Chap. 13), succors and heals all her children, black and white. She provides sanctuary not least of all to the slave Eliza, whom she gives her "motherly" seat and calls "my daughter." To underscore the point, Stowe declares:

." 'My daughter' came naturally from the lips of Rachel Halliday; for hers was just the face and form that made 'mother' seem the most natural word in the world" (Chap. 13).

The home of this robust, Christian mother seems holy:

> This, indeed, was a home, – *home,* – a word that George [Harris] had never yet known a meaning for; and a belief in God, and trust in his providence, began to encircle his heart, as, with a golden cloud of protection and confidence, dark, misanthropic, pining, atheistic doubts, and fierce despair, melted away before the light of a living Gospel. (Chap. 13)

The guiding spirit of this living Gospel is Christlike Rachel. Stowe declares in her climactic image of this maternal savior: Rachel Halliday "never looked so truly and benignly happy as at the head of her table. There was so much motherliness and full-heartedness even in the way she passed a plate of cakes or poured a cup of coffee, that it seemed to put a spirit into the food and drink she offered" (Chap. 13). Transforming ordinary food into a sacrament, Rachel Halliday, in a scene that calls to mind Christ's ministry at the Last Supper, suggests how restorative, how spiritually nourishing, mother rule might be.

Certainly, the argument implicit in Stowe's portrait of the Quakers is that matriarchy not only creates a safe, humane stopping place for George, Eliza, and Harry in their flight from slavery, the nightmarish but logical extreme of patriarchal capitalism. It also represents America's salvation. A year after the publication of *Uncle Tom's Cabin,* Stowe commented in *A Key to Uncle Tom's Cabin* (1853) on the ambition "to be above others in power, rank and station" and asserted: "Jesus Christ alone founded his empire on LOVE."[27] Stowe's Quakers, choosing democracy over aristocracy (the true identity of any system containing slavery within its boundaries) and, in economic terms, cooperativism over capitalism, provide a model for America's reconstitution on the Christian principle of love as opposed to power, a principle practiced in this life, in Stowe's opinion, by mothers, not fathers. Although less radical than her younger sister, Isabella Beecher Hooker, who along with Victoria Woodhull believed that the matriarchal millennium – an era of "maternal government"[28] – would soon be upon America (and that she, Isabella, would be Christ's vice-re-gent in this new dispensation), Harriet Beecher Stowe nevertheless looked to motherhood not as a refuge from the world, a sphere to be kept forever separate and above the dirty, usurious world of masculine commerce and nation building, but as the imperative model for America's re-formation. She offered no political pro-gram. Essentially a theologian and preacher, she foresaw change resulting from spiritual reorientation.[29] She raises the question of action in *Uncle Tom's Cabin* and concludes: "There is one thing that every individual can do, – they can see to it that *they feel right*. . . . The man or women who *feels* strongly, healthily and justly, on the great interests of humanity, is a constant benefactor to the human race. See, then, to your sympathies in this matter! Are they in harmony with the sympathies of Christ? or are they swayed and perverted by the sophistries of worldly policy?" (Chap. 45). For Stowe, change must begin in the individual human heart, and from that reorientation (fundamentally a religious conversion) will flow new behavior, new priorities, a new nation. Naive as this may appear to many late-twentieth-century readers and critics, it was not only strategically realistic (Stowe, as a woman, had access to two agents of change: literature and religion) but also com-pletely consistent with Stowe's belief in the superiority of maternal values. Violent revolution cannot be the answer in this book, even though Stowe does deal with the issue of violence sympathetically in the character of George Harris and goes on to explore it further in her next antislavery novel, *Dred, A Tale of the Great Dismal Swamp* (1856). Stowe's program in *Uncle Tom's Cabin* is basically spiritual. She seeks to convert those in power – white men (and the women with influence on them) – away from the patriarchal institution, slavery, which she associates with the devil, toward a new social ideal, one associated with the mother-Christ and man-ifest miraculously in the little girl Eva, the black man Tom, and the strong Quaker mother Rachel Halliday. Indeed, the image of Rachel Halliday's power as a rocking force strong and unchanging at the center of the Quaker social structure appears early in *Uncle Tom's Cabin* to show us that ideal made real, to show us the pos-sibility made flesh of that "mother's love" of Christ that Stowe believed could transform America into a just society.

This idea of mother rule shows up frequently in the work of white women writers after Stowe. Louisa May Alcott, one of Stowe's most important successors, carries the myth in several directions. In *Little Women* (1869) she looks backward and inward: to the impressionable world of childhood and the private world of the family, the home itself. Of course, officially *Little Women* supports patriarchy – it shows the correct training of little girls to be good wives. In fact, however, Alcott's book is subversive. It celebrates a time and place when women are free of men. The novel (like Stowe's) is based on the idea that there are two worlds: the world of war, which is father's, and the world of home, which is mother's; and between these two realms – one male and one female – there is a vast separation, an enormous gap. What we then see is that women exist very well without men. In *Little Women* Alcott gives us the world of mother rule, strong and self-sufficient. Indeed, as Nina Auerbach argues, independent female community is the true subject of *Little Women*,[30] Alcott's hymn to Marmee, her hymn, that is, to mother.

After *Little Women* Alcott attempts to fuse her ideal of mother rule with the culture's ideal of patriarchal marriage when she makes Jo, as headmistress of a school, the chief authority figure in a world that blends home and work. This vision of matrifocality and cooperativism, Auerbach theorizes, may very well have come from matriarchal ideas first encountered by Alcott as a girl in rural Massachusetts. "The school she [Alcott] shapes at Plumfield, which is also family, farm, and cosmos, bears a faint resemblance to the Shaker community which thrived in opposition to her father's own short-lived Fruitlands in Harvard, Massachusetts. Essentially matriarchal in its worship of its founder, Mother Ann Lee, the celibate Shakers lived according to principles of sexual equality and cooperation."[31] That some such salvific, woman-centered community was Alcott's real dream is clear from her novel *Work* (1873), begun before *Little Women* but not completed until several years after that novel was published. Realism gives way to fantasy in this flawed but interesting novel. With its heroine named *Christie*, the story Alcott tells, called a "feminist romance" by Elizabeth Langland,[32] envisions radical matrifocal re-formation of work and family, and the conclusion offers us utopia. When the book ends, Christie, a widow saved from killing herself by a woman named Rachel, lives happily in a new world. She, her daughter, and her former husband's mother and sister dwell as one family in an imagined, ideal community committed to profit sharing rather than competition.

If the name Christie, like Stowe's Eva, requires us to read Alcott's *Work* allegorically, it is likewise no accident that her better-known novel about female community, *Little Women,* opens on Christmas Day. Using the Civil War as context (this image of fratricide haunts *Work* as well), Alcott presents us with her female utopia on the day marking the birth of the world's savior. At one level Alcott, like Stowe, dreamed of women's alternative morality redeeming nineteenth-century culture from its disastrous masculine obsession with violence, competition, capitalism, and death.

Variations on these themes recur in the work of Elizabeth Stuart Phelps, Sarah Orne Jewett, Charlotte Perkins Gilman, and even Willa Cather. An excellent case in point is Phelps's enormous bestseller, *The Gates Ajar* (1868). Focused on a female theologian who is the mother of a little girl named *Faith,* the novel offers a treatise on matrifocal theology only thinly disguised as fiction. Phelps's heroine argues against the patriarchal definition of heaven as a place in which we lose personality and "rise above" personal relationships to some high state of abstraction, becoming disembodied, impersonal entities endlessly engaged in glorifying some all-encompassing and equally bodiless divinity. Against this abstract, masculine fantasy of heaven, Phelps's maternal theologian offers a personal heaven in which the relationships we cherish in this world remain ours forever. Bonds of love and succor – that network of relational dependence that sustains women and defines female culture in this world – *The Gates Ajar* argues, will not disappear in the next. How could paradise *be* paradise, Phelps's book asks, if the very best we are capable of here – abiding, loving relationships – is to be cast out as trivial, meaningless? This novel is not a domestication of heaven (as condescending critics often describe it) but a maternalization of Christian theology. Phelps redefines heaven vis-á-vis women's values that take seriously compassion, subjectivity, emotionality, and, above all, personal connectedness.

Refusing to abandon this brief in her next novel, *The Silent Partner* (1871), Phelps commemorates the martyrdom of one of her female characters with "two logs . . . caught transversely, and hung like a cross,"[33] and in the last chapters applauds the conversion of the young mill woman, Sip, into an evangelical preacher. Quite obviously, *The Silent Partner*, a book about the Industrial Revolution and female community, draws on the image of the female Christ and the ideal of the woman savior.

Translating this symbolism into a more secular context is Sarah Orne Jewett's 1884 novel *A Country Doctor*. The book implicitly argues against the increasing masculinization of medicine, a healing ministry at which the heroine's father excels principally because he is more in touch with its ancient maternal roots than its modern scientific intentions. Deciding to follow in the footsteps of her ambiguously named father, Dr. Leslie, Nan Prince (also an androgynous name) elects to become a physician, and the book ends with an image of this young woman sacerdotal and transported. Jewett shows all of nature in sympathy with Nan's decision to become a physician – her decision to bring healing back to its female source – and then ends with a triumphant image of her heroine: "The soft air and the sunshine came close to her; the trees stood about and seemed to watch her; and suddenly she reached her hands upward in an ecstasy of life and strength and gladness. 'O God,' she said, 'I thank thee for my future.' "[34] This image of divinely sanctioned female power and healing celebrates for a secular audience the essential icon of woman as savior.

Even more important in this tradition is Jewett's masterpiece *The Country of the Pointed Firs* (1896). Published the year Harriet Beecher Stowe died, *The Country of the Pointed Firs* recasts the midcentury myth for a new generation. In a figurative sense, Sarah Orne Jewett was the daughter rather than the sister of the authors I have been discussing; born in 1849 (she was two years old when Stowe began serializing *Uncle Tom's Cabin*), she wrote for a significantly different sensibility than did Stowe, Alcott, or the early Phelps. Nevertheless, in contrast to our post-Freudian assumption that each generation must wrench itself free from the previous one intellectually and artistically, Jewett was a nineteenth-century – a pre-Freudian – daughter, one who, as Carroll Smith-Rosenberg reminds us,[35] loved her mother(s). She sought continuity, not rupture. The myth of the woman savior so dreamed of by earlier writers such as Stowe and then Alcott and Phelps (and, as I will explain shortly, Harper and, paradoxically, Wilson as well) was shared also by Jewett. Because she was writing at a different time in history, she could no longer advance the myth as a serious political idea, as her predecessors had. The era of utopian experiments had waned. She could no longer imagine, like Mother Ann of the Shakers, that society might actually be reshaped – reformed – matrifocally with mothers and maternal values rather than fathers and patriarchal principles at its center. (Likewise, Jewett's contemporary and Harriet Beecher Stowe's grandniece, Charlotte Perkins Gilman, could not argue real politics but only science-fiction politics when she drew upon the myth for her fantasy of matriarchal rule, *Herland* [1915], early in the twentieth century.)[36] In 1896, Jewett, taught by history that the matriarchal millennium of Stowe's half-sister Isabella Beecher Hooker was not just around the corner, does not develop the myth politically – that is, as a real or even a possible program for widespread social reform – but metaphorically. *The Country of the Pointed Firs* is less the story of how society might really be reordered by maternal values than of how one woman's life – every woman's life – might be restored by contact with the myth. In Jewett's book, the narrator (and, along with her, the reader) is brought into healing contact with the world of mother rule: the world of preindustrial (or extraindustrial) community in which women, not men, are the philosophers, farmers, healers, artists, navigators, and lawmakers. In terms that echo Rachel Halliday's world in *Uncle Tom's Cabin,* Jewett gives us the myth of mother rule made fact.

As Marjorie Pryse points out in her excellent introduction to a recent edition of the book: "The lost world in *The Country of the Pointed Firs* is not the world of shipping, but a world in which women were once united with their mothers and inherited their mothers' powers."[37] At the center of this drama of recovery stands mysterious Almira Todd, whose last name rhymes with god and whose first name brings to mind the Latin word for soul, *alma.*

Appropriately named, this female savior – a large, motherly woman – welcomes Jewett's world-weary narrator into a peaceful matrifocal community where she undergoes a spiritual rebirth. She learns that art is communal, physical, female – the opposite of what she believed when she arrived at Almira Todd's house from the city with her sharpened pencils and disciplined, solitary work habits. At the communal celebration that ends the book, the Bowden family reunion, there is no written, no Miltonic, language (such as Captain Littlepage drearily introduced earlier in the narrative). Rather, to conclude the rural feast, the assembled company – the narrator included – eat together pies and cakes on which have been baked and iced celebratory words. This, Jewett implies, is "literature." Delicious, corporate, maternal. The narrator leaves the country of the pointed firs a changed woman. She has participated, literally, in a feast of female language that fortifies her (recall the spiritually nourishing food and drink dispensed by Rachel Halliday at the head of her family's table in Stowe's novel) as she prepares to depart the mother realm to reenter the outer world of men and print.[38]

Willa Cather, Jewett's friend and literary daughter, reiterates this matrifocal myth in *The Song of the Lark* (1915). Cather has her female artist, Thea Kronborg, descend into Panther Canyon, a womb in the earth from which she is reborn because she comes into spiritual union with Native American mothers who also climbed and descended the ancient winding water trails. The knowledge that those Native American women, Thea's spiritual foremothers, made art from the earth long before white men set foot on the continent restores Thea's creativity. In the womb of the earth – at the breast of her foremothers – Cather's artist is fed, just as Cather is fed by Jewett and Jewett by Stowe. In other words, preceding and enabling Cather is Jewett's *The Country of the Pointed Firs*, which is in turn a transformation of the earlier female vision articulated by Stowe: the midcentury Christian allegory of a mothering savior.

The Country of the Pointed Firs, translating an earlier vision into its secular variant, contains an idealized functioning matriarchy into which Stowe's earthy, bountiful Rachel Halliday might comfortably stride. The underlying energy and the essential fable remain unchanged. From *Uncle Tom's Cabin* in 1852 to *The Country of the Pointed Firs* in 1896 to *Herland* in 1915, mother rule operates as the ideal. It is an ideal that contains a vision of human community that places the group before the individual, cooperation before competition, love before progress. Given fantastical – science-fictional – realization by Gilman early in the twentieth century, it is an ideal that, whether Christian or secularized, asserts in the face of capitalist, masculine progress women's belief in the superiority of alternative matrifocal values.

3

Least appreciated in this tradition is the work of black women writers, who reflect and remodel the maternal argument of *Uncle Tom's Cabin* in fascinating ways. Compared with white writers, the relationship of black women writers to *Uncle Tom's Cabin* is both more direct and more complicated. In important respects, Stowe's novel represented a model. If the first *Uncle Tom's Cabin* could change attitudes about slavery, might not a second galvanize public sentiment against racism in general? At the same time, Stowe's book was written by a white woman. A number of her assumptions – for example, the "solution" of black people going "back" to Africa to live – strike black authors such as Frances Ellen Harper or Pauline Hopkins as ridiculous. Their admirable black characters find it no more attractive to leave their homeland for that of their ancestors than a white counterpart might. Thus, in long fiction by black women before the Harlem Renaissance, there is a mixture of debt to and revision of Stowe's novel, ranging from Sarah Lee Brown Fleming's *Hope's Highway* (1918) at the most imitative end of the spectrum to Harriet E. Wilson's *Our Nig* (1859) at the least.

But cutting across the whole spectrum, it seems to me, and important to any understanding of black women writers in America before the Harlem Renaissance, is the way black women publishing before the 1920s brilliantly adapt and recast for their own ends and audiences Stowe's exploitation of maternal ideology. On the one hand, Frances Ellen Harper, Sarah Lee Brown Fleming, and Angelina Grimké tend to agree with Stowe. They appeal to a sisterhood of mothers and argue in favor of maternal values as the ethical alternative and logical corrective to racial injustice in America. Harriet E. Wilson, on the other hand, is more complex; she both inverts and echoes Stowe's strategy. White mother rule exists in *Our Nig*, and what we see is as bad as (if not worse than) white male power. The book implicitly jeers at belief in white mothers and Victorian maternal values as society's salvation. Simultaneously, however, Wilson's story operates as a sort of canny mirror of Stowe's. It is the Marie St. Clare tale retold, and it is horrible precisely because the mother so fundamentally outrages our sense of Mother. From this perspective, Wilson's novel, apparently so different from Stowe's, paradoxically shares the maternal consciousness of *Uncle Tom's Cabin*.

Let me emphasize that my purpose here is not to claim that the work of black women writers before the Harlem Renaissance all traces back to Harriet Beecher Stowe. Clearly, their work traces first and foremost to other black writers, though they were few in number, and to people in the black community, especially women, who had for generations been struggling against oppression. Rather, my purpose is to consider together the maternal argument Stowe develops in *Uncle Tom's Cabin* and that manipulated by black women writers who followed her, knew her work (as everyone did), and shared her problem: how to argue against the white patriarchal power structure.

The year 1859 should be recognized as one of the most important in American literary history. Not only was the first short story by a black author published in the United States – Frances Ellen Watkins's (later Harper's) "The Two Offers" in *The Anglo-African Magazine* – but also the first novel by a black woman – *Our Nig* by Harriet E. Wilson.[39] Both, in very different ways, have strong affinities with *Uncle Tom's Cabin*.

"The Two Offers" takes for granted the ideal of the "Moral Mother." Called "the sainted mother" by Harper, she is the figure who rises between her child and the "deeds of darkness" to which he or she might be tempted; and the work of this guide and savior – this "true poet capable of writing on the soul of childhood the harmony of love and truth" – is the creation of a holy home, which is "the altar upon which lofty aspirations are kindled." Mother-centered, this Christian home is the place "from whence the soul may go forth strengthened, to act its part aright in the great drama of life, with conscience enlightened, affections culti-vated, and reason and judgment dominant."[40] Reform of the world through reform of the individual is, in other words, the work of mothers for Harper, just as it is for Stowe. As Harper says: "If we would trace the history of all crimes that have o'ershadowed this sin-shrouded and sorrow-darkened world of ours, how many might be seen arising from the wrong home influences, or the weakening of the home ties?"[41] Like Stowe, Alcott, Phelps, and Jewett, Frances Ellen Harper, an ardent aboli-tionist and eloquent, indefatigable public speaker for the cause, clearly looked to mothers as the possible saviors of a society "sin-shrouded" and "sorrow darkened" by human evil. (This early story, which is not about slavery, dramatizes the crimes against women of drink, physical abuse, and abandonment.)

Between the publication of "The Two Offers" in 1859 and the appearance of *Iola Leroy; or, Shadows Uplifted* in 1892, Frances Ellen Harper concentrated on poetry. Antilynching work (she also campaigned for temperance) was too desperately needed to allow for longer literary projects. As she has Iola explain almost four decades before Virginia Woolf's statement on the subject in *A Room of One's Own* (1929), "one needs both leisure and money to make a successful book,"[42] and neither was particularly accessible to Frances Ellen Harper in the years she committed to direct political action. But with *Iola Leroy* in the early 1890s (until recently thought to be the first novel by a black woman in this country), Harper at last had both the time and the money to bring her literary and political talents together in a long piece of fiction. Significantly, she inscribed on the frontispage of this fiction, which emerged after literally decades of labor in the service of social reform:

TO MY DAUGHTER

MARY E. HARPER,

THIS BOOK IS LOVINGLY DEDICATED.

Iola Leroy at a number of points closely resembles *Uncle Tom's Cabin*,[43] which so impressed Harper that she wrote at least two poems based on the novel, "Eliza Harris" and "Eva's Farewell."[44] Harper's novel opens like Stowe's with slaves debating the question of whether to run away, and although most of the characters choose flight, a couple explain why they will remain on the plantation; specifically, Uncle Daniel, reminiscent of Stowe's Uncle Tom, supports the right of others to escape but explains that he cannot in good conscience violate his master's trust. Similarly striking is the parallel between Stowe's planter, Augustine St. Clare, and Harper's planter, Eugene Leroy (Iola's father). Harper's character is kind, sensitive, and spineless; like St. Clare, Leroy believes that slavery is wrong, but he participates in the system anyway: "So strong was the force of habit, combined with the feebleness of his moral resistance and the nature of his environment, that instead of being an athlete, armed for a glorious strife, he had learned to drift where he should have steered, to float with the current instead of nobly breasting the tide" (p. 86). This planter, like St. Clare, is paired with a blood relation (in St. Clare's case a brother, in Leroy's a cousin) who seems to be his opposite – cold, ruthless – but who is, in fact, his double; the evil relative simply illustrates, overtly and consciously, what his passive brother stands for. One may be warm and the other cold, but in the end, tragically, they are the same man, with the same sin on their soul. Given these parallels, it is not surprising that the death of Leroy's little girl, named Gracie, vividly evokes the death of St. Clare's. Like Eva, Gracie (also the daughter of a Marie) is too pure, too innocent, to live; and her death, though less protracted than Eva's, clearly reifies the system's evil: "Tears would fill the servants' eyes as they saw the dear child drifting from them like a lovely vision, too bright for earth's dull cares and weary, wasting pain" (p. 96).

However, the deepest connection between *Iola Leroy* and *Uncle Tom's Cabin* lies in their shared reverence for motherhood. Throughout Harper's novel, heroic mothers are glimpsed: Uncle Daniel's wife, Aunt Katie, has a "saintly" face (p. 28); black Aunt Kizzy, her child ripped away by slavery, is "a living epistle" (p. 47); the mother of an enlightened Yankee officer named Captain Sybil turns out to have been a Quaker who was adamantly pacifist and opposed to racism (p. 48); Iola's mother, accurately named Marie, has something in her face such as one might see "in old cathedrals, lighting up the beauty of a saintly face" (p. 69). Clearly, the ideal of the "sainted mother" articulated by Harper in 1859 in "The Two Offers" stayed with her through the century, showing up in this series of sacred images of mothers in 1892.

Yet it is not a matter of Harper, a seasoned political strategist, mindlessly reiterating midcentury values in a turn-of-the-century novel. Rather, as alert a propagandist as Stowe, Harper shrewdly recasts the argument in terms of contemporary ideology. Well into *Iola Leroy*, Harper introduces her most interesting character, Lucille Delany, a very black (as opposed to mulatta) young woman who is college educated, outspoken, and completely up-to-date. This character seeks to apply to the modern world maternal principles dear to Harper (like Stowe) since the 1850s. Laboring in the great cause of racial uplift,

> she conceived the idea of opening a school to train future wives and mothers. She began on a small scale, in a humble building, and her work was soon crowned with gratifying success. She had enlarged her quarters, increased her teaching force, and had erected a large and commodious schoolhouse through her own exertions and the help of others. (pp. 199–200)

Picking up this theme again at the end of the novel, Harper has Iola deliver a paper at a *conversazione* where important essays on "Negro Emigration" and "Patriotism" and a fiery poem called "A Rallying Cry" are read and debated. Iola chooses to talk about the "Education of Mothers" (p. 253). Arguing the need for "enlightened" motherhood (p. 253), which is moral motherhood updated for a generation whose god is science rather than ethics (hence the transformation of the domestic arts into domestic science in Progressive Era America[45]), Iola follows her paper on motherhood with an impassioned extended parallel between the suffering of black people in America and the suffering of Christ. So powerful is this extemporaneous speech that her audience calls her "angelic," pronounces her "strangely beautiful," and exclaims on how "the tones of her voice are like benedictions of peace, her words a call to higher service and nobler life" (p. 257).

Iola's transfiguration, her sanctification, in this scene entwining enlightened motherhood, the suffering of blacks, and the passion of Christ, marks the moral climax of *Iola Leroy*. Harper deftly adapts Victorian ideology for an 1890s audience. Enlightened motherhood replaces the old ideal of the "Moral Mother" (the "sainted mother") in *Iola Leroy*, yet the religious imagery and the underlying argument remain familiar. Motherhood, it is believed, can light the way to a new world. That the novel ends with Iola heading out, like her "sister" Lucille Delany, to train wives and mothers to work toward the salvation of their people should come as no surprise. It is the logical late-nineteenth-century realization of this book's commitment to life-giving, matrifocal values, importantly shared and exemplified by black men as well as women in Harper's vision, as the basis for social change.[46]

Another turn-of-the-century novel more obscure than *Iola Leroy* and overtly indebted to Stowe is Sarah Lee Brown Fleming's *Hope's Highway* (1918).[47] This novel, which mentions *Uncle Tom's Cabin* explicitly, shows an angelic little girl named Grace (an echo of *Iola Leroy*, no doubt) with blue eyes and cloudlike blonde curls asking her governess to show her "a man like Uncle Tom who was so good to little Eva."[48] This little girl grows up to become the central figure in a drama of social reform. She plays an instrumental role in the education of Tom Brinley, a black man who goes on to head Vance Institute, an academy that will help turn "his people's steps away from the rough road of ignorance into the happy highway of hope."[49] Although the book is not as skillfully conceived or interestingly written as *Iola Leroy*, it matters in the tradition I am tracing. Hoping to influence whites, it uses a female character as the access to sympathy with black people's problems (a device brilliantly collapsed by Stowe into one figure, feminine Tom, as well as manipulated by her in various ways in her treatment of the bond that develops between Eva and Tom). Also, Fleming's novel, although the idea is more fully exploited by Stowe and Harper, suggests that female, and specifically maternal, love offers the foundation upon which to build a new social order.

Our Nig, published seven years after *Uncle Tom's Cabin* came out in book form, complicates the story I am telling in fascinating ways. In contrast to the work of Stowe or Alcott or Harper, there is in this book no nurturant maternal world. The black heroine's white mistress is vicious, sadistic, a torturer; and there is no balancing portrait of some gentle, sisterly, *effective* white female, let alone savior, in this angry book. There are women who comfort and aid Wilson's heroine, Frado. One of her mistress's daughters,

Jane, is kind to the abused black child; another family member, Aunt Abby, a sort of Aunt Ophelia figure, likewise sympathizes with the child; and there is a teacher who encourages Frado, as well as a kindly matron in town, Mrs. Moore, who takes her in when she leaves the home of her cruel mistress, Mrs. Bellmont. But this collective portrait of sweet femininity pales next to the portrait of vicious mother rule at the center of the book in Mrs. Bellmont. *Our Nig* jeers at the myth of the mother-savior and the idea that there exists some powerful, subversive, subterranean community of sisterly love among women, grounded in maternal values and standing outside the capitalist system. The most powerful person in *Our Nig* is a mother, and she is a "she-devil."[50] Here is no warm hearth and motherly rocker, as pictured by Stowe in her Rachel Halliday sequence. Instead, at the heart of this matriarchy, located in the dark crawlspace of this house's ell, above the kitchen, is a torture chamber. Hidden away from sight but existing at the very center of the white matrifocal world Wilson pictures sleeps a small black girl bloodied by the female hand that rules the house. This vision of white mother rule is not pretty. In *Our Nig* Wilson offers a bitter, and very important, challenge to middle-class feminine ideology in the decade preceding the Civil War. Domesticity is no sanctuary from capitalism in this book, much less an alternative model for the reorganization of society. "Home" in *Our Nig,* whether it is Mrs. Bellmont's or the one from which Frado was initially cast out by her own mother (also a white woman) because of poverty, manifests rather than contradicts capitalist values, which find their most hideous but nonetheless purest expression, of course, in slavery.

Yet at the same time, I would argue, the myth of the mother-savior, of the superiority of maternal values, does inspire *Our Nig*. Wilson draws on the myth even as she mocks it. For the monstrosity of the white mistress and the viciousness of her treatment of the book's black heroine derive their horror, in large part, from the fact that this is *not* the way it is supposed to be. To see a white man torturing a black woman is horrifying but, at some level, not surprising; aggression and even cruelty have long been part of the culture's definition of masculinity. But women are not supposed to be violent. Women are supposed to be nurturant, peaceful, cooperative, caring – that is, all the qualities of the ideal Victorian woman, typified by "Mother," off of which Wilson so brilliantly plays her story in *Our Nig.* In other words, the ideal of mother love explicit in *Uncle Tom's Cabin* operates implicitly in *Our Nig.* Where Stowe parades its presence, Wilson laments its absence; where Stowe uses its existence to suggest utopian possibilities, Wilson uses its nonexistence to show the hell-on-earth suffered by the Frados of America.

Indeed, this mirror imaging between *Uncle Tom's Cabin* and *Our Nig* functions very specifically. The story Wilson tells echoes – even imitates – the most important antistory about mothers in *Uncle Tom's Cabin:* the Marie St. Clare narrative. Wilson, writing out of her own experience, which produced both rage and terror, reiterates not the positive but the negative mother story of *Uncle Tom's Cabin,* echoing its essential features so deliberately that, had *Our Nig* been more widely read, it surely would have evoked the earlier novel for many readers and stood, defiantly, both as confirmation and as revision of that inflammatory first text. For in retelling the Marie St. Clare story in her own terms and *not* couching it in some positive over-story about mother love (as Stowe does), Wilson indicates, implicitly, which of Stowe's tales is truer from her point of view. And it is not the tale of mother-as-savior.

The echoes and inversions of the Marie St. Clare story in *Our Nig* are striking. Both give us a vicious mother, a spineless father, a starchy but kindly maiden aunt who is a relative of the father, a dying child who calls others to Christ as she/he leaves this earth, and a black protagonist who is persecuted by the wicked mother and befriended by the child who dies. The parallel between these two sets of characters – Marie/Mrs. Bellmont, Augustine/Mr. Bellmont, Aunt Ophelia/Aunt Abby, Eva/James, Tom/Frado – is very strong. Most obvious is the correspondence between Marie St. Clare and Mrs. Bellmont. Although Marie is lazier than Mrs. Bellmont, both are the complete antithesis of the loving Victorian mother. Mrs. Bellmont is "self-willed, haughty, undisciplined, arbitrary and severe" (p. 25). To provoke her temper is "like encountering a whirlwind charged with fire, daggers and spikes" (pp. 24–5). As satanic as Marie St. Clare, who routinely sends slaves to be beaten by others paid to do her bidding, Mrs. Bellmont directs her fury toward breaking her one slave, Frado, body and soul. Significantly, the particular torture she likes to inflict involves propping the child's mouth open with a block of wood while she whips her, an act designed to render the child literally speechless: without voice.

The resemblance between Augustine St. Clare and John Bellmont is equally pronounced. Although Bellmont, like St. Clare, appears kind and compassionate, he may actually be worse than his wife, for like St. Clare, he has the authority to change the system he lives with, but refuses to do so. John Bellmont's characteristic response to his wife's abuse of Frado is to take a walk. (The strategy recalls Stowe's Shelby when Tom is sold.) After witnessing Mrs. Bellmont kick Frado across the floor, Aunt Abby accosts John:

> "Why do you have it so, John?" asked his sister.
> "How am I to help it? Women rule the earth, and all in it."
> "I think I should rule my own house, John," –
> "And live in hell meantime," added Mr. Bellmont.
> John now sauntered out to the barn to await the quieting of the storm. (pp. 44–5)

Similarly, " 'I shall not punish her [Frado],' he replied, and left the house, as he usually did when a temper threatened to envelop him," at which point, of course, Bellmont's wife proceeds to beat Frado senseless (p. 34). John Bellmont, like Augustine St. Clare, gives lip service to change but acquiesces in the regime around him. Through his cowardice, Bellmont, like Pontius Pilate washing his hands of the crime before him, silently abets the victimization of Wilson's "martyr" (p. 83), Frado, at the hands of the "she-devil," Mrs. Bellmont.

Completing this series of striking parallels is the way in which Wilson's bond between a black girl and a white man echoes and inverts Stowe's bond between a white girl and a black man. Where the white girl, Eva, befriends and bolsters the spirit of the black man, Tom, in *Uncle Tom's Cabin*, in *Our Nig*, flipping the pattern, the white man, James, befriends and bolsters the spirit of the black girl, Frado. Moreover, James's death, like that of Harper's Gracie in *Iola Leroy* thirty years later, clearly evokes Eva's. As James, who has represented what little shelter Frado has had (p. 67), fades and dies, Frado, following his wishes, becomes a Christian; she finds herself able to receive the "compassionate Jesus" (p. 85). This early death of a gentle white person, the prolonged deathbed scene, the emphasis on a deathbed conversion, the love between man and child, the misery into which this death will plunge the black protagonist: all clearly echo Stowe's famous scene in *Uncle Tom's Cabin*. But where Wilson, writing from experience as well as imagination, bursts the bubble is in showing no significant change arising from this poignant scene. In the final analysis, Christian conversion does not affect the issues Wilson dramatizes. In *Uncle Tom's Cabin* Eva's death inspires Tom, whose death in turn inspires George Shelby, the son of Tom's first owner, and causes him to renounce slaveholding. In *Our Nig* James's death inspires Frado, who goes on to have a miserable life regardless.

Little is known about Harriet E. Wilson.[51] She wrote *Our Nig* to make money to support herself and her child. The book did not sell well, her son died, and she and her creation fell out of sight until the book's reissue in the early 1980s. What we can say is that the book she left speaks to a painfully ambivalent and very instructive perspective on the ideal of mother love so complacently idolized in Victorian America. On the one hand, in its portrait of Mrs. Bellmont, *Our Nig* flings the ideal of benevolent mother rule in the face of middle-class white America; the Bellmont household is, for all intents and purposes, a matriarchy, and what we see represents a nightmare of cruelty and abuse. On the other hand, behind and inspiring this portrait of maternal abuse is a longing for mother love, indeed for the mother-savior, which is intense. That hunger for the mother denied Frado, in the book Wilson herself wrote as a single mother desperately trying to support herself and her child, is poignantly shown in the language Wilson uses in one of the few other examples we have of her writing, a letter addressed to a woman who took her in and nursed her to health at a critical point in her life. Writing from the poorhouse, where she was forced to go to give birth to her child, Wilson sends her friend this fantasy: "I could see my dear little room, with its pleasant eastern window opening to the morning; but more than all, I beheld *you*, my mother, gliding softly in and kneeling by my bed to read, as no one but you *can* read, 'The Lord is my shepherd, – I shall not want,' "[52] Also from this letter: "I opened my precious little Bible, and the first verse that caught my eye was – 'I am poor and needy, yet the Lord thinketh upon me.' O, my mother, could I tell you the comfort this was to me."[53] That this passion for her friend as mother reflects more than a figure of speech is clear from one other fragment of information provided by another friend who recalled seeing Wilson while she was living with "mother Walker": "Never shall I forget the expression of her 'black, but comely' face, as she came to me one day, exclaiming, 'O, aunt J_____, I have at last found a *home,* – and not only a home, but a *mother.* My cup runneth over. What shall I render to the Lord for all his benefits?' "[54]

One of the latest pieces in this tradition, Angelina W. Grimké's play *Rachel* (1920), was commissioned by the NAACP in 1916 as part of its antilynching campaign. The play was written by the black grandniece of the famous midcentury white abolitionist, Angelina Grimké of South Carolina (the playwright's father was the nephew of the elder Angelina, who publicly acknowledged her black relative and helped finance his education). The plot of *Rachel* is simple. Grimké names her heroine for the Old Testament heroine blessed with motherhood (Stowe's Rachel also evokes this biblical figure, of course) and then denies her character the experience. First, Grimké's Rachel Loving learns that her father and brother were lynched; then she sees how racism maims the spirit of children she loves, making them wake up in the night screaming with fright or reducing them to catatonic self-loathing. Though she longs to marry and to have children, she vows never to do either.

> You God! – You terrible, laughing God! Listen! I swear – and may my soul be damned to all eternity, if I do break this oath – I swear – that no child of mine shall ever lie upon my breast, for I will not have it rise up, in the terrible days that are to be – and call me cursed.[55]

Rachel thinks of what she will miss: "Never to know the loveliest thing in all the world – the feel of a little head, the touch of little hands, the beautiful utter dependence – of a little child" (p. 63). But she quickly steels herself. Casting to the floor a vase of flowers, from which she has grabbed some rosebuds that she tears apart and grinds under foot, she cries: "You can laugh, Oh God! Well, so can I. . . . But I can be kinder than You. . . . If I kill, You Mighty God, I kill at once – I do not torture" (p. 63).

Although the rage of *Rachel* recalls *Our Nig*, the strategy of the piece evokes Stowe. To combat the racism that was mounting at the turn of the century, a situation epitomized by the increase in lynchings, Grimké plays on her audience's reverence for motherhood. The one thing Rachel wishes to do in life is raise children, and she would be superb at it: patient, pious, cheerful, selfless. She would perfectly exemplify the Victorian ideal of motherhood by now (one and a half decades into the twentieth century) enshrined in the popular culture as the highest calling of woman. (Simultaneously, this Victorian ideal had developed deep fissures by the turn of the century, as I will discuss shortly.) Much as the motherliness of Stowe's Tom identifies him with a set of values cherished by the audience she hopes to reach, and thus manipulates sympathy in the direction of a character usually dismissed by whites (buffooned, scorned), so Rachel's "natural" aptitude for motherhood allows Grimké to exploit her viewers' emotional attachment to the by now traditional ideal of Christlike motherhood. The strategy encourages her audience to see in this drama about racial injustice not only the tragedy of one woman but also the passion of Christ.

Clyde Taylor explains that by the turn of the century the tradition of the black messiah, rooted in traditional black religion in America, had "acquired new energy."[56] Taylor cites W. L. Hunter's *Jesus Christ Was Part Negro* (c. 1901), James Morris Webb's *A Black Man Will Be the Coming Universal King* (1918), Marcus Garvey's "call for a black God, a black Christ and a heaven populated by black angels," Countee Cullen's *The Black Christ and Other Poems* (1919), and W. E. B. DuBois's *Darkwater* (1920), "whose strongest unifying thread is the vision of a returning, resolving black Jesus."[57] Drawing both on this tradition and on the female tradition I have been tracing, that of seeing in Christ the mother and in mother the Christ, Grimké offers in *Rachel* a grim revision of both themes. Born to the Mary of Grimké's play is a child (Rachel) who, like Jesus, sacrifices her own life for the sins of the world. But there is a twist. The bitterness of Grimké's evocation of this possible savior, this black maternal Christ, lies in the fact that finally Rachel is allowed to be neither mother nor savior. There is no redemption, only tragedy, in this play. What the playwright shows is that racism has become so virulent that there will be no mother-savior. Although Grimke's appeal to maternal values places her squarely in the tradition of women writers that I have been tracing, her bitter use of the tradition suggests a new era, one in which the faith of a Harriet Beecher Stowe, or even a Harriet E. Wilson, is no longer possible. In renouncing motherhood, Rachel not only indicts American racism. She also, though this is not a conscious aim of the play, brings down the curtain, for a long time at any rate, on an era of feminist idealism that for well over half a century sought to lead America, as Stowe put it, through that "mother's love" of Christ to a new order.

It is not surprising that the dream of the mother-savior dwindled and went underground around 1920, not to resurface in a major way until the next explosion of energy in the women's movement in the late 1960s and early 1970s. The ascendancy of science over religion as the supreme arbiter of truth (and with that the medical establishment's redefinition of mother as sick rather than saint, even though the behavior prescribed remained Victorian: passivity, self-sacrifice, and sensitivity), plus the failures of the so-called Progressive Era and the devastating jolt to optimism offered by World War I, produced a new and cynical perspective on the possibilities of social salvation and reform in general. In addition, by the early decades of the twentieth century the idea of female separatism, the concept that men and women appropriately occupy separate spheres, the masculine one public and commercial, the feminine one private and domestic, was giving way to the new ideal of sexual equality and integration (the idea that women should inhabit both the domestic and the commercial spheres) that was to find symbolic affirmation in the passage of the Nineteenth Amendment, which gave the vote to women in 1920. With the end of separatism came the end, in effect, of the argument holding up the maternal world as an alternative model: separate, superior, salvific. If women were able and eager to take their place beside men in the workplace, then the specialness of women was no longer such a compelling argument. Fiction by women about the revolutionary possibilities of matrifocal values gave way to fiction by women about the new social imperative of integration, books such as Kate Chopin's *The Awakening* (1899) or Edith Wharton's *The House of Mirth* (1905) or (looking at both race and gender) Pauline Hopkins's *Contending Forces* (1900). Testing life *beyond* rather than *by* the domestic realm became the mission of modern fiction by women.

The old-fashioned writers had a different agenda. Stowe, Alcott, Phelps, Harper, Jewett, Grimké, Wilson, to name some of the major figures, did not challenge America to let women into men's world. They challenged the nation to reshape itself in the image of motherhood. They confronted America with the possibility of wholesale, radical social reorganization, and they manipulated and shaped a complex mythology of female power and community that continues to nourish female literary tradition in America. When Nikki Giovanni writes, "I turned myself into myself and was /jesus,"[58] when Joan Didion writes of crucified mother–daughter love in a novel entitled *A Book of Common Prayer* (1977), when Ntozake Shange says at the end of *for colored girls* "I found God in myself/ & . . . I loved her fiercely,"[59] they write out of one of the oldest female literary traditions in America. *Uncle Tom's Cabin*, for all its distance from contemporary attitudes about race, religion, and the art of the novel,[60] articulates a powerful dream of alternative female community as the basis for social reform. That dream, symbolically embodied by Stowe in the brilliant trinity of salvific "mothers," Eva, Tom, and Rachel, may have radically changed, but it has not vanished.

The same year that Stowe's grandniece, Charlotte Perkins Gilman, published *Herland*, a fiction that imagines Stowe's dream of mother rule as a reality, Dr. Robert Warren Conant brought out *The Virility of Christ: A New View*, subtitled *A Book for Men*. So prevalent was the feminine Christ by 1915, in Dr. Conant's view at least, that more than 250 pages of corrective argument were needed to assert the masculinity of Jesus, who was *not*, Dr. Conant explains, "meek and lowly" and should *not* be pictured "with an expression of sweetness and resignation, eyes . . . down-cast, soft hands gently folded, long curling hair brushed smoothly from a central parting – all feminine, passive, negative," with some insipid "appropriate sentiment, such as 'Feed my lambs!'" attached.[61]

The passion with which Conant insists on the masculinity of Christ (one thinks also of Bruce Barton's *The Man Nobody Knows* in 1925) speaks to the power of the feminine mythology tapped and exploited by Stowe, as does the following item published in a popular news magazine more than 130 years after Stowe stunned America with her maternal novel. At the Maundy Thursday services at the Cathedral of St. John the Divine in New York City in May 1984, the crucifix displayed bore a female Christ. One outraged worshipper is reported to have said: "It's disgraceful. God and Christ are male. They're playing with a symbol we've believed in for all our lives." Another was said to have felt it was "not at all blasphemous," that the crucifix reflected a mystic Christian tradition that "sees Christ as our mother."[62] *Uncle Tom's Cabin* had dramatized that idea more than a century earlier.

NOTES

1 For excellent discussions of popular women novelists in the nineteenth century, see Nina Baym, *Woman's Fiction: A Guide to Novels by and about Women in America, 1820–1870* (Ithaca, N.Y.: Cornell University Press, 1978), and Mary Kelley, *Private Woman, Public Stage: Literary Domesticity in Nineteenth-Century America* (New York: Oxford University Press, 1984). For examples of earlier twentieth-century views, which almost always denigrate these mid-nineteenth-century women novelists, see Helen Waite Papashvily, *All the Happy Endings: A Study of the Domestic Novel in America* (New York: Harper & Bros., 1956), or Fred Lewis Pattee, *The Feminine Fifties* (Port Washington, N.Y.: Kennikat Press, 1940).

2 The comments of these men can be found in *Critical Essays on Harriet Beecher Stowe*, ed. Elizabeth Ammons (Boston: G. K.Hall, 1980).

3 Sand, "Review of *Uncle Tom's Cabin*," ibid., pp. 3–6.

4 Jewett, "Excerpt from a Letter to Mrs. Fields," ibid., p. 212.

5 Fields, "Days with Mrs. Stowe," ibid., p. 301.

6 "Eliza Harris" and "Eva's Farewell," in *Poems on Miscellaneous Subjects* by Frances Ellen Watkins (Philadelphia: Merrihew and Thompson, Printers, 1857), pp. 9–11, 32.

7 Elizabeth Stuart Phelps Ward, "Mrs. Stowe," in Ammons, ed., *Critical Essays*, p. 284.

8 For the usual mid-twentieth-century argument, see, for example, Leslie Fiedler, *Love and Death in the American Novel* (New York: Criterion, 1960), R. W. B. Lewis, *The American Adam* (Chicago: University of Chicago Press, 1955), or Richard Chase, *The American Novel and Its Tradition* (Garden City, N.Y.: Doubleday, 1957). For a perceptive recent discussion of this masculine tradition in American literature, see Martin Green, *The Great American Adventure* (Boston: Beacon Press, 1984). Illuminating analysis of the masculine critical tradition in American literature can be found in Nina Baym, "Melodramas of Be-Set Manhood: How Theories of American Fiction Exclude Women Authors," *American Quarterly* 33 (Summer 1981):123–39; and Paul Lauter, "Race and Gender in the Shaping of the American Literary Canon: A Case Study from the Twenties," *Feminist Studies* 9 (Fall 1983):435–64.

9 "The Female World of Love and Ritual: Relations Between Women in Nineteenth-Century America," *Signs*, 1 (1975):1–28.

10 See, for example, the discussion of Stowe in Ellen Moers, *Literary Women* (New York: Doubleday, 1976), pp. 4ff.

11 Kathryn Kish Sklar, "Victorian Women and Domestic Life: Mary Todd Lincoln, Elizabeth Cady Stanton, and Harriet Beecher Stowe," in *The Public and the Private Lincoln*, ed. Cullom Davis et al. (Carbondale: Southern Illinois University Press, 1979), pp. 20–37.

12 See, for example, Phelps's remarks in Ammons, ed., *Critical Essays*, pp. 282–5.

13 Ruth H. Bloch, "American Feminine Ideals in Transition: The Rise of the Moral Mother, 1785–1815," *Feminist Studies* 4 (June 1978):105.

14 Sklar, "Victorian Women," p. 28. For a full-length analysis of Catharine Beecher's thinking and strategy, see Kathryn Kish Sklar's classic earlier study, *Catharine Beecher: A Study in American Domesticity* (New Haven, Conn.: Yale University Press, 1973).

15 Mary Kelley, "The Sentimentalists: Promise and Betrayal in the Home," *Signs* 4 (Spring 1979);436–7.

16 Baym, *Woman's Fiction*, p. 27.

17 All references to *Uncle Tom's Cabin* come from Harriet Beecher Stowe, *Uncle Tom's Cabin*, ed. Kenneth S. Lynn (Cambridge, Mass.: Harvard University Press, 1962).

18 Charles Edward Stowe, *Life of Harriet Beecher Stowe Compiled from Her Letters and Journals* (Boston: Houghton Mifflin, 1890), p. 154.

19 Barbara Welter, "The Feminization of American Religion, 1800–1860," in *Dimity Convictions* (Athens: Ohio University Press, 1976), p.

84. Contrasting interpretation of the feminization of religion in nine-teenth-century America can be found in Ann Douglas, *The Feminization of American Culture* (New York: Alfred A. Knopf, 1977).

20 Welter, "Feminization of American Religion," p. 85.

21 Harriet Beecher Stowe, *My Wife and I; or Henry Henderson's History* (New York: J. B. Ford, 1871), p. 37.

22 See Welter, "Feminization of American Religion," pp. 88ff.

23 Ibid., pp. 87–88.

24 For a detailed discussion of this typology (Eva as a second Eve), see my essay "Heroines in *Uncle Tom's Cabin*," in Ammons, ed., *Critical Essays*, pp. 152–65. This essay also provides a full discussion of some of the ideas I bring up about Tom, including the question of Stowe's racism and her concept of true manhood.

25 Forrest Wilson, *Crusader in Crinoline: The Life of Harriet Beecher Stowe* (Philadelphia: J. B. Lippincott Co., 1941), p. 275.

26 Harriet Beecher Stowe, *Religious Studies* (1877), in *The Writings of Harriet Beecher Stowe* (Boston: Houghton Mifflin, 1896), pp. xv, 36.

27 Harriet Beecher Stowe, *A Key to Uncle Tom's Cabin* (Boston: J. P. Jewett & Co., 1853), p. 229.

28 Wilson, *Crusader in Crinoline*, p. 571.

29 As the historians Ellen Carol DuBois and Linda Gordon remind us in a piece on nineteenth-century feminists' views on sexuality, the impor-tance of religious culture may be the hardest factor for a modern audience to appreciate. See "Seeking Ecstasy on the Battlefield: Dan-ger and Pleasure in Nineteenth-Century Feminist Sexual Thought," in *Pleasure and Danger: Exploring Female Sexuality*, ed. Carole S. Vance (Boston: Routledge & Kegan Paul, 1984), p. 35.

30 Nina Auerbach, *Communities of Women: An Idea in Fiction* (Boston: Harvard University Press, 1978), pp. 55–64.

31 Ibid., p. 71.

32 Elizabeth Langland, "Female Stories of Experience: Alcott's *Little Women* in Light of *Work*," in *The Voyage In: Fictions of Female Develop-ment*, ed. Elizabeth Abel, Marianne Hirsch, and Elizabeth Langland (Hanover, N.H.: University Press of New England, 1983), p. 113.

33 Elizabeth Stuart Phelps, *The Silent Partner* (Ridgewood, N.J.: Gregg Press, 1967), p. 278. Recent discussion of Phelps's work can be found in Mari Jo Buhle and Florence Howe, Afterword to *The Silent Partner* (Old Westbury, N.Y.: Feminist Press, 1983), pp. 355–86; and Carol Farley Kessler, *Elizabeth Stuart Phelps* (Boston: Twayne Publishers, 1982).

34 Sarah Orne Jewett, *A Country Doctor* (Boston: Houghton Mifflin, 1884), p. 351.

35 Smith-Rosenberg, pp. 10, 14–15.

36 I am indebted for the Stowe–Gilman connection to Dorothy Berkson, whose detailed examination of the link appears in an unpublished paper, "Deconstructing Patriarchy: The New World of Women's Culture in the Fiction of Harriet Beecher Stowe, Charlotte Perkins Gilman, and Marge Piercy." Also see Berkson, "Millennial Politics and the Feminine Fiction of Harriet Beecher Stowe," in Ammons, ed., *Critical Essays*, pp. 244–58, for an excellent discussion of matrifocal themes in the fiction Stowe published after the antislavery novels.

37 Marjorie Pryse, Introduction to *The Country of the Pointed Firs* (New York: Norton, 1981), p. xiii.

38 I discuss in detail matrifocal themes in Jewett in two other essays: "Going in Circles: The Female Geography of Jewett's *Country of the Pointed Firs*," *Studies in the Literary Imagination*, 16 (Fall 1983):83–92; and "Jewett's Witches," in *Critical Essays on Sarah Orne Jewett*, ed. Gwen Nagel (Boston: G. K. Hall, 1984), pp. 165–84.

39 Identifying "firsts" is always risky. A couple of years ago, *Our Nig* was unknown to the general scholarly community, and it is possible that future discoveries will displace either or both of the titles I cite here. Nevertheless, at this time, "The Two Offers" and *Our Nig* are to the best of our knowledge unprecedented and therefore of major importance historically as well as literarily. I should add that it is possible that *Our Nig* should be read as autobiography rather than as a novel. Since we know almost nothing about Harriet E. Wilson, it is difficult to say just how fictionalized the book is. However, even if it is entirely autobiographical, the parallels to Stowe's novel remain and bear analysis.

40 Frances Ellen Watkins [Harper], "The Two Offers," *The Anglo-African Magazine*, 1 (1859):311.

41 Ibid.

42 Frances Ellen Harper, *Iola Leroy; or, Shadows Uplifted* (College Park, Md.: McGrath, 1969), p. 262. For a perceptive discussion of this novel within the context of black women novelists in America (as well as mention of the relation between *Uncle Tom's Cabin* and the black literary tradition), see Barbara Christian, *Black Women Novelists: The Development of a Tradition, 1892–1976* (Westport, Conn.: Greenwood Press, 1980), pp. 3–5, 25–30, 19–22.

43 Deborah McDowell mentions but does not develop this idea in a bril-

liant article on Harper and Alice Walker, "'The Changing Same': Generational Connections and Black Women Novelists," forthcoming in *New Literary History.*

44 See note 6.

45 See Susan Strasser, *Never Done: A History of American Housework* (New York: Pantheon, 1982), chap. 11.

46 For the views of other black women during this period, see the excellent collections, Bert James Loewenberg and Ruth Bogin, ed., *Black Women in Nineteenth-Century American Life* (University Park: Pennsylvania State University Press, 1976); and Dorothy Sterling, ed., *We Are Your Sisters: Black Women in the Nineteenth Century* (New York: Norton, 1984).

47 Sarah Lee Brown Fleming appears in *Black American Writers Past and Present: A Biographical and Bibliographical Dictionary,* vol. 1, ed. Theressa Gunnels Rush, Carol Fairbanks Myers, and Esther Spring Arata (Metuchen, N.J.: Scarecrow Press, 1975), p. 299. Another novel explicitly linked to Stowe's and mistakenly identified (in my opinion) as the work of a black writer is Andasia Kimbrough Bruce's *Uncle Tom's Cabin of To-Day* (1906). Although Andasia Kimbrough Bruce (Mrs. William Liddell Bruce) is cited in *Black American Writers, 1773–1949,* ed. Geraldine O. Matthews et al. (Boston: G. K. Hall, 1975), p. 130, and her novel is reprinted from the Fisk University Library Negro Collection and appears as part of the Black Heritage Library Collection of the Books for Libraries Press (Freeport, N.Y.: 1972 rpt.), she is probably not an Afro-American author. The perspective, plot, point of view, and argument of *Uncle Tom's Cabin of To-Day* suggest that she was a white writer, and she is not noted as an "American Negro author" in the Schomburg Catalog of the New York Public Library (which does list the novel). For those reasons, I do not include her in this discussion. (I wish to thank Ann Allen Shockley, Associate Librarian for Special Collections and University Archivist, Fisk University Library, for her assistance on this question.) Another writer I do not include, beyond an occasional mention, although she was black and is very important to our understanding of women writers in America at the turn of the century, is Pauline Hopkins. Her best-known work, the novel *Contending Forces* (1900) (Carbondale: Southern Illinois University Press, 1972, p. 101), although insistent on women as leaders, does not really develop the paradigm I am discussing.

48 Sarah Lee Brown Fleming, *Hope's Highway: A Novel* (New York: Neale, 1918; AMS rpt, 1973), p. 24.

49 Ibid., p. 156.

50 Harriet E. Wilson, *Our Nig; or, Sketches from the Life of a Free Black* (New York: Vintage, 1983), p. 22.

51 See Henry Louis Gates, Jr., Introduction to *Our Nig,* pp. xi–lv.

52 Appendix, *Our Nig,* p. 135.

53 Ibid.

54 Ibid., p. 133.

55 Angelina W. Grimké, *Rachel: A Play in Three Acts* (The Cornhill Company, 1920; rpt. College Park, Md.: McGrath, 1969), p. 63. A good introduction to Grimké can be found in Jeanne-Marie A. Miller, "Angelina Weld Grimké: Playwright and Poet," *College Language Association Journal* 21 (1978):513–24.

56 Clyde Taylor, "The Second Coming of Jean Toomer," *Obsidian* (Winter 1975):39. See also Wilson J. Moses, *Black Messiahs and Uncle Toms: Social and Literary Manipulations of a Religious Myth* (University Park: Pennsylvania State University Press, 1982).

57 Taylor, "The Second Coming," p. 39.

58 Nikki Giovanni, "Ego-Tripping," in *Re: Creation* (Detroit: Broadside Press, 1970).

59 Ntozake Shange, *for colored girls who have considered suicide, when the rainbow is enuf: a choreopoem* (New York: Macmillan, 1977), p. 67.

60 For an excellent discussion of *Uncle Tom's Cabin* in light of mid-nineteenth-century aesthetic expectations, see Jane P. Tompkins, *Sensational Designs: The Cultural Work of American Fiction, 1790–1860* (New York: Oxford University Press, 1985), pp. 122–46.

61 Robert Warren Conant, *The Virility of Christ: A New View* (Chicago: n.p., 1915), pp. 12–13.

62 "Vexing Christa," *Time,* May 7, 1984, p. 94. For a discussion of this idea's appearance long before the modern era, see Caroline Walker Bynum, *Jesus as Mother: Studies in the Spirituality of the High Middle Ages* (Berkeley: University of California Press, 1982).

Notes on Contributors

Elizabeth Ammons, Associate Professor of English at Tufts University, is the author of *Edith Wharton's Argument with America* (1980) and the editor of *Critical Essays on Harriet Beecher Stowe* (1980) and *Selected Short Fiction of Rose Terry Cooke* (1986).

Karen Halttunen is the author of *Confidence Men and Painted Women: A Study of Middle-Class Culture in America, 1830–1870* (1982). An Associate Professor of History and American Culture at Northwestern University, she is writing a book on the Gothic imagination in nineteenth-century culture.

Robert B. Stepto is Professor of English, Afro-American Studies, and American Studies at Yale University. He is the author of *From Behind the Veil: A Study of Afro-American Narrative* (1979) and the editor of *Afro-American Literature: The Reconstruction of Instruction* (1978) and *Chant of Saints: A Gathering of Afro-American Literature, Art, and Scholarship* (1979).

Eric J. Sundquist teaches American literature at the University of California, Berkeley. He is the author of *Home as Found: Authority and Genealogy in Nineteenth-Century American Literature* (1979) and *Faulkner: The House Divided* (1983), and the editor of *American Realism: New Essays* (1982).

Richard Yarborough teaches English and is a Faculty Research Associate with the Center for Afro-American Studies at the University of California, Los Angeles. His essays have appeared in *MELUS, College English, Georgia Review,* and *Black American Liter-*

ature Forum, and he is currently completing a book on the nine-teenth-century Afro-American novel.

Jean Fagan Yellin is Professor of English at Pace University. The author of *The Intricate Knot: Black Figures in American Literature, 1776–1863* (1972) and the editor of Harriet Jacobs's *Incidents in the Life of a Slave Girl,* she is currently completing a book entitled *Women and Sisters: The Anti-Slavery Feminists in Nineteenth-Century American Culture.*

Selected Bibliography

Although the critical literature on *Uncle Tom's Cabin* is slight compared to that on the works of other major writers of the period, a number of recent books and essays have given Stowe and her novel more serious attention. In this case, however, works on the history of slavery and social reform are of crucial importance. Along with additional books and articles cited in the notes to the essays in this volume, readers may want to consult studies in the following selected bibliography. The standard works on Stowe's life and her composition of *Uncle Tom's Cabin* are by Forrest Wilson and E. Bruce Kirkham, and the standard text of the novel is edited by Kenneth Lynn.

Ammons, Elizabeth, ed., *Critical Essays on Harriet Beecher Stowe*. Boston: G. K. Hall, 1980.

Birdoff, Harry. *The World's Greatest Hit: Uncle Tom's Cabin*. New York: S. F. Vanni, 1947.

Blassingame, John W. *The Slave Community: Plantation Life in the Antebellum South*. New York: Oxford University Press, rev. ed. 1979.

Brown, Herbert Ross. *The Sentimental Novel in America, 1789–1860*. Durham, N.C.: Duke University Press, 1940.

Crozier, Alice C. *The Novels of Harriet Beecher Stowe*. New York: Oxford University Press, 1969.

Davis, David Brion. *Slavery and Human Progress*. New York: Oxford University Press, 1984.

Douglas, Ann. *The Feminization of American Culture*. New York: Alfred A. Knopf, 1977.

Faust, Drew Gilpin. *The Sacred Circle: The Dilemma of the Intellectual in the Old South, 1840–1860*. Baltimore: Johns Hopkins University Press, 1977.

Fiedler, Leslie A. *What Was Literature? Class Culture and Mass Society*. New York: Simon and Schuster, 1982.

Fields, Annie. *Life and Letters of Harriet Beecher Stowe*. London: Samson Low, 1898.

Selected Bibliography

Fisher, Philip. *Hard Facts: Setting and Form in the American Novel.* New York: Oxford University Press, 1985.

Forgie, George B. *Patricide in the House Divided: A Psychological Interpretation of Lincoln and His Age.* New York: W. W. Norton, 1979.

Fredrickson, George M. *The Black Image in the White Mind: The Debate on Afro-American Character and Destiny, 1817–1914.* New York: Harper & Row, 1971.

Furnas, J. C. *Goodbye to Uncle Tom.* New York: William Sloane, 1956.

Genovese, Eugene D. *Roll, Jordan, Roll: The World the Slaves Made.* New York: Random House, 1974.

Gossett, Thomas F. *Uncle Tom's Cabin and American Literature.* Dallas: Southern Methodist University Press, 1985.

Gutman, Herbert G. *The Black Family in Slavery and Freedom, 1750–1925.* New York: Pantheon, 1976.

Hersh, Blanche Glassman. *The Slavery of Sex: Feminist-Abolitionists in America.* Urbana: University of Illinois Press, 1978.

Kirkham, E. Bruce. *The Building of Uncle Tom's Cabin.* Knoxville: University of Tennessee Press, 1977.

Rourke, Constance Mayfield. *Trumpets of Jubilee: Henry Ward Beecher, Harriet Beecher Stowe, Lyman Beecher, Horace Greeley, P. T. Barnum.* New York: Harcourt, Brace, 1963.

Rugoff, Milton. *The Beechers: An American Family in the Nineteenth Century.* New York: Harper & Row, 1981.

Stewart, James Brewer. *Holy Warriors: The Abolitionists and American Slavery.* New York: Hill and Wang, 1976.

Stowe, Charles Edward, ed. *The Life of Harriet Beecher Stowe Compiled from Her Letters and Journals.* Boston: Houghton Mifflin, 1889.

Stowe, Harriet Beecher. *Uncle Tom's Cabin or, Life Among the Lowly.* ed. Kenneth S. Lynn. Cambridge, Mass.: Harvard University Press, 1962.

Strout, Cushing. *The New Heavens and New Earth: Political Religion in America.* New York: Harper & Row, 1974.

Taylor, William R. *Cavalier and Yankee: The Old South and the American National Character.* New York: George Braziller, 1961.

Tompkins, Jane. *Sensational Designs: The Cultural Work of American Fiction, 1790–1860.* New York: Oxford University Press, 1985.

Tyler, Alice Felt. *Freedom's Ferment: Phases of American Social History from the Colonial Period to the Outbreak of the Civil War.* Minneapolis: University of Minnesota Press, 1944.

Van Deburg, William L. *Slavery and Race in American Popular Culture.* Madison: University of Wisconsin Press, 1984.

Wagenknecht, Edward. *Harriet Beecher Stowe: The Known and the Unknown.* New York: Oxford University Press, 1965.

Walters, Ronald G. *The Antislavery Appeal: American Abolitionism after 1830.* Baltimore: Johns Hopkins University Press, 1976.

Wilson, Edmund. *Patriotic Gore: Studies in the Literature of the American Civil War.* New York: Farrar, Straus and Giroux, 1962.

Wilson, Forrest. *Crusader in Crinoline: The Life of Harriet Beecher Stowe.* Philadelphia: J. B. Lippincott, 1941.

Yellin, Jean Fagan. *The Intricate Knot: Black Figures in American Literature, 1776–1863.* New York: New York University Press, 1972.